The Women's .

JOAN KIRNER grew up as the only child of parents active and respected in the community, who were determined to give her the good education they had not had. After graduating from the University of Melbourne, she became a secondary teacher. Her thirty-five years of community activism began when her first child went to school in a class of fifty-four children. With other parents she organised a local, state and national parent lobby for better education. In 1980 she was made a Member of the Order of Australia in recognition of her contribution to community services. In the same year, she entered the Victorian parliament, where she eventually became Minister for Conservation, Forests and Lands, Minister for Education and Minister for Women. Between 1990 and 1992 Joan Kirner was the first woman Premier of Victoria. Her activism continues as co-convenor of EMILY's List Australia, a financial, political and personal support network to help more women committed to equity, choice and diversity enter Australian parliaments.

MOIRA RAYNER is a lawyer and human rights advocate. She grew up in New Zealand, graduated in Law from the University of Western Australia, and later gained a Master of Arts degree in Public Policy. She chaired the Social Security Appeals Tribunal of Western Australia and was the first woman to chair that state's Law Reform Commission. Between 1990 and 1994 she was Victoria's Commissioner for Equal Opportunity; in 1994 she was appointed a hearings Commissioner of the Human Rights and Equal Opportunity Commission. She chairs the Board of Directors of the National Children's and Youth Law Centre and the Council of the Financial Services Complaints Resolution Scheme, in Sydney. She was a high-profile elected delegate to the 1998 Constitutional Convention in Canberra. Her first book, *Rooting Democracy: Growing the Society We Want*, was published in 1997, and she writes regularly for the press, including *The Big Issue* and *Eureka Street*, and is in demand as a public speaker and social affairs commentator on radio and television.

To Susan Jolly-Brogan – a young leader who died too soon

The Women's power Handbook

JOAN KIRNER & MOIRA RAYNER

Illustrations by Judy Horacek

VIKING

The authors and publishers wish to thank copyright owners for the use of extracted material in this book.

The 'Damn Feminists' cartoon by Judy Horacek, on page 157, first appeared in *Women Against Violence*, no. 3, November 1997.

Viking
Penguin Books Australia Ltd
487 Maroondah Highway, PO Box 257
Ringwood, Victoria 3134, Australia
Penguin Books Ltd
Harmondsworth, Middlesex, England
Penguin Putnam Inc.
375 Hudson Street, New York, New York 10014, USA
Penguin Books Canada Limited
10 Alcorn Avenue, Toronto, Ontario, Canada M4V 3B2
Penguin Books (N.Z.) Ltd
Cnr Rosedale & Airborne Roads, Albany, Auckland, New Zealand
Penguin Books (South Africa) (Pty) Ltd
5 Watkins Street, Denver Ext 4, 2094, South Africa
Penguin Books India (P) Ltd
11, Community Centre, Panchsheel Park, New Delhi 110 017, India

First published by Penguin Books Australia Ltd 1999

10 9 8 7 6 5

Cover designed by Nikki Townsend, Penguin Design Studio
Pages designed by Leonie Stott, Penguin Design Studio
Illustrations by Judy Horacek
Typeset in Minion by Midland Typesetters, Maryborough, Victoria
Printed and bound in Australia by Australian Print Group, Maryborough, Victoria

National Library of Australia
Cataloguing-in-Publication data:

Kirner, Joan.
   The women's power handbook.

   Bibliography.
   Includes index.
   ISBN 0 670 88777 3.

   1. Women. 2. Assertiveness in women. 3. Power (Social sciences).
   I. Rayner, Moira. II. Title.

305.4

www.penguin.com.au

Contents

Acknowledgements

Many people have helped in the research and preparation of this book and the stocking up of the women's power 'tool box', not least of all the many women and men who have worked with us over thirty years or more of activism – too many to name. We thank them all.

We acknowledge the enormous contribution of our families, especially Joan's husband, Ron, and her children, Mike and daughter-in-law Sally, David, and Kate. Kate and David convinced Joan that she should write down what she was constantly telling them (she suspects that it was in the hope that she would stop telling them). Moira's debt to a feminist father and a powerful mother is apparent in everything she does.

Others worked on this book too. Janet Dalgliesh was a tower of strength and information; she shared our early meetings, brought food and wine, made tapes and kept records, and did the research that resulted in our 'Chart of Australian Women's Achievements'. Janet, inspired by the work of Teya Antonio-Wright, also did the substantial work for the section in Chapter 3 on 'Controlling Your Finances', a crucial element of women's access to power and control over their own lives. We are very grateful to her.

We are also indebted to the women who let us quote them, including Jenny Beacham, Dame Beryl Beaurepaire, Larissa Behrendt, Lisa Bellear (Goernpil), Linelle Gibson, Poppy King, Kate Lundy, Fay Marles, Mary Owen, Misha Schubert, Roberta Sykes, and Glen Tomasetti.

Research and advice was also provided by (in alphabetical order) Gillian Beer of the National Centre for Social and Economic Modelling; Bruce Davidson, Parliamentary Librarian, Parliament of Victoria; Ellen Kliemaker, Women's Officer, Victorian Trades Hall Council; Megan Peniston-Bird, Education Officer, Parliament of Victoria; Hoa Pham and Fatima Tawfek, Islamic Women's Welfare

Council; and Zora Valeska, the librarian of the Melbourne office of the national law firm Dunhill Madden Butler.

We both feel very fortunate in having the chance to work with each other, respecting and sharing each other's values and, most of all, expressing and enjoying each other's wicked sense of humour. Judy Horacek, who did the illustrations, added a further layer of meaning to our work, and we thank her for it. Our agent, Fran Bryson of AMC (Aust.) Pty Ltd, 'almost managed' us into completing the book, with good humour and patience. Our publishers at Penguin – Julie Gibbs, Executive Publisher, who started the project off so enthusiastically, and Clare Forster, Publisher, Books for Adults – and our editors Lesley Dunt and Meredith Rose were remarkably understanding and supportive.

We thank Penguin Books for publishing works that reflect and enhance the power of women, and for believing in us and this book.

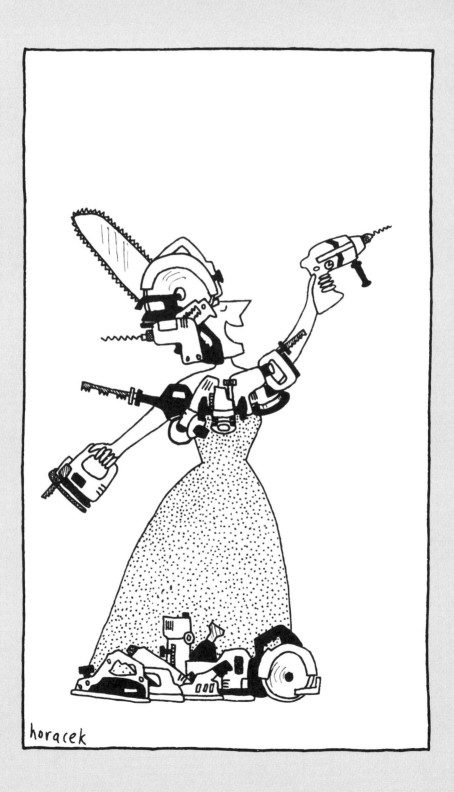

horacek

Introduction

When Moira Rayner was a child her parents told her constantly that she could do anything she wanted and advised her to aim high and to be herself. Her father, in particular, wanted her to be self-reliant. His own father had died unexpectedly, leaving his mother unable to cope with four young children. Typically for the time, the husband had managed the money and everything else. He had appointed business friends from his lodge to be the trustees of his estate and had obviously expected them to help his widow. They didn't. She had no financial skills, was pitifully lonely and searched fruitlessly for support. When she died, young, Moira's father was convinced she had just given up on what seemed an impossible struggle.

He was determined that this wouldn't happen to his daughters. After Moira's marriage broke down he came round with a gift: a little toolbox filled with what she would need to do her own household repairs.

This book is intended to be your toolbox, whatever your present situation. We believe that women can and should shape their own lives, and their community too. A community worth living in has to include women and reflect women's experiences just as much as men's. Women have a different view of the world: our biological, social and emotional experiences are different from men's. Yet most of the important decisions in public and private life have until very recently assumed that men's lives and expectations are the only ones there are. Many women want to make a difference and our world a better place. They need power to do it, but it isn't easy for women to be powerful in what has been a man's world for thousands of years.

Joan Kirner was one of the first Australian women to attain the office of state Premier, from 1990 to 1992. When she first entered the Victorian parliament in 1982 there were still very few women in it, but there were enough Labor women to gather in groups of three or four in Queen's Hall, and as a result some of the men dropped into irritating habits. The crusty older blokes would walk past and remark, 'Hello, hello, hello, this looks dangerous. What are you lot plotting?' This became tedious. So Joan and her colleagues waited for the most tiresome of the old codgers to walk past and make this remark again, and then all the women replied in chorus, 'Your downfall!' From then on he greeted them normally, and by name.

Moira Rayner is a prominent lawyer and human-rights advocate. She was the first woman to chair the Law Reform Commission in Western Australia and she was Victoria's Commissioner for Equal Opportunity from 1990 until 1994. In February 1998 she was elected as a Real Republican delegate to the Constitutional Convention in Canberra, where two-thirds of the delegates were men. When one of them, Bruce Ruxton, well-known president of the Victorian RSL and a likeable curmudgeon, walked by her little group of women delegates in the lobby during the convention and said, 'Hello, hello, what are you lot plotting?' they all cried, 'Your downfall!' and silenced him.

That's why we have written this book. We want women to speak up, talk back, laugh, and make a difference. We know how easy it is to be shut up, shut out, and shunted aside.

One of the greatest mistakes women can make is to assume that good intentions and hard work will be rewarded. They won't. You need power, to make a difference. To claim power and make it work properly, women need the right tools and the skills to use them. Women need power over themselves and their circumstances. They need the power to influence others, the power to communicate and to act as part of a group. Women need to be strong in themselves before they can take other people with them. Individual women need other people, because many voices cannot be shouted down and a critical mass of 'others' will change a culture much more effectively than a chorus of individual complaints.

Power has the ability to attract, intrigue or scare. Henry Kissinger, a rather plain man who happened to be US Secretary of State during the Nixon and Ford years, said in 1976 that power was the ultimate aphrodisiac – he couldn't explain otherwise how he attracted so many beautiful women. For some women, power is a dirty word. Many women are profoundly un-comfortable with being seen as strong, or standing out from the crowd. Women have traditionally been rewarded for 'feminine' behaviour – really, for being submissive, supportive of others, or delicate or needy; making others feel good by helping them. Other women are sensitive about power because they feel that it can be easily misused. It can be; it can be used in a democratic way or an autocratic way, for good or for evil. In today's society, power is exercised more for the individual than for the common good. We talk about the responsibilities of power in this book too, but power never stays stuck in the one place for long. Power, like victory, is always on the move.

Power takes various forms. There is the Mahatma Gandhi kind of leadership by moral example, of which there are plenty of Australian embodiments – indigenous leaders like Lowitja (Lois) O'Donoghue and the late Mum Shirl, for instance. There is the power to inspire others, such as the kind of inspiration Nelson Mandela gives to a divided and turbulent South Africa. There is the power of the community – people power. Power doesn't have to be visible in order to be real; in fact it is often most effective when it is exercised on the quiet. Invisible power can also be misused. It can ignore inconvenient views or protests; it can ridicule people and thereby ensure that they are not taken seriously; it can withhold or doctor information, restrict discussion and debate, or threaten reprisal if dissenting views are expressed. It can marginalise groups of people, and can make individuals feel guilty, inadequate, ashamed, or responsible for things like unemployment, crime, family breakdown.

Having power is about setting your own agenda, not reacting or responding to or resisting others'. When we talk about power in this book we're not talking about bullying or bossing or behaving like bastards. We're not talking about it in the old 'I win, you lose' way, either. There is still a difference between the way most men use power and the way most women use it. A lot of male power is power over people – 'do this' or 'do that' power. The way we are most likely to see power exercised by women is through networking: acting collectively, persuading, consulting and influencing. After all, any woman who can get her teenagers to do their homework is exercising real power – and she knows that threats, ultimatums or even force don't get

it done. In our experience, women with power don't flash it around, they don't like showing it off. We also believe that women look for 'win–win' outcomes.

Knowing you have power means being able to negotiate from a position of strength. It means getting done what you want to get done, what you want to achieve for yourself and others. When we talk about using power in this book, we mean using it in a democratic way: empowering others. Power as a verb and not a noun. We don't recommend women gain power by taking away others'. We have some ploys for preventing ourselves from doing that. We believe that power is meant to be shared, that it is for both the individual's benefit and the common good. Power can't be bought but it may have to be fought for, and it does have to be claimed. It is becoming more important for women to claim power as unemployment and the gap between rich and poor grows.

The Women's Power Handbook has practical suggestions to help women deal with problems even when whole systems are loaded against them. It is not a theoretical book or a feminist treatise, nor does it cover absolutely everything, but we have drawn on the experiences of many women, not just our own success (and failures). We have some wide experiences to share, because we have both either had power or been seen to be influential, and we thought it was time to share our knowledge and experience. This book will help you to work out what you want, communicate it, get others to work with you, and advance your cause.

Included in our how-to advice is getting over fear, staying true to yourself, knowing your own values and keeping them intact, managing your finances and your personal life, balancing home and work. There are ways for working out the unspoken rules in groups whose culture is not friendly to women and for making them work for you. We have also responded to the many requests made of us for help in managing meetings – at work, on committees, councils, boards or delegations – where women are often made invisible or inaudible, ridiculed or just plain outmanoeuvred. We advise on how to negotiate work conditions and wages, deal with discrimination and harassment. Powerful women have to process a lot of information and use a lot of energy – we suggest ways of managing this, and of being politically and media-savvy, forming alliances, networking, finding a mentor and being one. There are tips on speaking in public; using radio, television and newspapers; becoming politically effective through community action; and, one of the ultimate steps to power, getting into parliament.

Above everything else, we stress the hardest thing of all: remembering to keep having fun and to maintain a healthy sense of humour.

The Women's Power Handbook is not another book of interviews with successful women about how they 'made it'. It is not simply a self-help book on building self-esteem or assertiveness, although it does include advice in those areas. Nor is it a recipe book for succeeding by becoming honorary blokes. It is an instructional book for women who want to be responsible for their own lives; a manual to enable them to tune and run the machinery of their private, public and political lives.

We want women to use power in their own way, and to be proud of it. We want women to use their power to protect and promote what women care about, because we believe that when women have as much power as men, it will make the lives of all women, men and children better.

chapter 1

Getting started

Without power, women's needs and hopes and plans are always secondary to somebody else's. That is no way for modern women to live. They need to make their full contribution to society, in every part of their lives. They need to be in a position to be able to make their own choices and to achieve things for themselves.

Virginia Woolf wrote in *A Room of One's Own* that 'Women have served all these centuries as looking-glasses possessing the magic and delicious power of reflecting the figure of a man at twice its natural size.' But we have changed. Women are breaking that mirror. We are responsible for our own fate, no longer prepared to be treated as children; we have a clear vision of our own. To invert a famous saying of one of the fathers of the Christian Church, St Paul: once we saw through a glass darkly; but now face to face.

Women sought 'liberation' in the 1960s and '70s because the most important power of all is the power to direct and control your own life, and they couldn't. Paradoxically, we believe women can control their own lives only by seeing that individual power and personal freedom depend on having the kind of society that respects women as a group, one that includes and understands women's experience.

You can't have individual freedom without a community based on respect for the rights of the disadvantaged. Women have been disadvantaged, now they are breaking out. They know what disadvantage feels like; they should be willing to share their gains with others. We believe that by women claiming and sharing power, it is more likely that everybody will win.

How do we do that?

1   **start with yourself**   To feel powerful you need first to respect yourself and have a clear sense of who you are. It also means feeling able to take the next step – changing what you don't like about yourself. In a complex and insecure world, marked by growing inequality, many things seem beyond our control or influence. Such feelings of powerlessness can lead to alienation, simplistic solutions, or useless blaming. We've learned that making a difference depends on assuming you have power, and then others will believe you have it. This book is about taking back the reins.

2   **claim your place at work**   You need to feel valued in your work, whether that's in your home, in someone else's workplace, or, as is increasingly the case, in your own business or as a contracted worker. Nobody owns a job for life any more – arguably, nobody owns a job – but you have skills and knowledge

that you can take and apply anywhere. Power means knowing how to use what you've got to the best advantage.

3   get with your community   Individual and community understanding, advocacy and activism are essential strategies for overcoming personal powerlessness, and making governments listen and change. Community-based advocacy can give those who thought they couldn't influence or participate in decision-making the power to make a difference. But it depends on individuals becoming part of a group, collectively understanding and using power properly.

Both of us were trying to make a difference in something that mattered very much to us, personally. We learned that leadership stems from holding clear, deeply felt values and advocating them passionately, and that making a difference for yourself requires you to make a difference for others.

4   remember that power shifts   Power has wings. It can take off and alight anywhere. It shifts constantly. When you have had real power and lost it there are other ways to claim and use power. You can use your past role and knowledge and relationships with people to make connections, to embarrass people, to be a mentor and to influence, even if you don't have the power to control anyone or anything (except your own life). Yes, it becomes harder. The staff go, and the welcoming doors close. You may find yourself blacklisted in a changed government, business, professional or union structure. You have to find another door. But there is always another door.

When you lose your power base it is tempting to despair. A premier can improve things for women as a matter of government policy across the whole spectrum of public life. An equal-opportunity commissioner educates the public about their rights and responsibilities under anti-discrimination laws, and provides an opportunity for redress when someone believes their rights have been trampled on. Such roles give you an opportunity to influence public opinion. They mean you are of interest to the media. When you own a public position, you give journalists a handle to use. It encourages them to approach you for comment and report it. When you don't have that label any more, they stop doing so and you wonder what you can do.

This is not unlike the way many women feel when their children or their husbands leave home, and the way many men feel when they retire. They lose a rather simple definition of life and what its purpose is. Losing apparent power can be devastating, but it can be liberating too. It can provide an opportunity to do something completely different and very satisfying. Losing power is not the end of the world. It always opens another door. And it is a lie that opportunity never knocks twice. It's always, always tapping at the window. You just have to listen.

FIRST LESSONS IN POWER

Some people believe that I was born a politician, that I plotted and planned my path to the top. Not so! I grew up believing in social justice, but it wasn't until our first child was going to be in a class of fifty-four children in prep that I said, 'Oh no, not my child!' and decided to fight for his entitlement to a good education. Unbeknown to me I had started my political career. The local mums and I banded together to fight for more classrooms and more teachers and I learned my first political lesson – that if you want to change something for yourself and your child, you have to change it for others. So for me there has never been a conflict between the individual and the collective. My experience is that greater and more lasting power comes when individual and collective together benefit.

Joan

Power has limits. There is a vast difference between power, liberty and licence. With power comes the responsibility to use it for proper purposes and in an ethical way. Power is not a licence to abuse others. There is real power in exercising a freedom, such as the right to say whatever you wish. That does not give you licence to promote hatred of vulnerable people. The use of power – personal or political – must be based on a system of values. The most important point is this: if you have power and use it to make change, you have to be prepared to accept responsibility for the consequences of that change, then build again on what you've changed. You can't just walk away from something you've started.

RULES ABOUT POWER

Above all, woman-power is about finding balance. But the rules can be broken down into:

1 being centred This is a shorthand way of saying that to be effective you have to be clear about what you want and why, who you are, and what you value. People respond to clarity and vision. This does not mean becoming egotistical or big-headed. It is not tied to a particular job either.

2 self-confidence This is an essential prerequisite. You have to believe that you can effect change, that you have the ability, the right to try, and the will. You must believe that you are worthy of power. Self-confidence is the key to implementing the practical tips in this book.

3 understanding the three levels of power These are power over yourself (self-discipline, self-possession, steadiness under fire); power to influence others (persuasion, example, encouragement); and power to communicate and act as part of a group (political power).

4 working your way up While this is not a self-help book, claiming your personal power is essential if you are to have any political power. Starting where you feel comfortable, you can actually make a difference. You can't become Prime Minister overnight. You shouldn't try to take your first political action at the top. Start at a level just above where you feel comfortable, and the likelihood that you'll feel effective after you've done it will be stronger.

5   not being afraid of power   Women need to be willing to claim political power – whether at work, in 'real' politics, or in the community. Women should not be deterred by those who say that they are selfish or are asking for special privileges. Nor should women be jealous of or possessive about power. Women who have experienced discrimination and powerlessness should be willing to share power, when they have it, with others. Some women have achieved brilliantly by their own efforts, but it has taken tools like affirmative action, equal-opportunity programs, and anti-discrimination and sexual-harassment laws to enable so many women to achieve what they have today. These tools took away powerful obstacles to achievement – and they *are* powerful tools for women, otherwise nobody would be trying to take them back. Attempts to sideline affirmative action and equal opportunity with charges of political correctness must not be allowed to undermine women's power. A lot of women say, 'We don't want to be political.' But by that very argument they *are* being political. They are handing their small piece of power as a person, and a citizen, to someone else.

6   getting beyond wanting approval   By definition, 'nice' girls have only personal power. They depend on other people to do the things they want, to achieve their desires for them. But this is seldom effective. Good wives tried to influence their prominent husbands to include women in the original constitutional conventions that established our political framework – women were still excluded. Powerful women make their own decisions; they have independent opinions and express them freely, and they act positively to get what they want for themselves and for others. Powerful women act politically, in this sense.

Politically powerful women are still criticised and challenged; their efforts are obstructed, and attempts are made to marginalise them – though these can be used as opportunities, rather than hardships – far more than men. Why? Because the characteristics of a powerful woman are not traditional feminine virtues. They are leadership qualities.

Many people – some women, as well as men – feel uncomfortable with powerful women. We agree with Eva Cox, a well-known Australian social commentator and academic, who explains so well in her book *Leading Women: Tactics for Making a Difference* why it is time that these people gave up this view, and why those cultures of the institutions of politics, business, trades and professions which discourage women from leading must be changed. These cultures developed over hundreds of years to accord with men's career patterns and men's privileged social position, and they are remarkably persistent, reflecting that history and those expectations in the modern age.

Women are, often unconsciously, encouraged to fit the masculine model, or to aim lower, to be satisfied with smaller gains and lesser rewards, and to keep their influence where it is more acceptable – in the private sphere within the family; in personal relationships and social networks; and at work in supportive roles, working away in back rooms.

So you must be political! Power is political, whether or not it is associated with a political party. Every human transaction – family relationships, work, partnerships, contracts – is political. If you give away your individual power, someone will take it and use it, and maybe against you.

PRESENCE

People often talk to me about their perception of my power. Somebody said to me the other day, 'Even though you're not Premier any more, when you walk into a room you are noticed, even though you probably don't realise it. You always look comfortable, as if you've arrived.'

I gained a sense of self from my mother. I learned my sense of purpose from community activity. If you've got those two things, and the ability to communicate, to convince others, you have everything you need to claim power, whether you realise it or not.

Joan

THE WAY WE WERE

We have come a long way in the last fifty years, as this extract from the *Sun News-Pictorial* of 13 October 1942 illustrates:

SYDNEY – Irene Melva Vail, 20-year-old W.A.A.F. who is stationed in Melbourne, was ordered to return to her husband within 42 days by Mr Justice Street in the Divorce Court yesterday.

Mrs Vail had enlisted without the consent of her husband, it was claimed in court.

Mr Justice Street questioned whether he had the right to order the wife's return when she had taken the oath of enlistment but said he could not believe that the Defence authorities would take a wife without her husband's consent and hold her from her matrimonial duties.

Malvern Keith Vail, 23, of Hurlstone Park, said he was married last January when on three days' leave from the Army. On being discharged he discovered his wife had joined the W.A.A.F.s in Melbourne.

Twenty years later, things weren't much improved. In the 1960s girls were taught 'home science' or 'home economics', which included how to look after their husbands. 'Plan to have a delicious meal ready after work, to show that you've been thinking about him,' teachers would say. His return was to be a Homecoming: freshen up your makeup, put on a show, be light-hearted, attractive and interesting, for the hunter's return to his haven of rest. Clean, primp and hush the children so that they acted their parts as 'little treasures'. Typical advice of the day, in magazines and at school, was to tidy and dust, minimise noise, and greet the man of the house with a warm smile, never with problems or complaints. If he was late for dinner, so what? That was a trivial manner, given his real, working responsibilities.

One piece of classic advice, from a long-forgotten teacher, was: 'Make him comfortable: have him lean back in a comfortable chair or suggest he lie down in the bedroom. Have a cool or warm drink ready for him. Arrange his pillow for him and offer to take off his shoes,' the book advised. 'Speak in a low, soft, soothing and pleasant voice. Allow him to relax – unwind. Listen to him: you may have a dozen things to tell him, but the moment of his arrival is not the time. Let him talk first. Make the evening his.'

The housewife of the early 1960s was being told to behave like a nineteenth-century Japanese geisha. What could be more calculated to drive a modern woman into a state of deep depression?

Working women of the '60s were subjected to similar pressures to meet men's expectations. Sarah Maclean, in her 1962 book *The Pan Book of Etiquette and Good Manners*, advised the career woman that the essential for getting ahead was to possess 'an easy and pleasant manner and a capacity for fitting in', which ran 'a very close second to efficiency'. A competent employee, she warned, 'may be passed over for promotion because she has a gauche manner and a prickly personality'. When she applied for a job (the interviewer is assumed to be a male) she should be well groomed, and 'if you can manage to look attractive as well it will help your interviewer to feel you'd be pleasant to have around'.

The real killer is in her advice about the men in the office. On the one hand, the female employee should expect none of the old-fashioned courtesies: 'As far as they are concerned you are simply a colleague,' Maclean asserted. As soon as you enter the office you forfeit your feminine privileges. You do your own fetching and carrying, open your own doors and if you go out to lunch with him or for an after work drink you will probably be expected to pay your share.' But on the other hand: 'If you ever come across a man who regards you as a woman first and a colleague second, be aware before you plunge headlong and remember that if it comes to the point when you never want to see him again, *you may have to resign your job.*' (Emphasis added.)

And what about the so-called office wolf? We would call them sexual harassers nowadays. In 1962 Maclean believed he was 'fortunately a rare phenomenon'. Her advice for dealing with this rare bird takes the cake: 'But if your boss tells you one day that his wife doesn't understand him and follows this up with repeated invitations to dinner, there is obviously no respectable future for you in the firm and *your only course is to hand in your resignation.*' (Emphasis added.)

Not any more, thanks to anti-discrimination and harassment laws. That sort of nonsense – the behaviour and the advice – was tolerated by women for far too long. Many women have been and still are bullied out of their jobs by sexually voracious bosses and colleagues. These days such a sexual predator can either behave himself or leave his own precious job.

Such notions of subservience and submission were, quite rightly, challenged by women when feminism started its rise in Australia during the 1970s. The changes in the lives of women born since 1945 – the 'baby-boomers' – have been truly astonishing, thanks to dramatic advances in science and technology, government policy and law, but most of all to the struggles of many women working together at every level.

POPPY KING AND A SENSE OF HISTORY

I often think about why I was able to do what I've done. I am no genius. So what is it? I have realised that the only unusual quality about me, the thing that separates me from others, is that I believed I could do it. That has a lot to do with my mother, who always taught me to believe in myself. I never questioned the role of women. To me, women were powerful individuals whose abilities went far beyond that of pretty homemakers. They had thoughts, opinions and ideas and they deserved respect. They were decision-makers as well as emotional caretakers. It was when I came into contact some years later with the work of Dr Anne Summers that I realised it was not enough for me to believe in this, but that society needed to change. Through Anne's book, *Damned Whores and God's Police*, I began to understand that many of the things I took for granted were a result of feminist crusaders who had come before me, women who had fought for equality, not only with an individual perspective but for society as a whole. When I read Anne's book I felt a baton had been passed to me as part of a new generation, that although women had come a long way there was still much to fight for. That we must continue to look beyond the micro to the macro, and at institutional as well as individual change.

Poppy King

Poppy King created a cosmetics empire and has survived great financial problems with grace and distinction, to remain chief executive of Poppy Industries.

When women start to stand on their own feet, when they look for power in their own right, they are often told that women are equal now, that feminism is a movement whose day has passed, even that equal opportunity has gone too far. These are the last bellows of the dinosaurs. The truth is, it hasn't gone far enough yet.

There have been significant achievements in the struggle for equality between women and men in this country. We have documented them in 'A Chart of Australian Women's Achievements', given at the end of the book, because they need to be remembered, and celebrated. These achievements were hard fought for. They need to be built on. They are a firm base for moving forward. But in a society where male power is still dominant, where equity has not been achieved in politics or business, where market ideology dominates all decisions, and social justice has become a pejorative term, these achievements are at real risk. Young women, especially, need to know these achievements, and the struggles that have taken place to ensure gender equity, so that they keep moving forward and make sure they do not allow themselves to drift backwards. Women who don't know the facts about women's achievements may take them for granted, and assume that they are secure.

Add to the chart; women's history is largely unwritten and we may not have recorded it all – we won't have recorded it all. Use the chart as a reference.

WHERE WE ARE NOW

An AGB-McNair survey of Melbourne women published in the *Age* in February 1997 found that 65% thought feminism was relevant to their lives; 79% did not think that a sexually harassed woman should try to deal with it herself; 93% of women under 26 expected formal procedures for dealing with sexual harassment to be in place; and most young women, in particular, were optimistic about their lives. They have reason to be.

Australian women today are likely to live far longer lives than their mothers or grandmothers – unless they are Aboriginal or Torres Strait Islander women, who still die, on average, about nineteen years younger than other women. Women live longer than men, though the lifespans of both men and women have increased over the past decade. Over the past ten years, too, women's health programs have developed nationally, as a result of Commonwealth and state government health policies, and the recognition that women do have specific problems which have been long overlooked in traditional medical practice and research.

Australian governments have adopted institutions designed to improve the standing and well-being of Australian women – the Commonwealth's Office of the Status of Women, for example, and the New South Wales government's Department for Women – and, over the years, women-specific policies and programs. More women are employed in senior positions in governments – partly as a result of affirmative-action policies designed to eliminate past discriminatory patterns – than in private enterprise.

The extraordinarily high incidence of domestic and sexual violence against women has led to changes in the past ten years in criminal laws, court procedures and the law of evidence in order to improve the way in which that violence was dealt with. Sexually assaulted and battered women who strike back still find the legal system and traditions formidable obstacles to justice. Underlying attitudes have not, it seems, really changed so much. The Australian Law Reform Commission noted in its 1994 report 'Equality Before the Law: Justice for Women' the prevalence of domestic and sexual violence towards women. Historically, violence towards women in the home has not been regarded as 'real' crime by police. In 1992 a South Australian judge told a jury to consider whether a husband's 'rougher than usual handling' of his wife, whom he was charged with raping, was really violence. We cannot be complacent about women's advancement if judges, policy-makers and opinion leaders still hold to ancient stereotypes of women.

Most women value their role as mothers – and think that

it is grossly undervalued. The structure of families has changed a great deal over the past twenty-five years, with greater diversity, more single-parent families – overwhelmingly led by women and often in poverty – more long-term and short-term de facto relationships, and more women, and men, living alone. Of Australian families in 1996, 14% had single parents: 85% of these were headed by women and 70% had one or more dependent children. In two-parent families, 59% had both parents working. The influx of married women into paid work has blown apart the traditional expectation that the breadwinner should be a male and the homemaker female. The sheer scale and social significance of this change can be likened to that of the Industrial Revolution more than two hundred years ago. Today many women who work pay others (mostly women) to do most of their domestic chores. They spend a lot less time in the kitchen than they used to (one-third of our total household bills go on ready-made meals), and spend much more on personal services, such as house-cleaning, child care, and hairdressing.

Girls are staying longer in education and completing the final years of high school. Thirty years ago they were more likely to leave early for handmaiden-style jobs. Now girls are far more likely than boys to go on to Year 12 (in 1995 nearly 78% of girls went on to Year 12 compared with only 66.7% of boys). There are far more female students at all levels of tertiary education, and more women than men take higher education and postgraduate positions – though male students outnumber females at doctorate level and above.

Women have gained some control over their own bodies through access to contraception and, until 1998, through the interpretation of abortion laws which protected them from moralistic judgements and being labelled as 'killers' if they did not wish to continue their pregnancies to full term. In 1998 prosecutions of two Western Australian doctors for terminating pregnancies led to a mighty battle over liberalising draconian criminal anti-abortion laws. The tactics of right-to-life opponents showed how deeply opposition remains to women's rights to make decisions about their own reproductive health.

The Western Australian Criminal Code had always made 'procuring a miscarriage' a major crime. In most states abortion was illegal but judges interpreted the laws liberally to permit the termination of pregnancy in the interests of preserving the mother's health and well-being, and in Western Australia up to 8000 pregnancies were terminated each year in reliance on those judicial interpretations. The Western Australian parliament then changed the statute to reflect the common law in 1998. Abortion is now regulated primarily as a health, not a criminal, issue (unless the woman has not given 'informed consent') in Western Australia.

Women are increasingly financially autonomous, and have substantial purchasing power. In 1995 they made up 43% of the paid workforce, although 42.5% of the female workforce worked part-time, and part-time or casual employees earned less than full-time workers and were less able to negotiate working conditions that suited them rather than their employers. Just 57.5% of women worked full-time, usually because of family and home commitments (most women still take the bulk of responsibility for family care). The number of women holding full-time jobs in the workforce is going down all the time, in part because the availability of affordable childcare is drying up, in part because of the trend to casual or contractual work. More and more women are the family breadwinner: in 1985 just 21% of main family breadwinners were women, but by 1995 this had risen to 33%.

Between 1985 and 1995 the average income of women increased by 85%, compared to an increase of 68% for men. But this is misleading: most women still earn less than men for similar

work, mainly because they are not able to earn above-award payments, or work overtime because of family responsibilities, and
they earn less than men to begin with.

The purchasing power of women has certainly increased,
though. In 1995 single women aged 20–24 had the highest participation rate in the workforce of all female groups, according
to the Australian Bureau of Statistics, though they earned just
under the average income. Women of these ages were more
likely than those in other age groups to have a credit card, own
valuable jewellery and have superannuation. Twenty-seven per
cent of single women aged 25–40 owned their own home and 18%
were paying off their own mortgages. Between 1990 and 1994
the number of women living alone who were first-time home
buyers doubled. In 1994, 91% of single-parent home buyers
were women. Women buy 40% of all vehicles registered to
individuals. They make 70% of all household purchase decisions;
47% of women, compared with 50% of men, have a major credit
card, and 17%, compared with 8% of men, have a department-
store card.

In 1996 women owned one-third of small businesses in
Australia, and they are expected to own half by the year 2000.
They spent $4 billion a year on office products.

Women are really up there, financially, if they are not
indigenous women or from non-English-speaking backgrounds,
if they have a good education and if they come from the relative
comfort of our middle class. But there is still a long way to go
for many other working women who receive low wages and little
recognition of their skills. For those without paid work, or on
pensions, or who are single mothers, it is a major challenge to
achieve any power, let alone economic power.

All these changes have come about primarily because of
women's increased participation in the workforce. Yet financial
products and services are basically still designed for men's

lifestyles. Women's financial needs are different from men's, mainly because they go in and out of the workforce more often (biology at work), so they need to set their financial goals carefully and ensure that, if they're in a long-term relationship, their resources are used in financial partnerships with their husbands or partners, rather than relinquishing all financial responsibility as women used to do.

Women work predominantly in the health, education, entertainment/recreation, and wholesale/retail sectors of the economy. Australian industry is one of the most sex-segregated in the industrialised world. Where women have entered the professions they tend to take up the least remunerated segments of it: for example, women doctors are more likely to be GPs than specialists, and women lawyers are more likely to be solicitors or associates than equity partners in law firms. In 1996 only four out of 46 Federal Court judges were women (8.7%). Out of 53 Family Court judges, ten were women (18.9%).

In the late '90s far fewer women than men are taking up apprenticeships (14.9 per thousand compared with 111.4 men per thousand) and those who do tend to be in hairdressing. Women still cluster in clerical, sales or personal service jobs. A 1997 report by Dr Clare Burton into academic employment found that only 27% of all academics aged forty-five or over were women. Women also held only 27% of tenured positions but constituted 42% of academics on fixed-term contracts, including casuals or part-timers. Women with tenure tended to be in lower academic positions than men with tenure.

The story is much the same in education. Women are far more likely to be primary-school teachers, and far fewer women than men are principals of schools.

In 1996, 4% of all employed women were managers and administrators – 87% of these were childcare co-ordinators and 29% were in education. Of all employed men, 10% were managers and administrators. There are more women in management in the private sector – about 22%, if we are to believe the reports made to the Affirmative Action Agency – though they do better in the public sector.

Most worrying of all is the slip in women's achievement of equal pay for work of equal value in a decade of enterprise bargaining and the more recent emphasis on individual contracts. It seems, from a study done by Sara Charlesworth for the Human Rights and Equal Opportunity Commission published in 1997, that these systems overwhelmingly favour employers, and under them women are again earning less, with more limited career options, than men.

There are, as there always have been, wealthy women. However, the richest women are those who have inherited money from families. The most prosperous companies – those listed in the 26 May 1997 *Business Review Weekly*'s 'Rich List' – are run by men. Of 177 organisations, 154 were dominated by men. Surveys of boards of directors, conducted by Korn/Ferry International and the Australian Institute of Company Directors over the past five years, show little change in the representation of women. Only 4% of all boards have women members. But companies all say they mean to do better. One day.

Indigenous women have always been influential in their communities. The Aboriginal and Torres Strait Islander Commission (ATSIC) provides opportunities for indigenous people to determine their own future, though it is clearly less powerful under the Howard government. In 1996, 23% of ATSIC's elected councillors were women. Of 35 elected chairpersons of regional councils, seven were women (20%). Of the 18 commissioners of the ATSIC board, two were women (11.1%). Lowitja (Lois) O'Donoghue chaired ATSIC with grace and honour until she retired in 1997, but there are still no indigenous women in state or federal parliaments, although several have been endorsed candidates. While women from non-English-speaking back-grounds have always been influential in their own communities, it is only in the past two decades that they have taken the step into acknowledged leadership in the mainstream. Women like Helen Sham-Ho, Liberal MLC in New South Wales, Irene Moss, New South Wales Ombudsman and former Race Discrimination Commissioner, and Professor Mary Kalantzis have taken a high profile in broader public life, as have women whose parents were migrants, such as Jennie George, President of the ACTU, and many others in parliament, business, unions and the professions.

Since the 1970s women have used their legal rights to chal-lenge prejudice and discrimination, especially in employment. The bigger companies, and government, have become more aware of women's rights because of high-profile cases, and because they have had to report publicly on women's rep-resentation in their organisations to the Affirmative Action Agency.

One of the first great wins for women was Deborah Wardley's in 1984. Wardley complained that Ansett Airlines had refused to employ her as a pilot, even though she was a better-qualified pilot than the men they employed, because it believed its cus-tomers would not accept a female pilot. The Equal Opportunity Board found she had been the victim of sex discrimination and ordered her employment, on merit.

In 1997 Susan Dunn-Dyer won damages of $135 000 against the ANZ Bank by proving that she had been made redundant because of the insidious climate of sexism in which she worked as a money manager. She had been persistently disparaged as a 'mother hen' running a division of the bank described as 'the nursery'. But though she was compensated she didn't work for five years, while the managers who held these views furthered their banking careers.

Marea Hickie won too, in 1998, after she challenged her former partners in the law firm Hunt and Hunt for sacking her as a partner shortly after she returned to work part-time from four months' maternity leave. The Human Rights and Equal Opportunity Commission ruled that Hunt and Hunt had unfairly assumed that a part-time partner was not committed to her career.

The more obvious discrimination (deciding that some jobs are men's jobs or girls' work) is less common as a result of such cases. But cultural discrimination (failing to see someone's merits because of their sex) and indirect discrimination (applying men's expectations to the careers of women) are as common as they ever were. Successful cases get a lot of publicity but they are the tip of the iceberg of prejudice and negative assumptions about women's abilities, and the rate of complaints to equal-opportunity bodies continues to rise. The battle has not yet been won.

In July 1996, women made up just 15.5% of all members in the House of Representatives and the Senate in our federal parliament. In the 1998 election the ALP increased its proportion of women by 200%, to twenty-five: nine senators, sixteen members of the House of Representatives; the Liberal Party had twenty-four women (nine senators and fifteen members of the House of Representatives), more than double their numbers of two years before. When parliament sits in July 1999, fifty-six women will represent their federal electorates: twenty-three senators (30.3% of the total) and thirty-three members of the House of Representatives (22.3%). In state and territory politics there have been advances too: nationally, since 1987, the overall proportion of women in their parliaments has increased from 9% to 19%. While these are significant gains, they are still not enough. To achieve appropriate (equal) representation, women's numbers must more than double.

In July 1997 Australian newspapers reported that the nation

had been humiliated internationally by the United Nations Committee on the Elimination of Discrimination Against Women, in New York. The committee expressed its disappointment that Australia was no longer a leader on women's issues, and questioned Australia's recent record on women's health, industrial relations and anti-discrimination law. How, it asked, would the national government know about the status of women's health once responsibility had devolved to the states? What measures had been put in place to monitor the effect of enterprise bargaining on women? A coalition of women's groups, including the Australian Women Lawyers Association, the YWCA and the Women's Electoral Lobby, had told the committee that many of the federal government's budgetary measures had had the effect of encouraging women 'to move out of mainstream social and economic participation back into the role of family carer'. The committee was especially critical of cuts to the Office of the Status of Women, which had received a 38% funding cut; changes to the role of the Sex Discrimination Commissioner; and the effects of reduced funding for tertiary education and increased fees for most courses, which, of course, many women returning to studies after caring for children were unable to pay. The Workplace Relations Act was seen as undermining the system of industrial awards which had contributed to Australia's relatively good performance in pay equity for women, and as generally favouring traditional male working patterns, not those of women or men with domestic responsibilities.

The UN committee said that it 'was alarmed by the policy changes that apparently slowed down, or reversed, Australia's progress in achieving equality between women and men, such as in housing and childcare programs and in employment assistance'. It praised Australia as one of the few signatories to the UN Convention on the Elimination of Discrimination Against Women for its national women's health policy and moves to reduce domestic violence, but it criticised us over our loss of leadership and direction, the *Age*, 20 March 1997, reported in 'UN Report Slams Apparent Shift on Sex Equality'.

So where are women now? As ever, on the cusp of equality. What we have could be lost, overnight. Government policies can change, to the detriment of women, and so it is crucial for governments to hear women's voices and know that they have to be taken seriously.

AIN'T I A WOMAN?

That man over there say
a woman needs to be helped into carriages . . .
Nobody ever helped me into carriages
or over mud puddles
or gives me any best place . . .

And ain't I a woman?
I have born thirteen children
and seen most all sold off to slavery . . .
Then that little man in black over there say
a woman can't have as much rights as a man . . .

If the first woman God ever made
was strong enough to turn the world
upside down, all alone
These women together ought to be able to turn it back
and get it right side up again.
And now they is asking to do it
the men better let them.

Sojourner Truth
an African-American woman,
at a women's rights convention in Ohio, 1851

An Aboriginal woman, Eva Johnson, wrote a poem with a similar theme called 'Right to Be', which finishes:

Yes, I'm a woman and I know there's nothing that I lack
I'll progress with my learning till I finally get the knack
It's my independent thinking that makes me feel so strong
Our trust in solidarity means we can't go wrong

I don't want to be no second hand rose
I don't want to be your centrefold pose
I'm a woman and I'm Black and I need to be free
Being upfront and powerful is the only way to be

Eva Johnson

We believe, like Mary Wollstonecraft, that women do not wish to have power over men, but over themselves. That is what will strengthen our children, our democracy and our country.

chapter 2

What women need to be powerful

Freud, the originator of psychoanalysis, wrote in a letter to Marie Bonaparte, 'The great question that has never been answered and which I have not yet been able to answer, despite my thirty years of research into the feminine soul, is "What does a woman want?"' Surely any woman could have told him if he had asked her. We want to become what we potentially are, to develop our full human personalities. Freud couldn't see it because he could not see the world through a woman's eyes. He was as much a prisoner of his own blindness as women of his time and ours are of their invisibility.

Women cannot use power unless their experience is part of the political world. Women cannot achieve all that they want to unless they have power in those three fundamental aspects we mentioned earlier: power over themselves; power to influence others; power, through communication, to act as part of a group. If women are to realise their personal power, and achieve everything they are capable of, they need a supportive environment. Of course, it begins with ourselves, but there are some environmental necessities that all women must have, otherwise all the personal determination in the world will make no difference to our being able to realise our personal power. These include:

1   an independent, secure and reasonable income   This means, for most of us, access to reasonably paid employment (but we work to live, not live to work), a fair taxation system, superannuation, insurance and other financial security, including the right to own our own property and to share property jointly acquired through marriage. It means not being dependent on a husband or private income that women don't control.

2   good health   Until relatively recently women's particular health needs were neglected by the medical profession, including in the education offered to medical students and medical research. Women need access to information about how our bodies work, how the hormonal and other changes in our bodies and minds affect us as we age. We need good medical advice from providers who talk to and listen to women; we need sufficient information to enable us to participate in medical decisions and we need treatment that takes into account women's life experiences and lifestyles, and values them. Women who work and who want to be active in their communities have to feel well. We have to be fit, eat properly, exercise regularly, and not focus on our sexual attractiveness, our work or our families at the cost of our physical, emotional and psychological well-being.

3   control of our own bodies   This means, first and foremost, the power to decide whether and when we have children. All women need information about contraception and their reproductive system. It was no accident that the mass movement for women's rights, beginning in the Western world, came hand in hand with access to a means of contraception that did not depend on men's abstinence or approval: the Pill changed all women's lives. Control over our bodies also means being free from the fear of assault, including sexual assault. Women are, in general, much physically smaller than men and more vulnerable to sexual threat.

4   shared responsibility and help with childcare   Fathers are important in their children's lives, and should share them equally. In the 1980s it was assumed that 'superwomen' could have it all – career, husband, children, time for recreation and sport or the gym, and cordon bleu cooking as well. But over the past decade, women with children are increasingly having to work part-time, which inevitably affects their income and their capacity to advance in their careers. It is a simple fact that women cannot compete on equal terms unless childcare responsibilities are shared – not by nannies, or older women who cannot work, but by everyone.

5   access to information and education   A proven way to keep women powerless is to restrict or deny outright their access to education. This is counter-productive. International research has established that there is a direct correlation between educating women and reducing the number of children they bear, and thus increasing the affluence of their families. Educated women use information for their own benefit, and can also choose how to use it for their family's benefit. The community pays for the loss of free, quality educational opportunities that were made increasingly available to women throughout the 1970s and '80s.

6   equal rights protected by law   Traditional attitudes to women have often been implied in our laws and sometimes even expressed in our laws – as 'divine' laws. In Australia it was only recently that discrimination against women was made unlawful –

under state anti-discrimination laws in the late 1970s and when the Commonwealth's Sex Discrimination Act was passed in 1984. It has been a long battle for women to gain the right to own and control their property, to get an education, including going to university and being awarded the degrees they earned, and to enter the professions and the business world on terms of equality. Anti-discrimination laws have been very effective in challenging old assumptions and practices because they offer some redress if rights are taken away, threatened, or diminished. They are necessary, but not sufficient. It is now up to women to claim their power and their rightful place in public life.

7   our own space   Some people need privacy and isolation – what Virginia Woolf described as 'a room of one's own' – to explore their personal needs, apart from their families. Some people, like Joan, prefer to work surrounded by other people, which they find provides affirmation and renewal. Moira finds writing to be a profoundly anti-social activity and best done in solitude, but needs constant stimulation to provoke new ideas that will get her to think. What is important, however it is realised, is the social and emotional space that derives from respect for women's interests and activities. It's okay to have a different approach, to meet different needs. There are as many variations as there are women. Our message is this: women must work out what they need, then go out and get it. We must use our own networks for information, for support, and in our actions.

There are some personal assets we must have too, or we will never have an equal share in power of any kind.

A CASE STUDY
KATE LUNDY

Kate Lundy was elected a senator for the ACT when she was just 28 years old, after a career in the construction industry and unions. In 1997 she joined the ALP's front bench as Shadow Parliamentary Secretary for Sport and Tourism, after less than two years in parliament. Writing in the book Talking Up, *she says:*

My interpretation of feminism is very personal, and its development has contributed significantly to my sense of self. My life experience is one of manual work, motherhood and politics. I never anticipated a representative role in the Australian Parliament.

I am not a lawyer, academic or businesswoman. My formal qualifications consist of a Year 10 Certificate, scaffolders' licence and hoist drivers' ticket. I have managed to balance a family and work, and this balance is my measure of personal achievement.

I am confident that my life experience has relevance to the context of my current work. However, this wasn't always the case . . . I asked myself what the hell I was doing, contemplating election to federal parliament.

Over a period of time, the answers came. I realised that my experiences and political opinions are as valid as anyone's. Diversity strengthens Australian society and if our parliments are to be truly representative, this diversity must be reflected there. I came to the conclusion that if a semi-educated labourer with two young children can be elected, then this was a positive reflection of our democratic system . . .

To be politically active, in whatever capacity, is to be empowered.

THE TOP TEN ASSETS OF SUCCESSFUL WOMEN

1   a clear sense of purpose   You won't succeed in anything unless you are clear about what you want to achieve and know how to measure whether, and how well, you have achieved it. Muddling through means not making a difference. It means making a muddle.

To be powerful you need goals, targets and rewards. Girls are often not encouraged, as many boys are, to dream of doing great things, yet these visions are what we build our futures on. Some of us were told to expect to be a bride, others to have a career. Very few parents encouraged us to envisage both at once.

You need to find your own vision and then plan to achieve it. List the dreams you have now, or used to have. (Moira used to dream of being a famous doctor saving poor benighted heathens from leprosy and civil war in some mythical savage country.) Write them down. Do you still want them? If not, discard them. Then write down the steps you would have to take to realise them. This is a reality check. (Moira doesn't want to be a missionary doctor any more.) Start where you are now. You may want a new job, a good school for your kids, a local council that listens to you as a citizen and a resident, or a better relationship – it doesn't matter what it is. Don't wait for the big challenge to come along: decide what you want to change now, and start small.

Be clear about your target and your focus. You might have lots of plans and dreams, but start with a small one. Too large a target can become a burden. Pick the one that seems the most achievable and satisfying. Then take one step at a time, and consciously praise yourself for every small achievement, every milestone passed. Each success motivates and energises you and increases your capacity to make a real difference.

Neither of us started out seeking power for its own sake.

We had a cause and we were sufficiently self-confident to try to make a difference, and we found that this was enough to start. Don't allow yourself to be distracted. If the task is to persuade a Minister to do something, don't address audiences of the already convinced. Above all, don't solve problems that don't need to be solved. There's a story about three aristocrats who are carted down to the guillotine during the French Revolution. The first man stumbles up to the scaffold and places his head on the block, the blade whistles down and stops a scrape away from his neck. The crowd roars, 'A miracle!' and he is set free: God could not have intended him to die. The second man is dragged to the block, tied down, and the executioner releases the blade. Whomp! And again it stops just short of the chap's neck. The crowd goes wild: can this be the hand of fate? He too is released. The third person is an aristocratic woman. She walks hopefully to the foot of the guillotine. By this time the crowd is humming. The woman casts her eye to the heavens in search of divine intervention, then, 'Just one moment,' she says to the executioner, pointing to the shining blade poised ominously above her, 'I think I can see what the problem is . . .'

2   confidence   One of the essentials of successful women, at work, in public and in private life, is having confidence in your own capacity to make a difference and in your ability to succeed. You need the confidence to trust your own judgement, to take risks, and to negotiate on your own terms; and you need confidence to believe that your own experience, ambition and needs do matter.

One of the best ways to achieve confidence is preparation: knowing the facts, thinking and talking over the strategies, and planning. Most victories are won not by geniuses, but by those who work meticulously and single-mindedly on their objectives. If you prepare well, including getting support from others, you will have the confidence to engage in the debate on your own terms, and the confidence to insist on shaping the future.

Having a purpose turns your engine on. Then you need energy to keep it turning over. Success creates that energy – just a spark ignites the fuel. A leadership trajectory is powered by confidence. We all have the potential, yet only some realise it. You have to believe that you have the *ability* and the *right* and are *worthy* of power – and you have to own this before you can use any of the practical tips we give you.

Many successful women were lucky in their choice of parents, who were supportive of their daughters' ambitions, political activism, creative assertiveness and womanhood, and who approved of their strength. But how do we become confident, in our own capacity, in our own image, if we didn't get this support as a child? Where do we get the confidence to stand up for things we believe in and value? What if the public mood seems to be apathetic or even hostile – if only we feminists would go away, resume our rightful subordinate places? Glen Tomasetti wrote a song on the occasion of the first High Court case on equal pay for women in 1969. Its chorus went:

> Don't be too polite, girls, don't be too polite;
> Show a little fight, girls, show a little fight.
> Don't be fearful of offending in case you get the sack;
> Just recognise your value and you won't look back.

Confidence is part of the male armoury of success and influence. Joan needed confidence more than ever when she became the Victorian Premier. Most mornings she would get up, stand tall, square her shoulders (padded, in those days) and say to herself, 'I *can* do it – I *will* do it.' Both parts of that statement are important. Too many women know the first but don't say or do the second. What Joan was doing was giving herself an internal appreciative audience. We all need one.

In Moira's last year of primary school her father arranged a little presentation ceremony for her, just before the break-up concert. Her parents gave her her first camera, and her father told her, 'We want you to know we are proud of you, and know you did your very best.' Moira realised later that her parents thought that she wasn't going to get an award she had set her heart on: she wanted to be dux of the junior school. She went to that last night's concert confident that she didn't need to win to be loved and appreciated.

You can create the same feelings by remembering the good experiences and by rewarding yourself for being you. It isn't hard to do: have a long hot bath, or get a really good massage, or sit in front of a fire on a dark, wet night. Do whatever it is that makes you feel good; sometimes that might be just talking to a good listener.

Moira once got a very good piece of advice from a good listener, a long time ago. She had just gone back to her home town after a long absence and a major personal trauma, and was welcomed by old friends and family and felt especially cared for. A friend suggested that she 'bookmark' this feeling in her mind; find some time, every day, when she could be alone for a few minutes, then make herself comfortable, close her eyes and be there again. This is a really useful thing to do when things seem dark.

Once you start to feel good about yourself, you will quite naturally start to feel competent, and you will find the confidence to believe that you really can do anything you want to. Believing in yourself and being sure of your purpose means that you can make reliable assessments about what is and isn't possible, and about the resources required to achieve it.

You need support in order to find and keep this faith in your abilities. You can't achieve everything on your own. You should work out who of your friends and colleagues and family feels good about you. You need to surround yourself with such people – not 'yes men' who will not tell you uncomfortable truths (you still need them, in moderation), but people who will give you an appreciative audience to complement the one within yourself. They will help you to feel able to go on and achieve your best.

It's worth listing such people in order of trust – those to whom you can tell anything because you know they will keep your confidence and will love and support you without question or judgement; then those who, just as importantly, will tell you what you need to hear, whose judgement and opinions you value. It's sometimes salutary to ask yourself whether you are in their inner circle or whether the relationship is one-way.

3   integrity You can't lie and cheat your way to success. Even if you do win, power never stays with anyone long, and if you've stuck the knives in on the way up, there'll be a fair few out for you on the way down.

Your values are what get and maintain power for you and ensure that it is properly used. Valuing yourself as an individual is important, but it is just as important to value other people. We need to be clear, publicly and privately, about our own values and we need to continually measure our actions against them. In public life, even if people may not always agree with you, it is important that they are clear about where you stand and respect your integrity and your principles.

Bella Abzug, a wonderful US Democrat politician, once said in a speech that she was fuelled by the power of the pain and passion of women for change. We each have our own values. Write them down and think about them, and carry them around with you, adding to them when you feel the need. Review them regularly. Keep going back to the source.

If we constantly question and apply our values to our work, we change the structures we work within. Mary Robinson, the former President of Ireland, said, 'As women lead they are changing leadership, as women organise they are changing organisations.' One of your key values should be to see being a woman as an asset, not a problem.

Spell out and live by your values. Guard your integrity – it is your most important asset.

I BELIEVE

My values, and I try to measure my actions against them all the time, are:

+ Women matter as much as men do
+ Women have the right to determine their own lives
+ Women's experience matters and should be valued
+ Women should be able to describe freely and share those experiences
+ Women's knowledge and experience should be part of decision-making at all levels
+ Women are entitled to a fair share of the infrastructure that creates equality and equity: education and training, employment, safety, health, family, resources and representation.

Joan

---

4   community/team focus   A successful woman, and a good leader, is a team player; she knows she is part of a community. No woman ever made it entirely on her own. At the least, she is at the end of generations of mothers, daughters, wives – and their supporters – who got her there. Women need to foster the ability to relate to people, to share successes, to reach agreed solutions contributed to by many and benefiting the whole. Working with other people is something women excel at. Women tend to have a consensus approach to decision-making, sharing ideas and strategies and insights. That approach strengthens the bonds between the individual and the community.

COMMUNITY OWNERSHIP

One of my most satisfying successes came while I was the Victorian Equal Opportunity Commissioner. We weren't having any meaningful contact at all with the Aboriginal population, and it defied credulity that they didn't have any complaints of race or other discrimination. I employed three Koori staff: I listened to their ideas, and gave them virtually carte blanche to come up with a strategy. They started regularly visiting com-. munities, setting up relationships, and then started giving them information and training – not just on discrimination law, but whatever they wanted to know, such as the duties of directors of Aboriginal co-operatives – along with documenting complaints, and investigating and conciliating disputes. It succeeded, and became a national model, because I didn't impose my ideas but let my Koori staff develop their own in consultation with the community.

Moira

5   information   A successful woman maximises her power by understanding the context in which she is working. She asks, and finds answers for, these questions: Who has the power to advance or block her cause? How, and by whom and by what, can they be influenced? What are her rights? What are the processes open to her? What can she learn from previous winners and losers?

A successful woman can sort out the necessary information from the irrelevant or marginally useful and see how it can inform and guide her plans for getting what she wants. A successful woman also knows that she must constantly test the accuracy of information and verify her facts. (You don't want to look stupid, do you?) A successful woman keeps records of meetings, promises, letters, phone calls, commitments and plans – a data base in chronological order. That way she can deal with half-truths and lies told by other people, and make them accountable too.

6   balance and commonsense   Most women intuitively seek out a balance in their lives between work, family, personal satisfaction and community good. Commonsense is the ordinary person's wisdom. It's also a term much misused to discredit people who challenge the accepted view of things. It was 'commonsense', men said, that women were too soft and vulnerable to be doctors, or lawyers, engineers or politicians, or to run their own companies. Women's commonsense, though, said that any woman could make judgements, learn, and apply their learning to everyday situations, even secret men's business. Just ask Janet Holmes à Court, a leading Australian businesswoman who successfully restructured her husband's business, now worth $260 million.

Logic – using your head as well as your heart – is essential too. It might seem logical to take one course, but when your heart says another, think of the two as partners and find the balance. Each is an ally of the other. To make good decisions you need the music as well as the words.

7   self-knowledge and self-discipline   A powerful woman is a leader too. And a good leader is consistent, reliable, does what she says she is going to do, follows up, and manages her time effectively. This last is really important. Anyone who is habitually late for meetings, or forgets them, or misses deadlines, is less likely to be taken seriously.

TRANSFORMING ANGER

I know my own strengths and weaknesses. For example, I get impatient and angry quickly, especially at particular things – bullying, for example. I have a natural tendency to cry too. I don't try to deaden these responses – they're an essential part of me, after all – but I can choose how and when to express them. I have learned to recognise and use such feelings as a source of energy, to drive my purpose on. And to apologise when I give in to them.

Moira

THE LATE JOAN KIRNER

I am consistent, reliable and I do follow up, but I am not a good manager of time. I've always performed best when I've left writing a speech or a paper or a book until the last minute. I am often late for meetings (though not for planes), and I have burnt the candle at both ends regularly since I was a young student. But I think, in some places, I'm still taken seriously, even though some friends tag me the Late Joan Kirner. Mea culpa.

Joan

8   imagination   Imagination means being aware of the future and your part in it. People who make decisions based on foreseen consequences are more effective. If you lose your temper now with someone who is your ally, instead of being strategic you will have no influence at all in the future. Imagination includes being able to put yourself in someone else's shoes and being able to plan for their response, and act accordingly. Imagination is also the space to dream of what's perfect – then do what is practicable.

9   a sense of humour   No matter how serious your situation, there will always be something ridiculous in your life. The best therapy of all – and a good leveller, if you are getting inflated ideas of your own importance – is a big belly laugh. Make a point of having one every day. You need to be able to laugh at yourself and at adversity. If you can't laugh you might cry, and only blokes can do this and get away with it (see Chapter 7).

Remember to enjoy your work. If it's too hard, you're probably doing it the wrong way.

10   humanity   Sometimes you can persuade yourself that you are more important, and even slightly less fallible, than other people. Well, you're not, and you'll make mistakes and you'll be beaten sometimes and you're going to have to deal with that.

A genuinely powerful woman can bounce back from adverse events or mistakes, and keep going. She is resilient. Girls tend to be more resilient than boys to great setbacks: women can deal with pain better not because they are stoics, but because they *deal* with it. Instead of ignoring that pain in her chest, a woman consults a doctor: too many men tough it out, then keel over on the footpath.

Resilience means coping, making sense of things, practising forgiveness, and keeping hope alive. We often make mistakes: our failures have to be faced, accepted and built upon. We may be disappointed in others, or disappoint them ourselves. Each needs to be faced, and come to terms with. Never despair.

You need to develop a keen sense of your own humanity and respect for others. Claiming equality is, ultimately, good for everyone. As Lillian Holt, the former principal of the Aboriginal Community College in Adelaide, said when she addressed the Centenary of Federation Advisory Committee in 1995, 'I believe talking about racism in this country is about collective healing, and we can all learn as a result of it. It is not about being anti-white, it is about being pro-humanity. For what has diminished me as an Aboriginal woman in this country has diminished all Australia: both black and white.' If women around Australia accept and run with that message, we will shape a better nation.

LEARNING BY DOING

Initially, I didn't have a clue that I was exercising power. I was just out to get some teachers and classrooms for my own children and I didn't know that in doing this I was making a real difference. First of all I went to the people I saw as powerful to get them to make the necessary changes. When that didn't work we created our own power, but I didn't know that was what I was doing, not in those terms. Then I started being described as a powerful advocate for the parent movement and I said to myself, 'Whoops! Powerful? Fantastic, I'll start using my power!'

Joan

PROFESSIONAL DEVELOPMENT

That sense of delighted recognition – that you have unconsciously, unintentionally, acquired some kind of power in the eyes of other people – is common to Joan and me.

I started getting involved with human rights because I was doing a lot of work with parents and their children, appearing in the Children's Court where lawyers really weren't very welcome, in the '70s and '80s. Then, to my surprise, I found that I had been described as the 'doyen of the children's movement', when all I thought I was doing was appearing for children, who were usually not represented at all. Then I started being asked to give talks, join committees, and do more and more. But it all began just because I was there, doing something I believed in.

Moira

TAKING OTHERS WITH YOU

Effective and lasting change requires taking people with you. To do that, you need to listen to others, communicate your values and views, negotiate agreements, and look for win–win solutions. It is possible to move forward when change is desired, pursued

and owned only by a few people, but lasting change requires
open communication, negotiation, and shared contributions
and benefits.

A CASE STUDY
JOAN KIRNER AND LANDCARE

In the 1970s, when I visited country schools and talked to
parents about the quality of education in rural areas, I
began to understand the needs of the people and their
commitment to the land. At the time neither I nor most of
the families I stayed with had any idea of the threat to
their productive land from creeping salinity, soil
degradation and water erosion. In 1985 my first visit as the
Minister for Conservation, Forests and Lands to towns along
the Murray River changed my understanding, fast. First I
heard the figures about lost agricultural production, then
I saw the devastation myself. I was on a bus trip, and we
Ministers were treated to talks at each area we visited. Each
new departmental officer told us how bad the land and river
salting was, and how it could be 'fixed' if we allowed their
area to discharge into the Murray River. Only one, a wildlife
officer, ventured to speak of an alternative way: a whole-
of-catchment approach.

Then we talked over a cuppa with the farming
community, wives and husbands, about the real problems.
I didn't know much about soil conservation and land
protection, but I knew enough to be clear that solving
one area's salinity problem by putting salt into the river
and thereby worsening the next town's problem was no
solution. I also knew, from my parent-club days and visits
to country areas, that it was the farming women and men
who were the real stewards of the land, and if we didn't
involve them in decisions about improving the land,

nothing would work. So I noted some farmers who might
be ready for a new approach and for projects that
matched my ideas. In early 1986, I asked the Department
of Conservation, Forests and Lands to develop a new
system of land protection, with the proviso that it:

+ Be community-based, not focused on individuals
+ Be integrated in its approach to land protection issues,
  from weeds to wild dogs
+ Be involved, whole-farm, whole-catchment land protection
+ Actively involve farmers and the wider community in
  describing the problem and owning the outcome
+ Adopt sustainable agriculture as its long-term aim
+ Use professionals as advisers, not the decision-makers,
  on community decisions.

The program built on these principles we called Landcare.
Cabinet agreed to fund Landcare. I was delighted, but I
knew I needed three things. The first was a partnership
with the Victorian Farmers Federation. I was fortunate that
Heather Mitchell was its president at the time, and she
didn't have any problem with working with a socialist-left
'greenie' Minister, because she was focused on the job, not
the politics. The second thing I needed was Cabinet
agreement and funding; I got that. And the third was a
network for spreading the program across the state.

The first group was set up in the Wimmera that year
and it demonstrated that good land practices generate
greater productivity, that they are important in both good
times and bad, and that they are a long-term investment in
the future, not simply an add-on.

On the national scene, Philip Toyne of the Australian
Conservation Foundation and Rick Farley of the National
Farmers Federation took up the Victorian 'Heather and Joan'
show, and argued with the federal Minister, Peter Cook,

that land degradation was Australia's biggest environmental problem and needed federal government commitment and more money. They talked, promoted, publicised, networked and negotiated, until in July 1989 Prime Minister Hawke announced the Decade of Landcare, supported by a $340 million program. The media loved the Farley–Toyne, NFF–ACF combination so much so that they credited them with its creation. Landcare Australia had arrived, with bipartisan support.

When all major parties agree on a policy – as they did on Landcare – there is the possibility of real change. The Landcare proposal has become part of the nation's political, social, economic and environmental culture. I'm proud of that.

Heather Mitchell's and Joan Kirner's success demonstrates that linking up like-minded people is the best way of strengthening your power base and making change. Take the example of community action. Getting information out quickly to a lot of people may seem terribly hard, but there is a simple way: the telephone tree. All this requires is a bit of organisation. When you have some information to get out, each woman rings, say, three to five people on her list. Those people then have their own lists of people to ring. So long as they understand the importance of making those calls, the information will get out faster than by jungle drums. The last person rung on the tree then rings the first caller to make the information loop complete.

A newer way of networking, but in principle no different from the telephone tree, is by computer. If you have access to the Internet, posting messages on websites and sending messages by email are the fastest ways of getting information out. You can set up a mailing list of email addresses and send one message out to the lot of them, asking those who get your message to pass it on to their own contacts. We need to use modern technology and be open to new ideas. Once, politicians stood on soap boxes, or on the back of trains visiting remote towns to get their messages across. Now the messages can be sent faster and better in new ways. The old principles apply to new methods: get accurate information out fast.

Another important aspect of taking people with you is seeing that the personal is political. You are neither alone nor a victim just because you are a woman. You will not be destroyed by an attack upon you that tries to say you are. Being female is often used as a weapon by an opponent. If you let them, this can shake your self-confidence – you can't change sex, after all, or not without so much difficulty as to make this an unrealistic option. If you let personal attacks get to you, you can be immobilised.

It's worth spending time developing your self-acceptance as a woman. We have both had to do this. Neither of us is, in accepted masculinist terms, pretty, yet we are both comfortable with how we look. We can deal with ridicule of our appearance – Joan having being portrayed for years in political cartoons as 'the polka-dot premier', Moira as a pink-plumed, grim-faced ideologue during the Constitutional Convention in 1998. These personal attacks are political. They are meant to shut you up or make you look silly, so that you will not be taken seriously. Don't take them to heart. Turn them to your advantage.

'YOU STUPID WOMAN'

It was in the Victorian parliament, on 10 May 1989. I was Minister for Education, and Jeff Kennett was the Leader of the Opposition. We were head to head on spending on government education. Jeff repeatedly interjected, saying very quickly and quietly across the table at question time, 'You stupid woman. You *are* a stupid woman.' (Hansard didn't pick it up because he didn't have his microphone on.) It was designed to upset me; instead, I decided to make his bullying tactics the issue. I demanded that the Speaker make Mr Kennett withdraw, and I put into Hansard that 'He just used an extraordinarily sexist term for this parliament. I find interesting the attitude of the Opposition to women in this place.' Mr Kennett refused to withdraw.

This was picked up by the major Victorian papers – the *Herald Sun* and the *Age* – and there were days of stories. I made it very clear that I objected to the allusion to women being too stupid for politics. Other women MPs on the Labor side said that they had been subjected to a campaign of sexist abuse too. Damien Murphy, the state political reporter for the *Age*, ran the other stories: that Opposition MPs had called me 'foreman material' and 'the best man in Cabinet' and that an apple had been left in my office with a note reading 'To JK: an apple for the teacher', signed by 'a secret admirer'. He also ran the story, on 11 May 1989, that Alan Stockdale, later Victorian Treasurer, had remarked on the cost of my clothes and at one stage referred to the ALP women MPs as a 'knitting circle'.

Of course, Jeff made things worse for himself outside parliament by denying he was sexist in terms that proved that he was. He told the *Age* that 'The Liberal Party had difficulty recruiting female MPs because more of our female members tend, I think, to spend more time at home bringing up their children'; that he was passing comment on my intelligence, not my sex, and 'if she can't wear it in the bear pit . . . she could think of another career'. It was hardly his fault I had been born a woman, he told the *Herald Sun*. 'What's the matter with the lady? For goodness' sake, she's in politics. If she wants to be in a nursing home, go to a nursing home, but if she wants to be involved in politics . . . then stop whingeing about it and get on with the job.'

The media backed me, wholeheartedly.

At that time Jeff's leadership was under considerable
pressure: not long after, Alan Brown replaced him as Leader of
the Opposition.

Joan

When we started writing this book we asked ourselves and some
of our women friends what was the highest compliment we had
ever received. Joan said that the best ever was from a woman
she didn't know who approached her shortly after she had lost
office as Premier and said, 'I want to thank you for what you've
done. Now my daughter knows that she can be Premier.'

A compliment of a different kind came in 1965. Joan had
telephoned a government department and overheard one bureau-
crat say to another in the background (there were no mute
buttons on telephones in those days), 'It's that bloody woman
again, what shall we tell her?' Joan has taken 'that bloody woman'
as a compliment ever since. It usually shows you are getting
somewhere.

Eva Cox has often said that being called a troublemaker
was her highest compliment. Bella Abzug once said that she
had been called argumentative, aggressive and difficult, but that
whatever they called her, they knew she was a serious woman.
Sometimes compliments are double-edged. In 1985 one of Moira
Rayner's fellow lawyers told her that, in his view, she wasn't a
woman lawyer, she was an honorary bloke. What he meant to
say was that he accepted her as an equal, professionally, but it
had a profound and discomfiting effect on Moira.

Mary Gaudron, Australia's only woman on the High Court,
said in September 1997 when she launched the Australian Women
Lawyers Association that the reason women lawyers were not
better represented in the profession, and that male lawyers had
not been improved by the consequent competition, was that:

for all sorts of reasons, women did not really dare to be different from their male colleagues, did not dare to be women lawyers. To be different, to challenge the codes of conduct derived, as often as not, from rules developed on the playing fields of Eton for the male members of the British aristocracy, would have been to invite ostracism, perhaps, even, the attention of the Ethics committee; to assert that women were different, with different needs, would have been construed as an acknowledgement of incompetence; to question the bias of the law would have been to invite judgement as to one's fitness to be a member of the profession. And thus, very many of us became honorary men. We thought that was equality and, on that account, we rightly deserved the comment of the graffitist who wrote, 'Women who want equality lack ambition.'

Note that four strong women identified what was intended as, or actually was, a snub or an insult by powerful men and called it a compliment. There is a lesson here. Even insults can be, unintentionally, a tribute. At the very least, they can be turned against a would-be offender. Joan's confrontation with Jeff Kennett in parliament made a difference, improving her community standing and damaging his. Turning a setback into an advantage is one of the key strategies we recommend for women. Our message is this: make your (feminist) values and the politics of being a woman part of your life. Your experience counts, and should be made to count. You have the right to make your own choices and be yourself. Take it, and use it. You will be rewarded.

horacek

chapter 3

Personal tactics

As you read through the suggestions in this chapter, bear these three principles in mind:

1   be prepared   All change will be met with resistance: face the resistance, and it often disappears.

2   accept yourself   You may not be perfect, but you are perfectible. Our self-image shapes how we behave, who we mix with, what we try to do and what we try to avoid. Self-image influences how much we like the world and it likes us, and how much we will succeed in life on our own terms.

The reason you want power is to make a difference, a real difference, and preferably quickly. But first you must accept yourself. You must be confident in what you believe, and in your capacity to make change: that is how you persuade others. You must stand up for what you believe in and value. You also have the right – the need – to be who you are. Who decides your self-image? You or someone else? Does it depend on others' approval? That would leave you tremendously vulnerable. Unless you understand and accept yourself, no-one can make you feel good and anyone can make you feel bad. One of the easiest ways to boost your self-image is to accept and give compliments and praise. Practise this.

3   give as well as demand respect   People deserve respect because they are people, each with something unique to contribute. If you give respect to people, by and large you will be respected.

BUILDING YOUR SELF-RESPECT

Treat building your self-respect as a task worthy of your time, thought and energy:

+ Deserve it. Know what you value: always act with integrity
+ Drop that false modesty and accept compliments
+ Recognise when your work has been well done – don't keep trying to improve it
+ Be self-aware, identifying your strengths and weaknesses, letting go beliefs that weaken you
+ Risk change
+ Overcome fear. Learn to call it excitement
+ Value yourself, privately and publicly. This does not mean overlooking your frailties and failings or becoming an egotistical monster
+ Build *constructive* criticism into your daily program
+ Keep close to you the people who will always tell you the truth, but with love
+ Learn how to identify the 'monkey chatter' – the inner voices that tell you you're no good or worthless – and the button-pushers, the triggers that make you react

badly. Recognising the voices means you are halfway past them, without suppressing them, because that only means they can bounce back at the most inconvenient time, when they are least expected

+ Polish your external image – know that people judge you by how you seem, and that if you seem confident you are likely to become so
+ Seek out positive people
+ Expect to be respected: respect others
+ Most of all, dream. What would you like to be? How would you like to change the world? Be specific.

BEING YOURSELF

Although people do judge by appearances, you're the best judge of yourself. Your image must be a true one.

Mo Mowlam, Britain's Secretary of State for Northern Ireland, is a breath of fresh air on image issues. A 1997 poll in the UK showed her to be more popular than her leader, Prime Minister Tony Blair. Mo says it as she sees it, and she dresses and acts as she likes. Initially, she was criticised. During the 1997 election campaign the tabloids attacked her for gaining weight, losing what they called her 'fanciable' status, and looking frumpy. They looked pretty silly when she revealed that she had had a benign brain tumour; the treatment had made her moon-shaped, her hair had fallen out, and her so-called 'mousy' hairstyle was a wig. Shortly after the election Mo drew gasps of admiration when she took her wig off during a meeting with journalists, explaining that it was too hot and making her itchy. She carried on the interview – bald.

Secretary Mo takes the same approach to her whole political life. During the Irish peace talks Protestant prisoners delivered an ultimatum to their party: 'quit the negotiations'. Mo went to see the prisoners, sitting down with men who, according to experienced prison officers, were some of the hardest to be found in any prison in the world. She told them that 'what you see is what you get', and persuaded them to withdraw their demands and authorise their political representatives to go back to the talks. The rest is history, made by a strong woman who didn't have to be slim to be powerful.

CHANGING THE RULES

Every group has its own habits, culture, practices, and unspoken rules for leadership and authority.

In his book *Intelligent Leadership* Alistair Mant tells the story of Imo, a young member of a large colony of monkeys under study by Japanese scientists. They wanted to learn how monkeys interacted socially, and how they learned. They did it by providing them with food in unusual ways, without disturbing their natural foraging pattern, and observing what they did with it.

Imo, just eighteen months old, was the first monkey to wash the sand from the sweet potatoes the scientists left for them. All the others painstakingly picked off the grains, but Imo promptly washed them away in the stream.

After a while another youngster copied this method. Then Imo's mother did. Very slowly, mainly amongst the young and within families, the practice grew. The young ones started, then were followed by their mothers, who in turn were copied by the new infants. But the powerful males at the top of the group's pecking order never adopted the practice. They never came into contact with the young ones.

Yet when the top male monkey was persuaded to try a new and delicious food, the top female copied him at once, and then the whole band of monkeys took to it within just four hours. Why? Because everyone watches a leader. Nobody attends to an Imo.

Mant finds three lessons in this story. The first is that young or lowly members of groups understand practical things very well. They see the detail or the task as it affects them, if not the big picture. They have much to teach. We should learn from them.

The second lesson is that you can't predict where real talent will be found. It is important to get clever and innovative people into top positions so that the group benefits from their ideas and energy – wherever they are.

The third is that sometimes the obvious is culturally invisible. Mant remarks that when he tells Imo's story to his executive audiences and invites them to speculate out loud why Imo's bright ideas were taken up so slowly, it doesn't take them long to point out that Imo's youth was a reason. It takes a lot longer for them to work out that Imo was female. She was impotent because she was never given the attention that the powerful, top-status male – and mediocre – monkeys got. As he says, 'There is no use in having cleverness about the place unless it is tapped efficiently . . . There are many reasons other than femaleness for the neglect of talent, but it is without doubt the most spectacular cause for waste of intelligence in organisations.'

A fourth lesson, and the crucial one, that we draw from the story is that if you're a woman you shouldn't wait to be noticed. Don't ever assume that your hard work, creativity, intelligence – even genius – will be recognised and rewarded. You can't change the world unless you're top monkey!

So how do you get to the top, and how do you stay effective? Start with working out what the rules are, see if you can make them work for you. And if you can't, work together, and write your own. Successful women write their own rules, based on their own and other women's experience.

A CASE STUDY
LISA BELLEAR (GOERNPIL)

Lisa Bellear is an Aboriginal poet, photographer and community activist with a string of positive achievements in academic and community life. She is a wonderful example of a woman claiming power on her own terms, for her own people and for all young women. Her tactics for success focus on the personal:

+ Know what you're dealing with – if it's an issue of policy, get it and read it. Ask for advice, and take it
+ Always look for support when you take up a cause, and surround yourself with people you care about, and who care about you – and if they're having a bad time send them a card. You know how they feel
+ Talk to people you can trust – look for healing when you hurt. Seek out teachers – they're everywhere. One of mine, the late Dinny O'Hearn, told me when I was a student that you have to have solid foundations
+ Look for role models, and ask them how they got where they are. Follow them around, go to meetings where they're speaking, even if you feel shy – just watch and listen
+ Be a role model, or a mentor, especially for younger people coming up
+ Celebrate achievements. It doesn't have to be much – writing an essay to commemorate the anniversary of the 1967 referendum recognising Aboriginal people in our constitution was one way. Just have a morning tea – it's no big deal. Have healing celebrations
+ Praise yourself – social workers know how to do it. Maybe nobody else will praise you
+ Know there is a glass ceiling, but think that if you lift yourself just a little, it'll break – it's that low

+ Work with what you can control. Write letters: this helps you to clarify issues for yourself, and if you want to take up an issue with someone write them a personal letter, so that the receiver won't feel embarrassed and will be more likely to respond
+ Try to publish articles, poems, stories that will be useful, or that will fulfil your need to be creative. There are many groups publishing newsletters often aching for work to publish, and lots of opportunities to build up a publications record
+ Write submissions – you can often get copies of publications and reports for nothing from people
+ Don't stress yourself. If you've got a paper to write, do it in plenty of time so you don't get anxious
+ Find ways to relax – that will free you up. Don't take on too many committees, either. Prioritise, and remember what pays the rent
+ When you're feeling vulnerable, hurt or sad, go where you'll be looked after. You need to be able to cry sometimes, and be human. Do it, but do it somewhere safe, where no-one will be jealous or judgemental. Be protective of yourself. Don't try to explain yourself to a taxi driver when you're feeling stressed
+ Become notorious. I did
+ Keep contributing, and always follow through.

A CASE STUDY

FAY MARLES

Fay Marles is well known in Victoria. She has spent decades in community activity, holding important public offices: President of the Alfred Group of Hospitals, Deputy Chancellor of Melbourne University, Deputy Chair of the State Trust Corporation, Director of the Victorian Mental Health Research

Institute, and President of the Committee of Management of the University of Melbourne's Key Centre for Women's Health in Society, among others.

Fay graduated in social work from Melbourne University, and at 25 was the first social worker appointed to the academic staff of Queensland University. Then, like most women of her era, she married, became pregnant and left the workforce. She brought up her four children in country Victoria. At 47 Fay won a Melbourne Univeristy postgraduate research scholarship. She gained her Master of Arts two years later and was appointed a senior tutor at Melbourne, then became a lecturer in the School of Social Work. At 51 she was appointed Victoria's first Commissioner for Equal Opportunity. She recalls:

I remember vividly being bullied at school when I was seven. It was a lesson. If you want to avoid such misery you must get with the strength and be part of a group. I have never been a bully, but very early I learnt the importance of power. When I analysed it later, I knew that I wanted to achieve change rather than power over people.

I have always planned whatever I've done and have rarely taken my eye off the big picture. I don't believe that opportunities just happen.

When I graduated, working towards social change was my goal, and I saw social research as the instrument. Later, with four children in a country town, I became opportunistic: I took chances as they came. For several years I was a country-based part-time social worker, but I was also an entrepreneur: I restored and sold old furniture and held exhibitions of antique prints.

Later the opportunity came to do a History MA on a research scholarship from Melbourne University, and from

there I went onto the university staff. The tutorship I
accepted was the least rewarding financially, but it was
heading me in the direction I had always wanted to go.
Later, in 1977, I had to make a choice. I was offered a
senior lectureship at Melbourne University at the same time
that I was invited to become Victoria's first Commissioner
for Equal Opportunity.

I took the Equal Opportunity job because it went to the
heart of my values. It was protecting the rights of women;
it was exciting; it was risky; and most of all it held the
prospect of effecting real change. I have never regretted it.
I found discrimination of a magnitude I hadn't previously
imagined, and I was part of changes that exceeded anything
in my previous experience.

I have always been clear about my core values, which
came directly from my upbringing and were reinforced by
my professional training. My personal rules for success are:

+ Be trustworthy – be honest with yourself and others
+ Know yourself; analyse your own values and assumptions –
  you are the instrument you are working with
+ Verify any assumptions you are acting on, particularly in
  relation to other people's motivation – different people
  can think very differently
+ Make yourself known, and make yourself available to
  those you need to get on with, such as corporate leaders,
  bureaucrats or politicians. For instance, I got my
  departmental head to introduce me to the businesses and
  other organisations I would have to work with and receive
  complaints against. It was much easier to have a
  confrontation against a background of goodwill and
  mutual trust
+ Write your own letters and speeches – they must
  communicate the real you

- ✦ Accept outside voluntary appointments if they in some way support your main job – this creates a support network and makes you less dependent on your immediate work situation
- ✦ Use your networks to assist you to negotiate at a top level
- ✦ Plan for the hard times – emotional and material – so that you don't find yourself trapped or helpless when adversity hits
- ✦ Get professional training on how to handle the media
- ✦ Identify your natural base of support and make sure you keep those relationships healthy, even if it demands time in a busy schedule – at some stage you will almost certainly need your friends. For me, they were in the women's movement, and I called on them time and time again
- ✦ Finally, listen to your intuition; it is an important source of knowledge. And never forget, an unexpected reaction signals something you do not know. Treasure your surprises: they have something to teach you.

SETTING YOUR OWN VALUES

Sometimes the organisation you work within or need help from, such as a political party or a professional group, has rules that fundamentally conflict with your personal values. What do you do about it? What if, to get the standing and influence you need, you have to rely on patronage and nepotism, arrangements that have nothing to do with merit, and are expected to return the favour?

You have to decide whether the big picture – your objective – is important enough for you to withstand this kind of deal-doing. You will always have to make choices. You won't do this unless you are clear about your personal values. Power

CAREER ADVICE No. 87

There's more to finding your own vision than just getting the right sunglasses

My god - the world needs more social justice as well as 100% UV protection

horacek

is about the art of the possible, which means compromising, but you can lose your soul if you're not very careful. So you must work out for yourself what your values are. You need to have an ethical system for making those tough decisions, or you risk becoming an entirely reactive individual.

'You move politics along by being able to inject a sense of vision about certain values,' Mary Robinson said when she was elected President of Ireland. 'Take, for example, relations on this island. If it's possible to project the values of pluralism, of respect for difference, of accommodating and finding space for difference, that should influence the policies of a political framework for peace and reconciliation.'

We believe that most women share some core values born of their experience:

+ Respect for difference
+ The need to build in, and take, time to reflect
+ Inclusion
+ People being valued not as consumers or shareholders, but as citizens.

BUILT-IN VALUES

I expect to have my values respected. They are so fundamental that I don't need to spell them out to myself any more. I know what I believe in:

+ All people are of equal worth
+ Everyone has an equal right to shape their own lives
+ Everyone has an equal right to be able to meet their basic needs
+ To achieve this, it is necessary to spread opportunities and life chances as widely as possible, to eliminate inequalities, to accept personal and political responsibility, and to promote community participation and ownership of decisions.

Joan

You have to determine your own values, but whatever yours are, work them out, write them down, practise them, and be accountable for them. Many people do not agree with our views – but very few don't know where we stand. Moira found it invaluable to reflect on different people's ethics checklists, such as the one in *Organisational Behaviour* by S. P. Robbins and others, then develop her own; we hope you find Moira's checklist just as helpful.

A CASE STUDY
MOIRA RAYNER'S ETHICS CHECKLIST

A few years ago, I had to make quite a few decisions
that tested my sense of right and wrong – my intuitive
understanding of myself as an individual in society. So I sat
down one terrible weekend when I had a very hard decision
to make, and I wrote some out. Now I've got the Rayner
Ethics Checklist on my electronic organiser for instant
reference. I'm constantly reviewing them, but right now
this is what they say:

+ Have I defined the problem properly? How do I know?
+ How would I describe the problem if I were in the other
  person's shoes or taking the other side of our argument?
+ How did this situation come about in the first place? Did
  I create it? If I did, should that affect my decision?
+ Where are my loyalties as a person and as a member of
  the organisation? Is there a conflict? Which is more
  important?
+ What do I hope to achieve by making this decision?
+ What is the likely result of my decision? (Be honest.)
  How do my intentions compare with this?
+ Could my decision injure someone? If so, have I a duty to
  protect them? Could it hurt me? Should that change my
  decision?
+ Could I discuss this problem with the people who will be
  affected by my decision, before I make it? If not, why not?
+ Further down the track, am I confident that the stand
  I am thinking of taking now will seem as defensible?
  If not, should I do it?
+ Could I disclose my planned decision, and reasons, to
  people whose authority or opinion matters a lot to me?
  (This could be my father, or the secretary of a
  department, or the chief executive of the company I work

for, or my professional body, or even the media.) If not,
what will it do to my self-respect to act anyway?

✦ If my decision, and my action, is understood, could it
have some symbolic effect? What would that be? What
messages would I be giving if my decision were
misunderstood? Are these consistent with my intentions
and my values?

I used something like these questions in July 1993 when
I had to decide whether or not to ask the Victorian anti-
discrimination tribunal, then called the Equal Opportunity
Board, to restrain the government from moving women
prisoners out of women's prisons and into K Division of
Pentridge (men's) Prison.

The problem was acute. As Commissioner for Equal
Opportunity I was required to protect the Act and its
principles, and the interests of those who were most
vulnerable to discrimination, until a public inquiry was
complete. I had decided, after an investigation into Barwon
Prison, that women suffer badly in prisons run for a
majority population of men. The Act required me to resolve
the findings of my investigation by negotiation. If I could
not, I had to refer my investigation to the Board for a
public inquiry.

But there were strong rumours that the government
was going to shut down Fairlea, the women's prison, and
move the women into Pentridge to save money. The Act did
not give anyone, explicitly, the right to ask for an
injunction to protect the women's interests in the
meantime – pending the public inquiry – but if nobody did,
the women could be moved and the prisons decommissioned
at any moment (and this probably could not be undone).

Yet the women prisoners could not take legal action,
either. If I did ask for an injunction, my act would be

controversial, get a lot of publicity, could be misunderstood as a political act – when I felt it was my statutory responsibility – and would be extremely unpopular with the government. There was a real risk that the Equal Opportunity Act would be changed and my office lose some of its power, or I might lose my job. Yet the values underpinning the legislation also required that I do something: what was the point of such a job if its values could not be implemented?

I could not confide in anyone. At the end of that weekend the decision was clear: my values and those of the Act required that I take the action. So I did. Everything I expected to happen did. Victorians supported the women's position, the government decided not to move the women prisoners into Pentridge, the Act was changed, and I did lose my job.

So, as you set off on your power trajectory:

+ Establish your values and stick to them
+ Make them clear to everyone around you, and build your credibility
+ Have a passion for what you believe: it will give you the courage to endure and overcome.

Having a well-known and consistent set of values is a very good protection against being seduced by others, or accepting power from others on their terms. The important thing to remember is that if you accept power from someone else you aren't being given anything. You will always be dependent on them. And whose agenda will you be following then?

KNOWING WHOSE RESPECT YOU REALLY VALUE

When you have hard decisions to make, you need to protect your self-respect. You need to imagine getting up tomorrow and asking yourself whether you respect yourself for the decisions or actions you've taken today. You need the respect of those close to you. You also need – though sometimes you may have to do without it – the respect of the community. It doesn't matter whether your enemy respects you, because that's not who you're doing it for.

Make a diagram of the people whose respect you value, showing:

+ You at the centre (a head-and-shoulders photo would be good)
+ Those you trust completely in the inner circle – Mum, Dad, your partner, a mentor, a counsellor or a role model, people who actually have a relationship with you, whose opinion you value
+ Those whose opinion, if asked, would be frankly given, and who would keep a confidence but who are not quite that close, in the second circle
+ Those who can help, but in limited areas, in the third circle.

Check the diagram regularly and update it. These are the people who will keep you on track, and sane. You are going to need them.

THE PEOPLE IN YOUR LIFE

Never forget that you have a family and that it is a shared responsibility to keep it together, whether that family is just your parents, a life partner, or includes children. Children can suffer a lot when parents get caught up in their own work or political responsibilities and forget about them. But they can also cope with a lot, so long as they know they are loved and respected. Children are resilient, but they are also very observant. They have very effective bullshit meters and can tell when you are insincere or using them.

Moira has an adopted daughter; Joan has three children, a daughter-in-law, and two grandchildren. Joan's children coped in a range of ways with her very demanding role. They are all impressive young adults now, involved in work, family and friends.

In our view children cope best when:

+ They understand what is happening and how it will affect them
+ They can contribute, or know why they can't
+ They feel at least in some way in control of the situation
+ They feel that they, or someone they know and care about, benefits from what you are doing
+ They are absolutely certain that they are loved for them-selves and that they are not wheeled out as showpieces when it's convenient for adults
+ The basic framework of their physical, emotional and intellectual lives is secure.

Children need reassurance that your job is not as important as they are, but you can still help them to understand that it is important for you to achieve something that is worthwhile for other people, as well as you. They need to feel that the family can still have fun together. And if you are a public figure, they need to know that they are not responsible for your acts. Children also need to feel secure about:

+ Getting to school, childcare, sport, music or appointments with their friends and family on time
+ Knowing who will be at home and away from home, and when
+ Knowing who they or their teacher can contact if there is a crisis or something goes wrong
+ Knowing that if they really need you, your partner or someone else they love and trust will drop everything and be there for them

+ Knowing that, if there are rules for their behaviour and contribution to the family, you abide by the rules as well
+ Knowing that there will be some protected family time and certain weekends and holidays, and that if something has to be changed there will be negotiations
+ Knowing that even if you are an important person you are still Mum
+ Feeling that, when they have two parents, both share responsibility for them and love them unconditionally.

Children won't cope if:

+ You try to buy their love instead of making time for them
+ You don't listen to them
+ You don't have consistent rules for their behaviour (and yours)
+ You tell them how they're feeling
+ You expect them to have quality time with you, but always at your convenience
+ You always give your work priority over their needs: some never get over it
+ They feel their lives are out of control, because yours is
+ They feel responsible for their parents' happiness. It's the other way around.

Think more widely about the people in your life. Your friends, your support network, the people you work closely with are tremendously important. When you are stressed and take it out on them you damage yourself as well as them.

If you have staff, remember that they're the ones who do the messy work and get things done. Never ask them to do things you won't, such as the washing up. If they're under pressure, pitch in and help, reorganise timetables or get extra help. It's also important to have regular events to show your appreciation and enable everyone to see each other in a different light; to say thank you for big and little services. And be aware of family needs, too. There's no point in illuminating the city if your own home's left in darkness.

SEIZE THE DAY

You have two options: seize your day or just cope with it. But anything is possible with the four Ps: purpose, plan, practicalities, and perseverance. This goes for your personal aims and your political ones too.

You can choose to:

+ Leave a cleared, organised workplace for the next day's work **OR** close the door and hope the pixies will fix it
+ Come home to the meal you cooked and froze on the weekend **OR** buy a high-calorie sweet snack, or whatever's available in the local takeaway on the way home
+ Eat a meal at the table, without TV, and share your household's stories of the day **OR** stay at work until the family mealtime is over and eat toast and cheese, miserably, in front of the TV
+ Tick off your achievements at the end of the day and list your tasks for tomorrow **OR** worry about the day you've just had, and the day ahead, and have one or two stiff drinks to 'relax'
+ Relax and pamper yourself a bit – take a hot bath, get a manicure or a facial, get some time alone – **OR** be a couch potato
+ Repack your bag and briefcase and set out clothes and accessories **OR** leave it till the next morning and guarantee you'll rush or forget something
+ Set the alarm (try music instead of a buzzer) for two hours before you have to leave **OR** wake up when you're ready and shout at everyone that they're late
+ Listen to the news as you do stretching exercises, take

Vitamin B-plus and drink water or orange juice **OR** jump out of bed seeing stars and have a black, black coffee to wake up

✦ Get half an hour's exercise – walk, jog, swim, whatever is your thing – **OR** run around the house doing the jobs you didn't do last night (this might still be good physical exercise but it's stressful)

✦ Start the day with a good breakfast **OR** eat something on the run, and leave terse instructions to your household as you head out the door

✦ If you have family responsibilities, check their arrangements for the day, making sure your kids have their lunches ready, and are secure about being collected from school or childcare **OR** get anxious calls from the kids and watch your blood pressure rise

✦ During the day, take time to stretch, talk to a friend, buy some flowers, gaze out the window and dream of the future **OR** keep up your pace all day and go flat out until you feel like collapsing, or do.

You have a choice: you can live a marvellous life, or you can be a martyr. And remember, if it's too hard you're probably doing it wrong.

BEING PREPARED

Shop rarely. Buy groceries in bulk and stock up. Use a list and stick to it. Have the supermarket deliver and do it once a month, unless you have a partner with the time and the will. You won't have time to do a weekly shop – unless of course you like it. Then you can add to the basics with little luxuries.

Fix it yourself. Learn to do the most basic of home maintenance and small repairs for yourself, rather than waiting for your partner to find the time to do it (causing unnecessary tension), or sitting at home all day waiting for the repairer to call. If you have a small toolkit you can do most of them, even if they are only temporary fixes. You will need a full set of screwdrivers, a light hammer, a drill with a masonry bit, pliers, shears, a variety of screws, nails and tacks (a staple-gun is very handy), a spare set of fuses, and a good all-purpose glue. You also need to know where the gas, electricity, water and phone connections are, and how to turn them off in an emergency. But don't ever try to fix your own electrical appliances.

Plan your wardrobe. Look at your timetable for all the days of the week, especially if you're travelling, and make sure you've got an outfit for the occasion and the climate. You can't wear your favourite suit if its hem is down or it's at the dry-cleaners. We set out our clothes the night before.

Simplify your life. You don't need to run three bank accounts, or to spend a day a month paying the bills. Wherever possible, collapse complicated arrangements into simple ones. Pay your bills on your credit card, for instance (but only if you have the discipline not to spend the cash in the meantime).

Have another look at your housework. Your home doesn't always have to be spotless. Just keep it as tidy and clean as you need it to be in order to find things and feel at home and relaxed. Your time is too valuable. If you have children and their room is a midden, shut the door on it and move in only when you can hear the rats scurrying. Children often use their room as the first place to assert their individuality. Don't fight the inevitable. God won't strike you down if you don't iron the underpants, and tea-towels are meant to look crumpled. Your household needs your time and attention, not you snapping and snarling because you're feeling ratty. Do the bits you like. Other household members will pick up their own dry-cleaning once they're down to the last pair of pants, and do their own washing if it's left to pile up. If those you live with say that they need to be shown how to do such intelligence-taxing tasks as using the washing machine or the vacuum cleaner, don't fall for it: this is a very useful campaign to avoid doing their fair share. (Moira's husband used to break at least one dish each time he washed up.) And if they can't cook? Well, you don't need to cook a three-course meal to prove that you love people – leave the makings of pizza in the fridge. Most of all, eat together, talk together, listen. Love and good company are the best spices.

If you have companion animals (dogs or cats especially) and a lot of out-of-hours meetings to go to, or you travel a lot, make a standing arrangement with someone to feed them regularly for you. You don't want guilt over a wandering cat being hit by a car to complicate your life. Make arrangements with a kennel you trust for those times when they need to be boarded – preferably one that picks them up and delivers them. The extra money is well worth it.

Write a 'to do' list at the beginning of each week and review it during the week, ticking things off as you go. This will ensure you don't miss anything and will give you a sense of reassurance and achievement.

WRITE EVERYTHING DOWN

Memory is a fallible instrument. If you keep everything in your head, it'll be lost some day and someone else's recall might appear to be more credible than yours. So keep a diary, or two, and records of what you've said and done.

You need an appointments diary, one small enough to carry everywhere. Write it up in pencil so that when you have to change something you can, without leaving a scribbled mess that you can't read. It might be useful to keep a copy of your diary at home for the family, so that they know where you are, or if you have a personal assistant, leave it with them. There should always be someone who knows where you are and what you're doing.

You should also have a workbook in which you keep notes of all the meetings you have, putting the date of those meetings at the top of the page and starting a fresh page for every day. If you're really organised, keep an index of important things in the front. If you do this you will have a record, not bits of paper and a faulty memory, of whom you talked with and when. And you can refer back to it. If nowhere else, this is where you should record successes, concessions, promises and agreements. Check it regularly so that you don't forget to follow up on what you said you'd do.

Get into the habit of taking notes, jotting down key points (not every word that's said) and details of agreements, tasks, dates, times, and who is to do what. Keep copies of letters, notes, telephone discussions and notices in a folder in date order. Ideally, your date-order folder would be cross-referenced to the specific files you keep on the particular issue. You'll also need a simple system of reminders for your important dates. Many software programs have this facility, but there is also a Luddite option for those who don't use computers. Keep a copy of letters you have to answer or do something about, or which you have written requesting others to do something, in a concertina file that has compartments marked with the numbers 1–31, one compartment for each day of the month. Then check the file daily to ensure that the appropriate action has been taken. This 'tickler' system is almost infallible.

When you have a meeting, offer to write the agenda and have it agreed on at the start of the meeting. That structures the discussion. If it's an important meeting, appoint someone – or volunteer yourself – to take the minutes. Then, you write up what the discussion was about and who agreed to do what. Most men don't realise how important such minute-keeping is and think it's inferior work. It isn't: it's a contemporaneous record, and if push comes to shove, it's evidence. Minute everything. Send copies of your minutes to the people who were there and ask them to review them straight away.

If you're starting out in an organisation, it's quite a good strategy to start as the secretary. By writing everything down you really have a lot of influence (you have to work hard for it too, of course). If you ever become the president or head of an organisation, make absolutely certain that the secretary is your friend.

ONCE AN ACTIVIST . . .

I found the transition from lobbyist to Minister quite hard sometimes. When deputations came to see me for lobbying purposes I would ask, 'Aren't you taking notes?' As a lobbyist, you should make sure that you set the agenda and take careful notes. People you're talking to may be a bit discomfited, but you can be absolutely sure that if they don't want to do what you want them to do, they would rather you weren't writing down what they are saying. I found that people who came to see me were so grateful, even though they had a right to do so, that they would sit there awed and the only person taking notes would be my adviser. One day I just got sick of it, put down the pen and said, 'How on earth are you going to remember what I said? Write it down, and then send me a note, we'll check it out and then we'll know what we agreed.'

Joan

TAKE RESPONSIBILITY FOR YOUR OWN HEALTH

If you're occasionally tired or sick or sad or overwhelmed, that's normal. But if it's how you're feeling all the time you need to check where and why you aren't looking.

+ Look after yourself **physically** – keep fit, eat and sleep well, make sure you get good medical advice and that you follow it

- Look after yourself **emotionally** – love your children and grandchildren, appreciate your parents, value and keep friends, but keep space for yourself as well
- Look after yourself **creatively** – don't crush yourself with possessions. (William Morris, the English designer, once wrote, 'Have nothing in your houses that you do not know to be useful, or believe to be beautiful.') Take time to enjoy beautiful objects and music and read wonderful books. Take the time to make something – cakes, quilts, poetry, a garden, whatever you enjoy. Take the time to dream
- Look after yourself **intellectually** – read, listen, analyse, and argue.

If you're tired or hung-over, you can't do anything much. Don't drink alcohol, other than the health-enhancing one glass of wine a day, during the working week – we realise this means that for some workaholics they can't drink at all. You don't have to be hung-over to be affected by the drinks you had the night before; they could be what's making you feel not quite up to it in the mornings.

Drink a lot of water, eat a lot of vegetables, never eat snack food or in-flight food for your main meal, and get some exercise every day – even if it's just a brisk walk first thing in the morning. If your work requires regular travel, invest in good walking shoes and a comfortable light tracksuit that you can take anywhere.

Find a good doctor – one you can talk to and feel comfortable with. A doctor can be much more effective if you are fully informed about your health, which is really the only way you can co-operate with any treatment. Read up about your condition and any prescribed medication so you can ask intelligent questions. A good doctor builds a relationship of trust. Don't waste your time with a patronising doctor (of either sex), especially one who says, 'I don't mean to patronise you, but . . .'

Most active women – at work, in politics or the community – get exhausted at times. You can deal with it by taking
time for yourself, daydreaming of success, doing good things for
your body (try a full night's sleep occasionally) and taking care
of your physical health. If you don't, you will pay.

When Joan finished up as Victorian Premier in 1992 and
the pressure of daily media appearances was gone, her physical
system simply collapsed. She put on weight, developed tendonitis,
had two falls and broke some bones, and couldn't get going
again for twelve months. The exhaustion just caught up with her.
When Moira finished up as Commissioner for Equal Opportunity
in 1994, she couldn't believe how dog-tired she was – so tired
she couldn't sleep. She kept going in other work – as a legal
consultant, writing books and a newspaper column, speaking –
and she too put on weight, had a couple of falls and broke her
ribs and an ankle, and then acquired diabetes.

It is no coincidence that we both had similar experiences.
We forgot to put into practice what we are now preaching to
you. So, from our own experience, we say that when after a
long struggle you're having an attack of 'I can't go on':

+ Take stock of your health
+ Fix up your underlying problems – weight, back, depression, or whatever – with daily exercise, physiotherapy,
  psychotherapy. See a chiropractor or a naturopath, or, if
  you have to, have surgery. Don't put it off
+ Rebalance your life. Joan and her husband bought an
  off-the-road van and now go away for short holidays and
  a two-month outback safari each year. Moira works from
  home one or two days a week (it's called the weekend)
+ Spend more time with the people you love – not nagging,
  or instructing or complaining, just being there
+ Learn to cook again
+ Reduce your activism to what you can manage

+ Say no more often, or charge for your services – and pass on the business you can't handle.

CONTROLLING YOUR FINANCES

Most women worry about money, and many don't manage their money properly. Yes, it would be nice to have a private income that just provided for your needs. You don't, and won't. It's crucial that you are able to pay the bills, and that you won't be in penury when you stop working. If you want to be powerful you need money, and you need control of your personal finances. Before you think about fund-raising, deal with your own attitude to money. The chances are it will be the greatest obstacle to raising money for a cause.

Good financial management is made up of two fundamental elements, neither of which is much use without the other: attitude and beliefs, and skill and knowledge.

ATTITUDE AND BELIEFS

The subconscious mind often contains beliefs that we're not consciously aware of, and which can be hard to change simply by an effort of will or a conscious desire. They manifest in our everyday lives and we can tell what they are by looking at the things happening around us. The good news is that they can be reprogrammed to clear out negative attitudes.

Subconscious programming is a result of information acquired in childhood, and programming about money is influenced by culture and upbringing. For instance, many English-speaking people tend to find discussions about money distasteful, whereas European families are more likely to talk openly about it. Many Asian cultures believe that money can only be acquired through hard work, while many Australians believe, against all the evidence to hand, that money comes from poker machines and lotteries.

Some of the symptoms of negative programming about money include:

+ A store cupboard full of canned food even when you live next door to a 24-hour supermarket (an obsession with scarcity)
+ Spending money as soon as you get it (because 'I might never get money again')
+ Overspending (same thing)
+ Abusing credit cards ('I'll never be able to save, so I'll buy it now')
+ A terror of setting budgets ('I don't want to face the reality of how little money I have')
+ Despising money ('it's the root of all evil')
+ Despising people with money ('all rich people are crooks/mean/greedy')
+ Not taking responsibility for making serious money decisions ('I'll just leave it in the bank until I decide what to do with it')
+ Giving total control of your finances to someone else ('I let my husband/financial adviser/children take care of my money')
+ Feeling trapped in a job you hate ('I can have either a good income or job satisfaction, but not both').

These beliefs sabotage your financial security. Is it likely that you will handle money well if you subconsciously believe all rich people are evil? Or that there is virtue only in poverty?

Some negative beliefs are common among women who were born before the '60s, who will often have unconsciously passed them on to their daughters:

+ Looking after money is not women's work
+ Women are naturally bad at figures
+ Women find money/finance/economics boring and therefore incomprehensible

- A woman's income in a two-income family is the second income, therefore it is trivial and doesn't need to be managed
- A woman's income is to pay for housekeeping and children's expenses, not to be invested
- Women's work is inherently less valuable, therefore it's okay for a woman to be poorly paid
- Only men who already have money can get rich by investing.

Although few of us subscribe to these notions at a conscious level, the reality of many women's lives suggests that those beliefs are still playing a significant part at an unconscious level. Beliefs about money are the reason some people on low incomes are able to pay off their houses and take overseas trips, while others earning four times as much are constantly strapped for cash. It is also the reason why four out of five big lottery winners revert to their previous financial status within five years of their big win.

Changing money beliefs can be done in any number of ways – there are many good books and courses on the market. You can do it through meditation, counselling, affirmations, timeline therapy, neuro-linguistic programming – the possibilities are infinite. Get help.

In addition to addressing subconscious beliefs, it is also important to take some conscious actions to improve your attitude to money:

- Take responsibility for your money. Begin to be in control a little at a time
- Focus on prosperity and abundance instead of scarcity and fear. Take pleasure in what you have and what you've achieved so far, no matter how small
- Work out what money represents to you. What does it enable you to do?

✦ Set clear goals which will motivate you to manage your money better. 'Why' is much more powerful than 'how' or 'should'

✦ Creative visualisation – as an exercise, regularly picture yourself setting and achieving your goals in a very specific way

✦ Be clear about your planning time and space

✦ Make a commitment and stick to it, but be kind to yourself when you fall by the wayside – guilt is not a useful habit

✦ Put your past money behaviour and habits where they belong – behind you – and focus on the present

✦ Make an agreement with yourself that your money will be of benefit to others. For example, supporting Australian-made products, giving to causes you believe in – this will help counteract the belief that money is evil

✦ Find a role model whose financial stability and integrity you admire. Find out what they did and learn from it

✦ Become a union member or a member of a business association which offers financial advise.

When Joan went to her financial counsellor for advice on converting her superannuation payout she was shocked to be asked, 'How long do you think you'll live?' Joan had never thought about it, but statistically, she learned, she'd make it to 86, another thirty years. So she was told, 'You'd better invest your super and go and get a job.'

SKILL AND KNOWLEDGE

Financial freedom means entirely different things to different people, but some basics apply to everybody. You can't have financial control without knowing where you are now and where you want to get to. There are two useful exercises to help you in this.

EXERCISE 1: WHERE AM I NOW?

This requires a pen and paper and an afternoon of facing up to the truth. It's much better to know where you stand financially than to lie awake at night worrying about it, so get it done as soon as possible.

First, write down your income, no matter how small or erratic, and your expenses – include everything. (If you don't know, there's your major problem.) If you are paid weekly, work it out weekly; if you are paid fortnightly, work it out fortnightly, and so on. If you are paid irregularly, work it out annually and then divide by twelve to make it monthly.

To complete the financial picture, also write down what you own outright (house, car, any other valuable assets), any savings you have (if none, that's okay), and what you owe. Now you have the figures to create a budget.

A successful budget should:

+ Be like a successful diet – not make you feel deprived
+ Be flexible, to allow for the unexpected
+ Be realistic. If you spend $50 per month on dog food, there's no point budgeting for $20 – the poor dog will starve
+ Allow some money for spending on things you enjoy, or you won't stick to it
+ Be designed for only a short period – for example, one month – so you can review it at the end of each period and monitor how effective it is. Keep records and receipts to allow for easy monitoring and reviewing, and make sure you do so regularly
+ Be divided into two kinds of expenditure – essential (mortgage, food, power) and optional (movies, trips, concerts)
+ Include in its essentials something inexpensive that makes you feel prosperous – flowers on the table, one cup of really good coffee every morning. This helps reinforce

your focus on prosperity rather than scarcity

✦ Include in its essentials an amount set aside before anything else, to be saved towards your goals – even if it's only $2 per week. You are now a person who saves money and, most importantly, you are in control

✦ Include a regular, truthful accounting of your credit-card spending.

If your budget is out of balance – that is, your expenses are more than your income – there are two possibilities. You need to spend less or earn more. If spending less is not an attractive option (you love the dog too much to give her away), and you don't have a way to earn more right now, then make a deal with yourself: spend less for a fixed length of time during which you will take action to enable yourself to earn more.

A CASE STUDY
KAREN DOE

After several years of working as a poorly paid art teacher, Karen (not her real name) took two years out of the workforce to study for her Master's degree. She lived in a tiny, cockroach-infested bedsit near Kings Cross while she studied full-time. She earned an erratic living as a waitress, usually on the 4 am breakfast shift, only finding out each Thursday whether she would have any work that weekend or not. During that period she managed to keep up her one love, sailing, by offering her expert services as unpaid crew on ocean-going yacht races. She gave up everything else – eating out, dressing up, going to shows, drinking good wine. At the end of the two years, she was offered a choice of jobs and is now head of the art department at a major Sydney secondary school, with real responsibilities, a good income and access to excellent teaching and art-room facilities. She never doubted that it was worth it.

EXERCISE 2: WHERE DO I WANT TO GET TO?

Money doesn't have any particular value in itself, only in what it can get you. So you are only likely to take action if you can identify some specific things that you really desire – goals. Write down a list of your goals, and remember that goals need to be:

+ Things you feel passionate about
+ Achievable, even if they take a long time
+ A mixture of short-term (up to three years) and long-term (over three years). Long-term goals should be broken down into manageable steps
+ Created with dates attached, or they are just wishes. But if you don't achieve them by the date you set, that's perfectly okay
+ Reviewed every few months to see if you still want them, and to see if you need to adjust the dates
+ Not set in concrete. If you find in a year's time you've lost interest in one, you can drop it. If goal-setting is difficult, try just writing out your dreams. Attach some dates and work out the steps to achieve them – they then become goals.

WHEN IT'S NOT ONLY YOU

If you're in a situation where joint finances operate, or you have responsibility for dependants, the basics are still the same: budgeting, goal-setting, saving. But you need to work out together where you are and where you want to go. Remember that, since people bring their own cultural and family beliefs about money to any relationship, ignoring this, or hoping it will sort itself out in time, is likely to be disastrous. It's much better to talk openly about money issues and cash flow before they create friction. Some practical tips:

+ Find a time to talk about money when nobody is feeling under stress

- Work out what you both/all believe is fair in how to manage joint finances. Look for common goals
- Think of it as a partnership or a small business, and try to keep emotional issues out of the discussion. If you can't discuss money without it turning into a fight, consider getting someone else to mediate for you – a neutral party, such as a counsellor
- If you have joint accounts, set a limit on what can be withdrawn without all signatories
- Joint investments should be in joint names, not one partner's only, in case of any future problems with the relationship
- Make sure you understand exactly what a partner might be asking you to sign, particularly in respect of things such as being guarantor, the power of attorney, and co-borrowing
- Any major assets you owned before going into the relationship will be better kept separate – the same goes for others in the household.

There is a common misperception that the person who does the bulk of the breadwinning should have all, or at least the final, say in how joint financial decisions are made. Remember that 'joint' means undivided shares, so they can only be equal. Whether you earn less or not at all, your contribution to the partnership is no less valuable. Without your contribution – managing the household, the children, aged parents; entertaining business or influential visitors – the breadwinner would have to pay someone else to do it or they wouldn't be able to earn a living. You should still make major financial decisions – buying property, for example – as equal partners.

Retain your independence where possible. Some sensible approaches include:

- Keeping your own bank/credit-card account, and managing it responsibly

+ Working out how you will manage joint finances. For example, all parties might contribute an equal amount, or a pro-rata based on what they earn. Whatever arrangement you have, it must be one everybody agrees is fair
+ Working out which expenses are joint and which are individual, and taking responsibility for your share
+ Expecting no less from your partner.

SQUEEZING THE TEATS OF THE SYSTEM

Managing money is like milking a cow: if you have the skill, with a little sensitive manipulation the bucket gets full; do it clumsily, and you'll get a tail-full of muck in your face, and no milk at all.

Learn everything you can about how the different elements of the financial system work, including banks and building societies, tax, superannuation, government benefits and schemes of assistance, investments, and, if you're going into business, different business structures and their benefits. Review where you keep your money. Look at all your bank statements and work out how much you spend in bank charges and how much interest you make. Have a separate account for bills. Total all your bills over a year (allowing for the unexpected) and put aside money to cover them. Never use it for other purposes; think of bill-paying as essential. Do some research on different accounts and find out how much each one will cost you. If you find the information confusing, just take it slowly and keep asking until you understand it. The key is to learn at a pace you feel comfortable with. You don't need to understand the All Ordinaries overnight, but once you've worked your way up to it, you'll have a much better idea of how money functions, and, more importantly, how your money can work for you.

If the thought of dealing with money scares you or seriously bores you, you can engage the services of a financial adviser. Be careful about choosing one – some are employed or paid by companies that sell a particular financial product, so their advice may not be impartial. Look for a financial adviser who is qualified, independent, and a member of a professional association, and who understands women's needs, and your needs in particular. You can find financial advisers through the Financial Planning Association of Australia, whose members have a code of conduct and a conciliation process for handling complaints free of charge. (As of October 1998 anyone with a securities licence has to belong to such a scheme.) If you know someone whose finances are healthy and who uses a financial adviser, get a recommendation from them.

If you do decide to use the expertise of an adviser, don't forget that you are still responsible for the control of your money. Use your commonsense and learn as much as you can from them. They should suggest options for what you can do with your money and give you their advice, but the ultimate decision is still up to you. A financial adviser is not a substitute for taking responsibility. Giving over control defeats the whole purpose of financial independence: to have power over your own life.

The final part of the financial system you need to come to terms with is credit cards. Everybody knows the accepted wisdom – pay them off as soon as possible and avoid overspending. If you have a credit card problem, it's probably a symptom of some negative subconscious programming. You need to do two things – address the programming, and get the cards under control. Some practical tips:

+ Get out the scissors and cut the damned things up
+ Leave them at home. That way, when you see something you 'must have' you have built in a cooling-off period. By the time you get home and back, you'll have had time to think

+ Put your credit cards into a container, fill it with water and put the whole thing in the freezer. This makes it impossible to get quick access to credit for impulse buying but isn't as drastic as cutting them up
+ Only have one card. Remember you're paying fees on them all, and you will be twice as tempted to spend if you have two
+ Keep a piece of paper with your most important goal on top of your credit card in your wallet. You'll have to decide each time whether you want to delay your goal by using the card
+ Work out what you could do without that would free up, say, $20 per week – it might mean taking lunch to work instead of buying it or giving up eating out once a week. Do it for a year and you'll have paid off $1040
+ Finally, remember this: if you really want to make a difference, get your own dollars together.

You determine the quality of your life by organising your finances and managing your time. You decide whether to spend money on a wonderful new suit and then worry about the credit-card bill, or to save for the gas bill. If you can't manage your own finances you will be constantly distracted from your big-picture aims by having to get in to pay the bill just before the electricity's cut off, for instance.

HAVE FUN

Hard work is one thing, but desperate struggle is a warning that your strategies are up the spout. It is absolutely essential to have some fun. And to maintain your sense of humour, to share it with friends and allies, and use it against your enemy if you will. It's a potent weapon.

THE JOKE'S ON JOAN

My government was under even more pressure than usual because of welfare authorities' raids on a religious sect to take away some of their children. I went to a conference the next morning and some quip was made, to which I replied: 'What's the difference between a social worker and a Rottweiler? The Rottweiler eventually lets the child go.'

Wow! What a reaction. The audience laughed (most of them). My adviser was aghast, social workers were up in arms, even the Commissioner for Equal Opportunity criticised me on the ABC, and Rottweiler owners threatened to march on Parliament House. Fortunately the Minister for Community Services, Kay Setches, had a sense of humour and a sense of balance. Apologies were demanded by the profession but not given. Stubbornly I insisted that social workers should have a sense of humour. I needed one when the joke boomeranged. Q: What is the difference between Joan Kirner and a Rottweiler? A: Rottweilers don't wear lipstick. I should have just apologised for the hurt and moved on.

Once I was out of the limelight I could let the real me loose on the public – playing 'I Love Rock and Roll' on 'The Late Show', in full leathers with a straight face and a great band. It was the best political thing I ever did but I did it for fun, and as a favour to a friend in the TV business, Jane Kennedy. I came across as human and with a good sense of the ridiculous. I didn't tell my husband though: we were watching television at home when it came on screen. Ron nearly died. 'What are you doing now?' he said quietly. My daughter Kate was similarly affected. But the public loved it. I still get people – especially young men – coming up to me in hotels and saying, 'You were terrific, Mrs Kirner, we love rock'n'roll too.'

Joan

PERSISTENCE AND COURAGE

Getting and keeping power is hard work, and you have to work at it for as long as it takes. Never give up the fight, whether you're winning or losing. Don't accept things without questioning, and don't believe the big lies that take power away from you: that 'It'll happen anyway, you might as well make the most of it' and 'You haven't got the power; someone else does, and there's nothing you can do' (another version of 'You can't fight City Hall').

Yes, it's true that sometimes you lose. The important thing is never to lose without giving it your best shot. If power does lie somewhere else, make 'them' wear the consequences of their decisions. Go down fighting – and live to fight another day, another way. Protect yourself, and learn to deal with criticism in a way that doesn't kill your optimism and sense of purpose. Deal with criticism politically, or professionally, and don't take it personally.

A CASE STUDY

THE POLITICAL IS PERSONAL

For the first six months of Joan Kirner's premiership Jeff Hook, a cartoonist with the *Herald Sun*, repeatedly portrayed her as a harassed housewife wearing a spotted dress. This was, at first, really distressing and infuriating for Joan and her family. Initially Joan took it all personally, and this was a big mistake (even wonder-women make mistakes). At one stage she even made a speech admitting that she really didn't like the cartoons. This just encouraged the cartoonist, and the editor of the paper, and they got worse. Joan felt that she was becoming their caricature. So one day she tackled the cartoonist and said, 'Why do you do it? I don't even own a polka-dot dress, and I'm certainly not harassed all the time.'

He said, 'Well, Mrs Kirner, I know how to draw Henry Bolte and I know how to draw Bob Hawke, or John Cain or

Paul Keating, but I've never had to draw a woman in power
before and I don't know how to draw you.'

She suddenly understood: he was getting a handle on
her. After this, she looked at her supporters and laughed,
and said, 'I've always known the personal is political.' There
she was, taking his cartoons personally, reacting to what
was, in fact, just another political attack. The editor and his
cartoonist were showing their own prejudices – their view
of how a housewife would cope – to get at her politically,
and she had let them do it. They didn't like her style of
politics and they got at her not by attacking the style, but
by attacking her personally.

So she stopped taking it personally, she showed herself
in the media in positions of control, visiting factories and
making speeches, and she developed and showed her sense
of humour with events like a fund-raising 'Spot on Joan'
concert. And she got her power back.

Have a clear idea of what constitutes strength, which is not
necessarily the same as being tough. Have a strong support
network of people around you, which helps you be strong and
have courage. Learn to deal with fear.

Fear is nature's way of saying you're at risk. It's a safety
mechanism, but when it freezes you and you can't take risks
that will achieve what you want, it's a negative. Confront your
fear. It is never as bad as you think it's going to be. And if it *is*
bad, stay in the moment, because the moment is soon over, and
you're still alive. Eventually you will have the power to say no
to things you don't want to do. There's an old saying: a brave
man dies but once, but a coward a thousand times. Courage is
about being scared to death and doing it anyway. Conquering
fear is not about posthumously winning the Victoria Cross. It's
about reaching above, reaching out, and jumping over your fears

and other people's prejudices – taking the next step because it has to be done. It means acknowledging your fear and doing something with it.

There are ways of dealing with fear:

+ Name it
+ Write down the three worst things that could happen and express them out loud
+ Visualise doing whatever it is you're afraid of, and practise it with friends if you have to
+ Involve yourself in activities directly related to your fear
+ Plan how to deal with the frightening thing, should it ever arise
+ Check it out with a friend – are you being foolhardy?

JAILHOUSE BLUES

Just before I moved on taking action in the Equal Opportunity Board to protect the interests of women prisoners, I rang an old friend whose opinion I valued. I could not tell her what I was thinking I had to do but I did ask her what she thought of the rumoured plans to move the women into the men's jail. Her reaction was direct: 'I think it would be cruel,' she said. 'Would you do everything in your power to stop it?' I asked. 'Yes,' she said. It was a reassurance to me, but acting was still my responsibility, and one I would be accountable for. I started preparing for the worst.

Moira

A CASE STUDY
FEAR OF FALLING

Neither of us is good with heights.

Joan found herself one day, as the Minister for Conservation, Forests and Lands, visiting a site – wearing high heels – where she was required to scale a couple of

ladders and walk across a catwalk high above the ground. She just had to do it: she could not let anyone know that she was afraid because the farmers were saying, 'What's this socialist feminist doing as our Minister?' and the workers were saying, 'She'll never come to much.' She had to prove that she had the right stuff. So she did. And once she had got used to such situations, she found that she could sometimes say, 'You go ahead, I'll just stay here.'

Moira was so afraid of heights that she felt sick looking out of the windows of tall buildings. In 1992, when she was in Queenstown, New Zealand, for a conference, she decided to challenge this fear, which was crippling her self-confidence. She booked in for a parapenting exercise – all you had to do was climb a small mountain, then walk off a minor cliff about five hundred metres above the ground wearing a parachute. The first moment, when there was air instead of ground beneath her feet, was the most terrifying, sphincter-relaxing moment in her life – and the split second later the most exhilarating. She reached the bottom alive and cheering and has never felt that gut-wrenching fear since. She's never bungee-jumped, either, and doesn't feel the need.

You will have to learn to deal with disappointments and setbacks on the road to power. With a sound values system and confidence in yourself, you can cope well and make positive contributions when you:

+ Lose a job – both of us have, and they were jobs we cared passionately about. There is always another way
+ Have to live with failure – especially when you didn't achieve something you cared passionately about. Remind yourself that you made the best decision you could at the time. If you really did your best, then you will have

to accept that you are not in full control of the entire universe

+ Make mistakes. As a young solicitor, Moira made a very bad mistake in her first court case, two weeks after she was admitted. Moira's cross-examination was so pathetic that her client lost the case when he should have won. He certainly would have won if she had objected to a copy of an account being admitted as evidence, and if she had done the proper preparation beforehand. The carbon copy of the account that had been tendered turned out to be forged. The magistrate learned of the perjury, reheard the case, found in favour of her former client, and very kindly took Moira out for morning tea and advised her to remember the point of law but to forget the pain and humiliation of her mistake and get on with her life and her career. She did.

The moral of the story is that even catastrophic mistakes can be turned to very good ends, and that you become more powerful, not less, with every experience, as long as you learn from it.

FEAR AND LOATHING IN GEELONG

After the collapse of the Pyramid Building Society, the city of Geelong suffered really badly – loss of jobs, collapse of businesses – and they all blamed the government. I had to go to Geelong to give a speech about the tariff debate. I got on quite well with the mayor at the time but he told me that, though he wanted me to come, he couldn't guarantee me safe passage. I thought, It's now or never: it's such a clear issue and something I know something about. I went.

When I arrived, there were about 5000 people – more than twice the number I had expected – and a sea of Pyramid placards. Understandably, they were very upset. I was the last to speak. There was a huge group of people who were pro-union standing behind the angry group with the placards. Anyway, when I got up to speak it was 80% boos and 20% claps, and the mayor had to appeal for a fair go. But by the time I had finished, I had turned it around. At the end of it I expected the placards to go up, but instead they were going down: I thought they were just getting tired.

The leader of the union group said afterwards, 'It worked, didn't it,' and I asked what he meant. He said, 'It's amazing how quickly those placards came down when we stood real close and said, "You'd better put those placards down."' And I'd thought it was my personal charm! But it was very important to face the people of Geelong as Premier, and from then on, though we didn't change the vote in Geelong, I've always been able to go there and be treated with respect. When I went down there recently to talk at an alternative rally to a One Nation meeting, my heartfelt speech inspired an offer of motivational work with the Geelong Football Club. Praise indeed!

Joan

DOING IT WITHOUT BECOMING A BLOKE

Don't assume that we think you have to adopt male or macho behaviour to be powerful. Whatever you do – whether it is in political activism, politics proper, business, or other employment – you will do it differently from men because your life experience is different. You don't need to adopt a protective coloration. It isn't necessary, to do your job, to play the negative corporate games so typical of traditional, male-oriented business.

Sue Vardon, Australian Businesswoman of the Year in 1996, said in the *Age* of 14 February 1996 that women don't have to follow bad behaviour, which she identified as boys' rules – 'such unconstructive behaviours as short-term planning and strategic thinking, hoarding of information and power by senior managers;

inflexible, rigid and complacent attitudes; poor people skills and lack of teamwork'. The values she espoused included teamwork, cross-functional integration, relationships, the resolution of conflict and the management of diversity. These skills do not belong exclusively to women, but companies would 'see that the decision to utilise these skills is commercially advantageous to them'.

Work your way up, and be willing to do it differently, because you are a woman. Don't engage in put-downs or offensive gossip about, or with, female colleagues or competitors. There is a time and a place for the one-liner – usually when the atmosphere is quite light-hearted and they're trying you out. Above all, smile as you deliver them. Don't get drunk with the boys. They really do have different standards for women and men. Be aware that your conduct will, anyway, be construed differently. If you accept lifts to or from work, or start going out with someone at work, gossip starts early and doesn't go away. Nor should you expect all women to be sisters. There is a distinct group of women who resent any expectation that they should have to think about the well-being of other women, or behave in politics or business or professions any differently from the men.

BEING A FEMINIST

Once you've decided that you are a feminist, you have decided that you want to make a difference. Should you call yourself a feminist? The decision is yours: you can be a feminist without demanding to be acknowledged as such. Glenda Jackson said on going into the British parliament, 'I'm a woman. I've worked in male-dominated areas all my life.'

Being a feminist is not about imposing your will on others, nor about one group of women deciding how another group of women should live or behave. Nor is it about receiving from men the rights women demand. It is about each woman making her own decision; listening to women, as well as acting: understanding what Mary Robinson called 'the small print of people's lives'; taking collective action to empower all women.

Feminism is about institutional change – reminding men they don't own the place, that there are rules – and it's about shared power, equal opportunity and justice, not taking away other people's rights. If you use the F-word, you must be able, by your own behaviour and intelligence, to deal with jokes and criticism based on negative stereotypes – that all feminists are humourless, touchy, exclusive, demanding, self-centred, victim-focused, combative. Even being assertive can become a negative. You may be described as hairy-legged, a dungarees wearer, judgemental of other women, a man-hater. You can demonstrate that feminists are none of those things by what you say and do.

When people say that feminism has gone too far, argue with them. Ask them what they mean. When they say that we don't need feminism or affirmative action because equal opportunity is mainstream now, point out that mainstream means men and women having equal access to power, money and status, and ask them to point out in which area of life this equality has been achieved. At the same time, acknowledge our achievements – we've given you this information in our chart of women's achievements.

Being a feminist means:
+ Being able to explain your views if they are under attack, and being willing to explain, and if necessary persuade others on, your view – or at least getting respect for yours
+ Asking yourself, How do I make a difference for women in my work? How will this affect women in the community? In committees? In business, in unions, in parliament, in Cabinet . . . ?
+ Lifting as you climb – that is, acting as a mentor to other women

- ✦ Looking at every issue in terms of gender balance
- ✦ Finding new ways to enable women to contribute to the common good in shaping their own lives.
- ✦ Being able to defend equal-opportunity laws. Having the right to make a complaint of discrimination does not mean that you have to complain, but it does mean that discrimination has to be avoided. Equal opportunity is better gained by policy and practice that takes women's experiences into account, so that they are treated on their merits and are not thought of as special or rather irritating demands for privileged treatment
- ✦ Being able to defend programs that are designed to

eliminate the past effects of discrimination, which is all
that affirmative action is, in this country. It is not about
setting quotas for women irrespective of merit and
potential and capacity, but setting targets, once it has
been established that women are missing out. Affirmative-
action reporting is designed to draw your attention to
the fact that women have missed out

✦ Pointing out, when an affirmative-action program is
challenged, that its objectives are clearly right – that is,
to use fully the talents of women in work, based on merit
that might have been overlooked or underutilised or
simply never developed. That makes sense, doesn't it?
And it makes financial sense, as well as moral sense.
Wasting talent doesn't do any organisation good, and
when women's viewpoints are ignored or trivialised, the
results are low productivity and poor decisions. Companies with good EEO programs significantly outper-
form those with poor EEO records. Good women leave
companies where they are subjected to anti-woman
prejudice and blocks on their advancement. What a waste!
Remember that equality is never to be taken for granted – even
though the girls leaving school today do assume they are equal
to men. Equality can be whittled away by those in power seeking
to retain their comfort zone. Look out for other women, and
men, left out by powerful cliques, including your own.

Young women no longer ask to be equal, they expect to
be. Keeping this so requires eternal vigilance. Misha Schubert, a
young journalist and a republican delegate to the 1998 Constitutional Convention, wrote in the book *Talking Up*:

No great feat has ever been achieved without strategy and
co-ordination . . . [I]nfluence comes with a strategy for its
acquisition, no matter how effortless power appears. At the end

of the day, a girl's gotta have a plan. We can't afford to be naive if we are going to take our rightful share of power. We need to learn the skills of public influence if we hope to retain and exercise our rights . . . In essence, we need to be co-ordinated, streetsmart and hard-nosed in our politics.

horacek

chapter 4

Skills for all situations

Power is exercised by groups against individuals or less powerful groups. You will be stronger if you act with others: many voices cannot be shouted down. A critical mass of 'others' will change the culture of an organisation much more effectively than a chorus of individual complaints. You need to get into the organisation, identify its culture, and decide what you want to change and why. Engage with other women, and sympathetic men, so that when there is a win others can build on it. Don't try to do it alone. You also need to understand the group defences and counter them, and if the culture can't be changed from the inside, get your own organisation and change it from the outside.

Mary Owen, one of the founders of the Working Women's

Centres, speaking at the annual dinner named in her honour on
3 April 1997, said:

> We are a disparate group – women are! We don't all have the
> same opinions on all matters, we may have different priorities,
> but we have one thing in common: we want to see that the
> opinions and priorities of women are given the same recognition
> as those of men. We don't want to be men, or to be the same
> as men. We don't want to be heard only on what are seen by
> men as women's issues. All issues concern women. Some affect
> women in a manner quite differently from the way they affect
> men – often to our detriment. That is why we want to be in on
> the decision-making.

A CASE STUDY
MOTHERS GETTING POLITICAL

Scene Victorian Federation of Mothers' Club Conference,
Assembly Hall, Melbourne, 1969. Four hundred women are
packed into the hall, women in hats and gloves who have
run the Mothers' Club Movement for years and created
effective and respected networks of school fund-raisers.
New young mums are sitting up the back at their first
statewide meeting of mothers' clubs, some with pre-school
children on their knees. Some of the mothers are
incredulous that, with the deplorable state of schools, this
potentially powerful gathering of women is concentrating on
issues like the bust sizes of girls' school uniforms, instead
of the lack of government planning or funding to meet the
education crisis.

Action One young mum lifts her toddler from her
knee (no occasional childcare in those days), gives her to
a friend to nurse and walks to the front microphone.
She gives a heartfelt speech on the urgency of parents

demanding more funds and better teachers for state schools.
She argues it's time for parents to start demanding a say in
the quality of their children's education. Unknowingly she
gives the media her first grab: 'It's no use just baking cakes
any more,' she says.

After the meeting she is asked to go on the State
Committee of the Victorian Federation of State School
Mothers' Clubs and she becomes its publicity officer. Her
life – and the life of mothers' clubs in Victoria – is never to
be the same.

Joan Kirner – the young woman in the story – along
with hundreds of other Victorian women, many of whom had
never taken any public action before, changed the Mothers'
Clubs Federation from a fund-raising network to one of the
most effective education lobby organisations in the nation.
They became a formidable women's collective for better
education.

After much discussion in clubs across the state, these
Victorian mothers decided to get political. They changed
their constitution, which had read 'The organisation is non-
political', so that it read 'the organisation is non-*party*-
political'. In making that decision they took the first
step to becoming effective lobbyists. They changed their
approach to the Minister for Education and departmental
heads, setting agreed agendas instead of going up for cups
of tea and a chat. Government became the apolitical party
to be both helped and challenged in its implementation of
education policy, instead of a powerful creature to be
obeyed, feared or thanked. Using the full power of their
diverse political views and connections, they made
education the priority of all MPs.

To this day, Joan says, she has never seen more
effective lobbying than country mums ensuring that their

local National Party members crossed the floor to support
Prime Minister Whitlam's School Commission Act in 1973.

GETTING INFORMATION

Once you have started on your course – whether it be getting
ahead in the company where you work, or changing a government decision that affects your neighbourhood or your school –
you need accurate information, or you'll be dismissed as a
whinger. You need every bit of information necessary for every
decision, or you may make the wrong tactical choices. You have
to earn the respect of the technocrats and the experts by being
well informed and inspirational, and so being taken seriously.

Sometimes the best way to get the information you need
when your knowledge base is pretty shaky is to ask a question
that gets your adversary talking. It is a very common tactic for
your opponent to suggest that you don't know what you're
talking about and to cross-examine you in order to reveal your
ignorance. Turn it back on them. Get in first by asking them
to share their knowledge. They'll be flattered, patronising, and
inadvertently helpful.

A woman once told Joan Kirner how she used the 'What
do *you* think?' tactic to good effect. She had written to the head
of the fire services criticising the privatisation of some of its
services and the casualisation of the labour force (this meant
the workers never knew when they were on and when they were
off, which had a bad effect on culture and commitment). She got
a phone call from the man wanting to know what she understood
by privatisation and casualisation, and where she had got her
information. She wasn't going to tell him the second and she
didn't know the answer to the first, so she said, 'What do *you*
mean by it?' And half an hour later he had explained exactly
what he had in mind. She and others then knew exactly what
they had to do to counter his plans.

Sometimes, if you sound as though you have the information, you get given more in a conversation: you are seen as being in the loop. The essential strategies for getting information are:

+ Acknowledge that you don't know everything yet
+ Seek out all the information you can on your own – facts, places, strategies and networks
+ Find the people who know what you need to know. This means that you need to have networks and mentors and the confidence to seek them out and use their advice
+ Use as many techniques as you need to get the information you need
+ Build up, maintain and retain your own research information. Newspapers are fine. Keep your own files of clippings and articles
+ If you want to build up a file on a politician, parliamentary libraries are invaluable. They have press clippings and Hansard on file (Hansard can also be searched on the Internet). You need a friendly MP to help you get research access. They're around.

Other sources of information include TV, radio, Acts of Parliament (obtainable from the Papers Office in parliament), reports of parliamentary and other committees (obtainable through members of party and select committees), Who's Who listings, websites and newsgroups, press releases, books and magazines, organisations and lobby groups active in the field, surveys and polls. And don't forget your network of family, friends, politicians, business associates, lawyers, unions, bureaucrats, other feminists, greens, minority groups, journalists and editors. You have to be up to date and you need to be able to do research on your enemy.

HOW TO BE A MINISTER ON THE FIRST DAY

It was 1985 and I desperately wanted to be the Minister for Education, but I knew I had little chance as a newcomer to Cabinet and with Premier John Cain sure that I was too close to the so-called interest groups of parents and teachers. I knew nothing whatever about Conservation, Forests and Lands (ranked well down in the Cabinet pecking order), and so that's what I got.

What, I wondered, was I going to do? I always had faint green credentials: I knew a bit about bushwalking, camping and parks (I did have a good pair of walking boots), but I really wanted to make a good impression with my new department. So I did a couple of things. I read up on Victorian national parks, so I could at least talk to one head of department sensibly. Then I selected three good political advisers: a man well versed in conservation who had been in the department; a woman who was a great political strategist and minder – a tough ex-politician – to watch my back and do the tough negotiations; and a long-time friend and secretary to charm, or guard, as the case might require.

I knew that, on my first meeting, I had to try to flush out those I could and couldn't trust. So I decided to have a round-table discussion with the senior bureaucrats, at that stage all men.

Next morning I called a meeting for that afternoon. At the meeting I gave some background on myself, and then I asked them to tell me the three things they did well and the three things they didn't do well. All performed exceptionally on the three things they did well. But two just couldn't think of anything they didn't do well or could improve on. Right, I thought, these are the guys I've got to watch; they will always protect themselves first and are unlikely to give me what is essential for good management – frank and fearless advice. By the end of the year,

both had left the department. It's important to know your allies
when the buck stops with you.

Joan

PLANNING

Nobody sets out on a successful expedition without knowing
where they want to go, without a map, or without a plan for
surviving on the way, including staged destinations and refuelling.
To achieve you have to plan. Getting what you want means that
you have to:

+ Define it
+ Believe you can achieve it
+ Set achievable targets
+ Plan how to get there – short- and long-term
+ Persist
+ Be flexible about how you get there – someone else may
  have a better way
+ Take others with you and let them know precisely what
  you are doing, why, and what their role is
+ Make allies and keep them
+ Celebrate milestones and have fun
+ Evaluate and review.

Planning means more than getting kids to school or yourself
to the job on time: it means being clear about your targets
and objectives, including others in the process, getting the right
things done on time and ignoring what's irrelevant. It means,
for a defined timespan, making this task your core business.

If you're part of a group that wants to make a difference,
you need to be clear about what difference you want to make,
where you want to go, how you are going to get there, and what
you will need to get there. How will you get the resources and
use them without wastage or burn-out? This all requires planning.
Planning, to some people, seems to take too much time. But if

you don't plan, there is no point in starting. You need to:
+ Identify real needs and demands, and what actions will meet them
+ Define what areas you will cover and what areas others will
+ Tell the outside world what you are doing and how
+ Keep track of what works and what doesn't, then discard, build and grow.

Some useful questions to bear in mind when planning anything are:
+ What do you or your group or your community want?
+ Who needs it?
+ Is anyone already trying to meet those needs?
+ What can you do that isn't being done?
+ Is the problem a symptom of some other problem?
+ What is the *core* issue that must be dealt with? What is peripheral?
+ What are the strengths and weaknesses of your strategies to address the issues?
+ How can you get resources?
+ What can you realistically tackle with the resources you've got now? What can you build up to?

Select the tactics with the best chance of success and check that they meet the identified needs, and then write down the objective for each one. Objectives need to be specific (for example, placing a leaflet in every house in the street), achievable and measurable. Eliminating discrimination against women is not an objective, it's a vision.

You then have to list, beside each tactic, who, when, where, and with what. And you have to agree on the signs of success. Ask yourselves, Why are we doing this? What will be different if it works? Who will know? How can we find out these things? In planning jargon, these are your performance indicators. Write them down too.

Keep reviewing your plan. Were the tactics right? Was the approach realistic? Did you overestimate what you could do in the time, with the resources? What could you do better, or differently, next time? Who else could you include in the task?

If you reach an impasse, think laterally and don't be afraid to change the whole frame of reference of your new plan. At the end of it all – or, if it's ongoing, at least every few months – assess what has actually happened. Circumstances might have changed, to which you didn't adapt. You can learn and move on but you must review and evaluate before you can do this. Don't despair because someone tells you there's only one way to do it. There isn't. Do what you find works for you or your group.

The major points to remember about planning are:

* Everyone has to do it – and take responsibility for it
* It has to be based on facts, not hope alone, though hope is essential too
* Every objective has to have a name (who's responsible) and a date or time beside it, so you can see who's doing it, or didn't do it
* You have to be able to measure, objectively, your failures and successes
* You have to marshal your resources to achieve a plan
* If you don't plan, you won't arrive.

MAKING ALLIANCES AND ACCEPTING HELP

Never try to change the world on your own. You're too vulnerable and you can be got at. You need to engage with friends, and even opponents, for the particular objective you're trying to achieve.

First of all, learn who you can trust. You should be prepared to be disappointed sometimes, and delighted and surprised at other times. There are some people you can work with on a single issue or particular activity or at a particular event. There are other, rare, creatures you can trust with just about anything. If you have formed a team – for a project, or a campaign, or a Great Purpose – you should not assume that being on a team means each person has precisely the same goal, or the same way of operating, or even that you will like one another. Know one another's limits.

Next, look for allies who are not on your team. You should not refuse to do deals with people you have not worked with before, or whose objectives you do not fully subscribe to. Everyone needs allies. You should not assume that a past adversary cannot become your friend – at least for this campaign.

Take help when it's offered – so long as you can live with the strings, if there are any. Remember your values, and whose respect you really value, as you practise the art of the possible:

+ If someone can't give you funds for your campaign, they might be able to give you skills or time
+ If a colleague can't vote for your proposition in a meeting, they might be willing to canvass others' voting intentions for you, and help you plan your tactics
+ If people are not able to give time or effort, then accept what they can give in terms of advice (lawyers are pretty good at giving you free advice)
+ When you form alliances, or when people do favours for you, be prepared to do something in return.
+ Have your values well thought out, and be sure of them, and see whether or not the favour asked fits with those values.

Sometimes strange bedfellows make good alliances. When Joan Kirner was Leader of the Opposition in 1993 and the Victorian government announced its decision to close down the Williamstown railway line in Melbourne, her ally was the Williamstown community, where she lived, but she needed to have the Minister of the time, Alan Brown, and the rail union and the media as allies too, to win. Joan and others worked hard at showing them all that everyone would benefit from saving the railway line, and they became allies in the cause.

Moira Rayner was astounded to find herself in strong agreement with a former foe over Bob Hawke's plans to introduce an Australia Card in the 1980s. The very man who had attacked her as a socialist zealot (untrue!) the year before rang and asked her to join with him in support of a civil libertarian campaign against the card. She agreed. And in 1998, when she was a delegate to the Constitutional Convention, one of her former critics, and a vigorous one too, the late Professor Patrick 'Paddy' O'Brien, became one of her colleagues in the Elect the President group of delegates, who wanted an Australian republic to allow people the right to elect their new head of state. The alliance lasted for the duration of the convention, and they were never 'enemies' again. You take your allies where you find them.

NETWORKING

Networking is central to power, particularly woman-power. Networking is, as Fay Marles recognises in the Case Study on pages 63–66, just making and using contacts. Personal networks really matter, whether you are in business, government, or politics, paid or unpaid. Write down all the networks you belong to. You'll be surprised how many you have: colleagues in the workplace; community groups; unions or professional organisations; local-government councillors and staff; sporting contacts (yours, your partner's or your children's); your family, friends and neighbours; local businesses; ethnic or religious groups; students and schoolfriends; people you meet at pubs and clubs; the Internet; cultural groups; local childcare or kindergarten; lollipop ladies; and the people who run the local shop. You are well connected! If you make connections with busy and influential people, the ones who can help you the most, don't ask for help

or favours unless you're really serious. Some points to remember
when networking:

- It is not egotistical to seek to be influential. It is necessary
- Your network may draw on people in political parties,
  or in the political movement you are a part of, or other
  women who are 'sisters', or community leaders
- You need relationships outside your particular sphere of
  interest because you never know when it is going to be
  necessary to call on them for help – all issues are multi-
  faceted
- There's no need to be exclusive about your networks –
  they could be from your sporting association, the library
  group, a church (if you go to one), business or service
  clubs, schools, Neighbourhood Watch, the local takeaway
- Networking demands that you don't 'use' people. People
  know when they are being used and they'll resist your
  requests next time you ask
- People want to do business with people they know and
  trust, or feel that they want to know and are prepared to
  trust
- People will often take someone else's recommendation
  for contacts
- Doing favours is the best way to develop your social
  capital – that is, the willingness of your neighbours to
  give you a hand simply because you need it. But be clear
  that in helping you don't expect a quid pro quo
- Share your experience and expertise with other women –
  be generous in all that you do, and they will respond in kind
- Get a business or visiting card. Just your name and contact details will do. You can get these done very inex-
  pensively. Take them with you everywhere. Give them to
  anybody you talk to about your cause, or you think might
  be helpful later. Give them to journalists

+ Keep a small pocket diary and always carry it with you. You can make arrangements and appointments on the spot. Don't lose an opportunity
+ Work out which groups or individuals have common interests. Identify the organisations that already exist in the area (you can help to revitalise them if they've gone a bit quiet)
+ Join groups. But don't join them straight away; you should make sure that it's the right group – at least two or three meetings as a guest should be enough to make that apparent. Be clear about what you want to contribute and what you hope to get out of the group. If you do join, go regularly or it's a waste of your time and theirs.

When you go to meetings, arrive on time (Moira does, Joan tries to). Wear a name tag – carry your own with you in case they don't have them – that's big enough to be read without someone peering at your breast. Wear it on your right side: that's where people look when they shake your hand or meet you for the first time. Keep an eye out for the people who seem a bit lost, and on their own. Talk to them: get a relationship going. Learn to make small talk (news is good, sport is always useful, but TV is a stinker).

Make a very big effort to remember names, or don't complain if people forget yours. Joan is renowned for remembering people's names. (Moira is notorious for forgetting her sister's name once.) Joan learned the skill early, as a new recruit teacher. Introduce yourself by shaking hands, asking the person's name, and looking clearly into their eyes, repeating their name and committing it to memory. Remember the pronunciation too. It's courteous to get names right. After the meeting, write down the names and contact numbers of those you need to remember, and where you met them, in your address book. Keep a file of their business cards. Write on the back where you met them and what their interests are, and add the name and contact number to your address book. If you meet the person again in a different setting, the chances are you may not remember the name but you should remember the face. So you can at least say, 'Haven't we met somewhere before?' It's no embarrassment if you haven't. Or shake hands and say, 'Good to see you again, but I've just forgotten your name.' Most people are impressed if you remember the setting you met them in, even if not their name.

The key to networking is earning the right to ask a favour, or be asked for a favour, and that comes from doing things for other people without always demanding something in return. Even if you don't get what you want, you should look for the opportunity to give help to others. What you give comes back: it's one of those laws of life.

MENTORING

It is a myth that a successful woman – or any person for that matter – is entirely self-made. This is especially true for successful women who take on work in non-traditional areas. Former Ford chairman Don Petersen was fond of saying, 'If you see a turtle sitting on a fencepost, you know she didn't get up there by herself.' All of us get where we are with a lot of support from a lot of people along the way. We learn from someone else's experience, then in turn can pass the information on.

The concept of mentoring comes from Greek mythology. According to Homer, Odysseus chose his friend Mentor as a guardian and tutor for his son Telemachus before going away to fight in the Trojan War. Today mentoring can be personal, or an organised process linking a less skilled and experienced person with someone from whom they will willingly accept advice, knowledge, analysis and feedback on how they can achieve their goals. A mentor is a person who agrees to share their knowledge and experience with you, so that you can access power. Then you can become a mentor too.

How do you go about finding a mentor? Follow people around and watch what they do. Talk to other women who have been mentored and ask them what their relationships were based on. What did their mentor tell them or show them or whom did they introduce them to that made a difference?

WOMEN MENTORING OTHER WOMEN

Over the centuries women have supported other women, particularly younger women, to advance their understanding of power and success. Often this is an informal process, not even a conscious one. I have lost count of the women, of all ages, who have claimed I was their hero or role model (usually at a chance or one-off meeting). My response is usually 'Thank you, but why?'

If a more in-depth conversation reveals that I can help her practically, I'll give her my card and suggest she contact me. That gives her a chance to think about whether she really wants to tell me more, and I know that when someone does ring they are serious about wanting to learn.

Joan

Becoming a mentor is not so easy: people may come to you, or they may be found for you and you may be asked to talk to them. Of course, mentoring is a two-way street, particularly if you are working with younger people. Their energy, enthusiasm and optimism as well as their expertise can rejuvenate your commitment and energy and set you off in new directions. That's our experience, anyway.

In 1998 Roberta Sykes, in the *Newsletter of the Black Women's Action in Education Foundation*, wrote the following tribute to one of her mentors who had also been a mentor to hundreds of others.

A funeral was held at St Mary's Cathedral on 4 May 1998 for Colleen Shirley Perry Smith, more widely and fondly known as MumShirl.

MumShirl was born to Isabell and Joseph Henry Perry on Erambie Mission in about 1928. From humble beginnings she overcame racism and poverty to become a national and highly respected figure, a scourge to bureaucrats and a saint to the poor and dispossessed.

In addition to her own accomplishments, which were many and included involvement in the Foundation for Aboriginal Affairs, Aboriginal Legal Service, Aboriginal Medical Service, and the Detoxification Centre at Wiseman's Ferry, MumShirl was also the powerhouse behind many other people finding their niche in life.

Any needy child, any starving adult, found help at her door. When it came to helping others in their time of need, MumShirl was colour-blind.

As Official Visitor, an honorary position, at prisons throughout NSW, MumShirl offered assistance, acknowledgement, advice and sympathy to any who requested to see her.

MumShirl had little time for material concerns, and shared her invalid's pension with the city's poor. She accumulated no wealth, and died in the modest surroundings in which she had always lived.

She did, however, accumulate a wealth of respect and a host of admirers, locally, nationally and internationally. MumShirl would no doubt have been pleased to see the thousands who came to give her their last salute. She will be sadly missed.

As well as personal mentoring, including the kind of mothering and support Mum Shirl gave to so many young men and women, there are some very effective formal mentoring programs. As Minister for Education in Victoria from 1988 to 1990, Joan Kirner set up a mentoring program in her department – and more than a decade on it still exists and continues to grow.

If mentoring is to work the support provided must be:

+ Voluntary
+ Matched – that is, it must work for both of you
+ Focused on particular goals agreed upon between well-intentioned people
+ A joint commitment
+ Available when most needed, and flexible
+ Non-judgemental
+ Confidential, unless otherwise agreed
+ Integrated into the work expectations of the person being mentored
+ Evaluated and reviewed regularly
+ Subject to termination by agreement without recrimination.

Before you embark on a mentor program there must be:

+ Open communication between the person wanting mentoring, the mentor and the organisation on the purpose and the process of mentoring
+ Training or advice for mentors
+ An agreed supervision and evaluation process
+ A commitment from the people concerned and from the organisation
+ Induction for all involved
+ Ways out agreed upon, if things go wrong.

Mentors need to be:

+ Willing to teach and to learn
+ Comfortable with the person being mentored
+ Prepared to dedicate quality time
+ On call, if needed
+ Good communicators
+ Good listeners
+ Organised, so that they can make timely interventions when asked or needed

◆ Practical

◆ Thanked.

Those being mentored need to be:

◆ Volunteers

◆ Prepared to listen, learn and teach

◆ Comfortable with the mentor

◆ Committed to implementing advice received

◆ Able to negotiate change

◆ Willing to be mentors themselves, when they're ready

◆ Rewarded.

Roberta Sykes was the first Black Australian woman to be admitted to postgraduate studies and won a Master's degree, then a doctorate, from Harvard School of Education in the US, without any government assistance. She felt she was morally obliged to share and pass on her success in postgraduate education to Aboriginal women, to set up a chain so that they did not have to go it alone as they sought the appropriate place to use their skills. She wanted a solid core of Aboriginal graduates providing support for each other.

Roberta set up a support network for Black Australian women in education, the Black Women Action in Education Foundation. One of the young women supported, Larissa Behrendt, wrote about this in the US journal, *Cultural Survival Quarterly*, in 1998:

Roberta Sykes had said to me: 'So, when are you going to apply to Harvard?' She had encouraged me through all stages of the application and fund-raising processes and she has remained a valuable resource to me while I have been away from my family. Roberta anticipated the tough emotional and intellectual struggles that I have faced while I have been here [at Harvard Law School studying for her law degree].

My acceptance to Harvard, and the role Roberta played in

that journey, is a lesson in the importance of mentoring in the education of Aboriginal children. Given the legacy of educational policies that denied Aboriginal children learning opportunities and directed them towards work as manual labourers, there are very few role models within the Aboriginal community (and still less of those success stories who actively support and encourage younger generations). I noticed how the lack of role models can impede the visions the Aboriginal children have about their future when I went to a careers day at a local high school. When asked what they wanted to do with their lives, I was surprised how many Aboriginal children replied that they wanted to be policemen. When I asked what the attraction to that profession was, a number replied, 'Because I'm interested in the law.' When I asked why, then, not be a lawyer, I was met with the response, 'I never thought of that.' With very few indigenous lawyers trained in Australia, there is little chance of meeting one.

HOW TO NEGOTIATE

The masculinist model of power is all about winning and losing. Most women know differently – the greatest wins are those where the differing parties feel that they have each achieved a win: a win–win situation. Our challenge is to make power and winning inclusive.

Most women have an instinctive feel for negotiation. We are physically unlikely to win a major physical stoush, unaided, against men. Socially, historically, our rights have been won through struggle, not dominance: they have been prised out of, not imposed by, powerful male-dominated institutions. Besides, any woman with teenage kids who can get them to take advice has negotiation skills as advanced as those of US Secretary of State Madeleine Albright.

Negotiation is a skill, done best when you are clear about what you are trying to do. It is a tool for getting what you want, without a major confrontation, and without using anybody.

Negotiation takes five steps: preparation, discussion, pro-
posing, bargaining, and agreeing. After this comes putting it into
effect, which often requires ongoing negotiation. It does not
necessarily mean sitting down, together, at a round table. Often
it means engaging with a range of people in private, then moving
on when various interests seem to have come to a point. If you
want to know more about negotiation, read G. Kennedy, J. Benson
and J. McMillan, *Managing Negotiations: How to Get a Better
Deal*. The outline that follows is from their model.

PREPARATION

**1   distinguish what you intend to get (if humanly possible),
from what you would like to get**   Have up your sleeve something that you know you can, and are willing to, trade relatively
easily (a bargaining chip). Be very clear also about what you
won't trade. Do this on the basis of the facts. Are you being
realistic? Talk it over with your friends and supporters, and
someone independent too.

2   do the same thing for the opponent   Do you know who
your opponents are, and what their answers to these questions
might be? If you do, you will be much better prepared for negotiating. Try to work out what the other side might consider
to be a win, and what their expectations are. For both of these
first steps, be very clear about what information you need and
what information you are willing to disclose (or think might be
disclosed whatever you try to do to prevent it). Consider what
concessions you might make yourself and what you might want
in exchange (trade-offs), in terms of what the cost to you might
be, and what the benefit would be to your opponent.

3   work out as many options as possible   You need as many
choices as you can find, to satisfy both sides' needs and priorities. This is good for your own flexibility, and also helps encourage

competitive negotiators to be more co-operative, setting up an expectation that you will agree, in spite of all the problems. But don't be stuck – if new facts come in, or attitudes change, there might be even more options available. Stay flexible.

4   work out your best alternative to a negotiated agreement   Think what the other side's might be. For example, during the 1998 Constitutional Convention it became obvious, in the second week, that there was no way that the republicans who wanted to elect the president could get the numbers in the convention to get their model up. The issue then became what the best alternative was. For some it was to get, at the least, agreement on a republican referendum in 1999, and work on it in the meantime. For others it was to scuttle the convention and trust that the Prime Minister would call a plebiscite on the broad question of a republic, hoping that the numbers for a 'real' republic would be better a few years down the track.

It's a good idea to think about the worst alternative to a negotiated agreement too. In this case, it was that the Prime Minister might decide not to hold a plebiscite at all, and the convention delegates would be lynched on the way home for failing to get their acts together.

5   make sure that you have the authority to negotiate, and know what limits there are   You could shoot yourself in the foot, creating major bad feeling, if your negotiations get to the closing stage and you pull out because you have to consult. Successful negotiation depends on the atmosphere and feeling of the time.

6   decide whether to have a negotiating team   Teams are really, really useful. You can divide up and take on different roles. One of you can be leader or spokesperson (it can change from time to time); another can be the observer (watching body language, sensing how well things are going, feeding it back); and someone else can take the notes and be the reporter (very important). You can share perceptions about how things are going. Different people can adopt differing tactics (soft cop/ tough cop), or slot in when personality clashes threaten to derail the negotiation. Having a team means that the responsibility is shared – along with the blame and the gains.

There are disadvantages. The worst is the need to keep the team together and the extra time it takes to prepare. The more people there are, the more important it is to focus, have a common aim and strategies, and be disciplined. There is nothing more damaging than having a well-intentioned team player break ranks at a crucial point.

One person should be responsible for the team, to ensure that everyone communicates properly and that they all feel part of the shebang.

7   decide on negotiating styles   There are ways and ways of negotiating, and sometimes it helps to know what the other side does. If it's a bullying style, decline to get into the bullying mode. Moira Rayner recalls going into a conciliation as the mediator, knowing that one side was going to be implacable and the other immovable – both of them fighting for a principle and both of them willing to die in the saddle, so to speak, as long as it meant the destruction of the other side. It became her job to make it clear to both that neither would achieve their aim.

Co-operative negotiating styles are all very well but sometimes they just aren't practicable. If you know the enemy has been engaged in negotiations before and they are confrontational or bullying, or threatening, try to head off a repetition of the same tactics at the beginning of your own negotiations by not starting in the same way. Refusing to fight back can lead to co-operation. You might have to revert to the gatling guns afterwards, but at least start nice.

8   pick the arena   You need to have a climate of negotiation, not petition or threat. Choose a neutral, comfortable and relaxed environment.

DISCUSSION

You need to have your 'argument' first. That doesn't mean a fist fight, but it does mean getting each side to hear what the other side wants and how it justifies it. This is an opportunity to exchange information, explore where the interests and barriers lie, and test assumptions. Don't get sarcastic or belligerent; don't pour scorn on the other side, or interrupt them, or shout, or talk over them, or threaten them. Or cry. They hate that.

Do ask the other side to justify their position – point by point – and listen without judgement or commitment to their proposals and explanations. Listen, give information and seek it, summarise the issues neutrally and look for clues about where their priorities really lie.

Always be sure of each side's assumptions before you start. In one mediation Moira discovered that the other side had assumed that her side wanted an apology for defamation so that they could publish it and destroy them politically. They were enormously relieved to know that the apology could be private and personal, so long as it was heart-felt and accompanied by the payment of legal costs.

PUTTING A PROPOSAL

A proposal is a suggestion that advances negotiation and moves people closer together. It may include compromise, or moderation of an existing position. Never interrupt if someone is making a proposal; not only is it rude, it sends a message that you are not sincere in negotiating. You can, and should, ask questions to clarify it afterwards. Summarise it fairly, before you respond. This shows you were listening. A proposal is stronger than an argument and it is best answered with a counter-proposal.

There are a couple of rules about proposals. The most important one is that you don't just state a grievance – you propose a remedy. The second is to always invite a response.

Package your proposals. Sometimes they are more easily accepted if they are wrapped with suggestions which address the other side's deepest fear. 'I'll buy your house, if you give me first option over your beach cottage as well.'

BARGAINING

A bargain is all about exchanging something of value for something else valuable. 'If you agree not to pour effluent into my drinking water then I will not proceed with my litigation.' 'If you keep my child's class sizes down to twenty-one or -two then I will ensure that the parents' group fund-raises for new library stock.' It's all about trading interests. Keep your issues linked until you get to closing, and always impose the conditions you intend on your offers before you make them.

REACHING AGREEMENT

Nothing is more calculated to drive someone crazy than, having accepted an offer, finding a new clause added. 'Okay,' they say, 'we'll keep the school open so long as the parents pay for the repairs.' Then the parents discover that they won't be allowed to do any of the repairs themselves, and must use the principal's brother-in-law's firm to do the work. This causes suspicion and resentment.

It's not easy to agree – there are many points at which an agreement can come undone – but if you do agree, then make sure you agree on what you have agreed. Write it down and sign it, there and then, even if you have to have a formal contract later on.

Remember, an effective negotiator is:

+ Well-prepared and well-informed
+ Clear-headed and flexible under pressure
+ Insightful, especially into the other side's heart
+ A really good communicator
+ A very good listener
+ Patient
+ Self-controlled
+ Persistent and determined
+ Possessed of integrity
+ Accountable to the team
+ Always aware of what they want to achieve
+ Ethical.

All these skills will serve you well as you seek out power and use it wisely. Without proper information you can be manipulated and lied to. If you don't plan, you won't achieve success. Nobody travels alone: making allies is essential to enjoying power. And networking is what women do best: we always do better as a group. Women need mentors; experienced women should be mentors to others. You need negotiation skills to solve household disputes as much as workplace ones; to finalise contracts; and to establish market prices. These skills will put you in a woman's proper place: in control.

chapter 5

Managing meetings

Women who want to make a difference go to a lot of meetings. That's where decisions are made, relationships formed, policies developed and performance reviewed. Meetings are important. You need to be able to manage them, influence their decisions, and control their outcomes. Good meetings are those that:

+ Have a purpose. Decisions are contemplated before a good meeting takes place. Know why you are meeting, what you hope to get out of it, and review after the meeting whether you achieved this – and if you didn't, have another way forward

+ Are held with plenty of notice and are therefore well attended by people

+ Happen at times that suit everyone, especially people who have family and other responsibilities. There is no need, most of the time, for meetings that interfere with family or household arrangements – those held in the early morning, in the evening, or on weekends. A critically important work meeting should happen during a working day

+ Do not move their times or locations from those planned without good reason

+ Start and finish on time, and where possible are over within an hour

+ Have written agendas, distributed before the meeting. Any changes should be asked for and agreed to at the commencement of the meeting

+ Document their decisions and distribute an action sheet afterwards so people know what they are expected to do

+ Start by reviewing the minutes of the previous meeting and checking if required action has been taken

+ Are chaired courteously, authoritatively, impartially, and in accordance with an established set of procedures

+ Allow genuine discussion and the polite exchange of views and sharing of experience – not the suppression of dissent, or rubber-stamping of decisions made beforehand by an elite group

+ Are not interrupted by telephone calls, visitors, or unnecessary departures to caucus in the toilets or to deal with unrelated business

+ Are based on respect for the other's point of view, but do not necessarily demand unanimous agreement. If the issues have been fully discussed, even dissidents can accept an outcome that is not their first choice

+ Are not punctuated by outbursts, raised voices, in-jokes, or belittling or abusive language. Nor do they allow the loudest, most forceful voice to intimidate others out of contributing

✦ Are occasions in which women and men participate equally.

There are ways of running meetings that exclude women from decision-making. Meetings may be called at difficult times for women with family or other responsibilities, and women are then made to feel bad when they can't come. Women members may be frozen out: they may not be introduced when they join a committee for the first time or come to their first meeting; they may not be chatted to informally, while the men are. There are some women who resent other women joining 'their' group, and they can freeze out newcomers too. And there are men who continually, even if unconsciously, defer to other men in meetings and ignore women's contributions. Women may be talked over, talked down to, ridiculed (subtly or very rudely), or left out of the pre-meeting that sorted out the agenda and choreographed the discussion and predetermined the outcomes.

There are ways of dealing with all these difficulties. The key is awareness. If you can't make any progress in a meeting, analyse what's happening. There are five strategies commonly used against women. To deal with them you need to identify the mechanisms used to keep power away from you, talk about them with someone you can trust, then find a way to neutralise the strategy – and plan on using it with your allies. You need not assume it's a plot. The most common problems in meetings arise from the group's culture. If you're on the outer, you need to be aware that there will be a range of conscious and unconscious responses to you from people who like the culture they are working within and don't want it to change, because it suits them. They'll resist you, even when they're being friendly and affable.

The way to overcome these obstacles is by making allies on

the committee. Work out which strategy is being used against you and get the other women to support you in countering it. It is particularly hard to change a culture that these strategies protect if there is only one woman on the committee, so do what you can to make sure you are joined by other women.

DEALING WITH BEING MARGINALISED

The five strategies used to marginalise women are:

+ Making women invisible
+ Making women ridiculous
+ Keeping women ignorant
+ Making women feel inadequate
+ Training Judas sheep.

The effects of all of these at once can be devastating. A woman who feels invisible, ridiculous, ignorant, inadequate or simply exploited may come to feel so unimportant and unvalued that she decides not to keep working for change.

A few years ago some Swedish women politicians published a quick 'do-it-yourself' on how women obtain real personal power, and some strategies for dealing with meetings, in *The Power Handbook*. This inspired us to write our own. We hope that you feel similarly inspired to add to our list. Talk your approach through with your women colleagues, and men who support you, before each meeting.

It is important to understand the strategies used to marginalise women and to agree beforehand on a signal for identifying each one, and on your counter-strategies. Your signals need to be visible, unambiguous to those in the know, and subtle enough for others not to notice. Passing notes takes too long and they are noticed. A wink could give entirely the wrong impression. Getting up and joining your colleague at the coffee table does give you an opportunity for a quick word but it's unwieldy and obvious. We suggest, therefore, that you develop

a code, using a hand signal or a word, to indicate the strategy being used against you.

For example, if the meeting is using the first strategy, making women invisible, you could stroke your eye or eyebrow with your thumb. If the strategy is making women ridiculous, stroke your cheek with your index finger, or point at something, or take off your left earring. The third strategy, keeping women ignorant, could be noted by shutting your notebook and tapping it with your middle finger. The fourth strategy, making women feel inadequate, you could show by holding up four fingers. For the fifth strategy you might hold up both hands, as if you were surrendering. There are many other possible codes you might feel more comfortable with, including verbal ones. Practise them; they not only trigger your counter-strategy but also build a feeling of solidarity.

MAKING WOMEN INVISIBLE

The first sign that this strategy is in place is when men are quite obviously not listening to what you have to say. They start looking through their papers, talking to one another quietly – or over you – or making witty irrelevant remarks. Or they excuse themselves and go to make a call or two, or disappear to the bathroom. More often than not, this is because they simply don't perceive what women say as relevant. Women do, often, see issues in different ways from men because they live their lives under different conditions. If men don't recognise women's views of a situation they will choose either not to listen or not to get involved, then use their superior numbers to make a decision that might not be the best available.

If you're getting the invisibility treatment:

+ Signal to your allies that the first strategy is afoot
+ Name it. Make it clear that you are aware of the method being used, and that you do not accept it
+ Insist on the meeting paying attention to what you and your colleagues have to say
+ Pause until the shuffling of papers and chatting has stopped, and tell the meeting that this is what you're doing
+ Pick up the idea that's being ignored and turn it into a motion, and move the motion yourself at the appropriate time. Organise a seconder. The mover and seconder of a motion must be recorded in the minutes, whatever the outcome of the motion

+ Insist that a vote not be taken until any absentees have
returned from their urgent visits to the bathroom or the
phone, or wherever

+ If they still don't understand, use similar tactics on one
of the men the next time round. Say what you are doing:
it will make your point

+ Train your voice. A low-register, distinct and clear voice
carries, and is not easily ignored.

Sometimes being invisible – letting others take your ideas as
their own – is worth wearing if it means your ideas get implemented. When Joan was a parent activist it was clear that the
Director-General of Education was prepared to broaden decision-
making at the school level to enhance professionalism and learning
relevance. He wasn't particularly keen to have parents as full partners, but he would, clearly, advocate parent participation if it was
seen to be part of his own strategy and his own idea.

To get the debate over decentralisation and devolution of
power in education off to a start, parents agreed to his view.
Then, as the debate continued, they intervened publicly and
shaped the debate in ways that eventually led to parents becoming
full partners in education decision-making. Letting the Director-
General think that the idea was all his had made the break-
through.

There are other ways too of making sure you are taken
seriously. During the 1960s Joan Kirner was often appointed to
committees as the only parent representative, and she found that
she was noticed for her novelty value but ignored when it came
to having her views taken into account. She developed tactics
for being noticed, which included:

+ Making media statements, or getting others to do it,
about what should be done or ought to be said at the
meeting. This sometimes produced an anti-Joan-Kirner
backlash but notice was certainly taken

✦ Ensuring that at least two other people, preferably including one in the power loop, raised the same issue she
did

✦ Circulating a short position paper, signed by herself and
influential others.

Joan also found that she wasn't getting the same treatment from
flight attendants and fellow passengers when she first became
one of the army of Whitlam change agents in the 1970s and
had to travel a lot. She was often one of a very few women
sitting up front in business class with the male secretaries of
departments, Ministers and bureaucrats, who would engage
her in little chats about family instead of policy. She used to
board the plane clutching the *Age* newspaper or a bundle of
last-minute papers to read. Then she realised that one piece was
missing in her power kit: she wasn't seen reading the *Financial
Review*. So she started buying it, reading it on the plane, and
the conversations turned like magic to the business and politics
of the day. Joan Kirner was in.

DID SOMEONE SPEAK?

In 1995 I was elected onto the Council of the Law Institute of
Victoria. During one of our meetings we were discussing a serious
problem. I made a suggestion. Nobody interrupted. Nobody responded. The chairman called another member to speak, and a
few more remarks were made by male speakers. Then a senior
member said, 'Why don't we . . . ' and repeated in his own words
exactly what I had proposed. The chairman said, 'That's the first
good idea anyone has had all evening,' and asked him to put it
as a motion. I said, 'Hang on, that's exactly what I said: am I
invisible, or what?' And everyone laughed.

The next morning I sent the chairman a copy of a *Punch*
cartoon by Riana Duncan that showed a group of men and a
solitary woman around a boardroom table, with the Chair saying:

'That's an excellent suggestion, Miss Triggs. Perhaps one of the men here would like to make it.'

Moira

MAKING WOMEN RIDICULOUS

Being funny at the expense of women is a profoundly successful way of keeping them powerless. The whole point is to denigrate women and their efforts. Jokes about silly little blondes and menopausal mothers-in-law, stories about mistakes that high-flying women have made, or about feminists – any joke that makes women feel uncomfortable falls into this category. Tolerating such jokes or laughing at them is fundamentally self-defeating. As Louisa Lawson, the mother of Henry Lawson, put it so well, 'The most powerful weapon that the proponents of mental inferiority [of women] had was ridicule. They could build upon a rich Australian culture of jokes and cartoons picturing women as stupid, shallow, loquacious, hysterical and incapable of logical reasoning ... habitual belittlement leads women to distrust themselves and silently tolerate jests against womankind.'

The Australian finance industry is a good example of a traditionally masculine one. There are still relatively few women in senior positions. One woman Moira knows, who eventually suffered a health crisis over increasing hostility from her male colleagues, admitted that she had herself engaged in anti-woman jokes to prove that she was no feminist and be accepted. On one occasion, of which she was bitterly ashamed in retrospect, she laughed at a mistake made by the first woman appointed to the Board of Directors of her company, along with the male manager who subsequently drove her out.

Another time, Moira was counselling a group of women financiers who had lost their jobs after a long period of victimisation. At the end of the session one of them told the group a long joke whose punchline involved describing the Premier as a portion of a woman's sexual anatomy: the woman had no idea how she had personally contributed to the anti-female atmosphere that had, indirectly, resulted in her losing her job.

This does not mean that you shouldn't crack jokes, only that you should never do so when the joke is at the expense of another woman. There are stacks of feminist jokes that are funny but not belittling of either gender. Add them to your repertoire, and take responsibility for one another's success in meetings.

If you find yourself or another woman being given the ridicule treatment in a meeting, you should:

+ Signal to your allies that the second strategy is afoot
+ Make it very clear that sexist jokes and habits of speech are unacceptable at any time. You don't win supporters by joining in
+ Stare, pointedly, in astonishment at the perpetrator of the belittling joke. Create an embarrassing silence. Turn to another woman and ask distinctly, 'What on earth is he trying to say?'
+ Deal with the subtle put-downs consistently. Men get tired of being corrected. One of the irritating habits of some defensive men is to make a big issue about titles, sighing deeply when 'chairperson' is suggested, or elaborately adding 'person' onto any other job description, whether or not it is gender-specific. This is meant to make women look unreasonable. We have been trying, for years, to ensure that women are not excluded by language. If they, or you, don't like 'chairperson', there are many other words – convenor, president, principal member, spokesperson. You may want to refer to a specialist dictionary such as *The Nonsexist Word Finder* by Rosalie Maggio. Make the point that we use words to

describe and manipulate our world and our business. The better and more precisely we use our language, the better we control our work

✦ Confront a chronic offender in private, should all else fail. Often, pride makes them more defensive in front of their peers. Besides, if you do it on their turf, other people might spring to their defence out of misguided friendship.

MAY I HAVE A QUICK WORD?

Once, I had a regular problem with a committee member who in meetings made a point of addressing softly spoken – so that only I could hear them clearly – smilingly delivered remarks about 'persons', and little challenging and irrelevant remarks about 'equal opportunity'. Or he would facetiously accuse me of harassing him when I spoke emphatically or critically.

I spoke to him in private about it and he was very pleasant. However, his next act was to appear to cringe elaborately when he saw me, and to make remarks about my being tough. This was preferable, though it irritated not only me but also his male colleagues, who then prevailed upon him to stop because he was making an idiot of himself and distracting them.

Round one to me.

Moira

KEEPING WOMEN IGNORANT

Withholding information and keeping people in the dark is a very effective marginalising tool. Men chat to one another and exchange information in changing rooms, pubs, clubs and toilets – without thinking that it's the Men's Room. Sometimes they do it deliberately, conferring before the formal meeting to decide what it will decide. This is a strategy you can emulate: never go to a meeting without having decided what you want

out of it. But if the men have done it well, the decisions are virtually foregone conclusions and the meeting only gets to ratify them. The women, if they ask for discussion on the matter, are accused of prolonging the meeting and not coming to a decision that is so obviously 'right'.

Women need to ensure that they caucus and organise their

numbers beforehand. They should help shape the agenda and define the process, and perhaps offer to be the chair or the secretary of the group meeting. But if you're in a meeting and realise that you're being given the mushroom treatment you should:

- Signal that it's on, with the agreed code for the third strategy
- Make sure that you have a copy of the organisation's constitution and rules, or its memorandum and articles, and understand its requirements. If they are not sufficiently clear, work up amendments that will make them so and get support for changing them at the next annual general meeting
- Become familiar with, and use, meetings rules and procedures. You have the *right* to discuss proposals, and to be given adequate notice of them, and to defer a decision until you have the information, especially if you are responsible for the outcome
- Not allow the chair of the meeting to regulate debate in a discretionary way. Leaving the conduct of meetings to the discretion of the chair can mean that women's issues are not heard, because they do not *have* to be
- Insist that important issues requiring more preparatory study be shelved, or discussion deferred until the next meeting
- Ensure that you get the information you need by other means, such as your own networks.

If there are no special provisions for your group's meetings, you can use other established conventions and rules for how meetings should be run. Learn them and practise using them. (*Joske's Law and Procedure at Meetings in Australia* is an excellent reference.) As a rough guide, put the following into effect:

- Motions should be put in writing and tabled *before* a meeting
- The person who proposes a motion must have a seconder before there can be any debate
- The proposer can speak in favour of the motion at the beginning, or wait until the very end. The seconder also has a right to speak in favour of the motion
- Speakers for and against a motion must alternate – one 'pro' then one 'anti', until you run out of speakers, with the mover and the seconder of the motion having the right to speak last, but not repeatedly
- If someone wants to amend the motion, they have the right to do so, with a seconder, and the amendment must be voted on before the substantive motion
- If the debate bogs down, or seems designed to protract the meeting, you may move 'that the question be put', and the motion must be voted on at once. If it succeeds, there is no more debate and the substantive motion (that is, what you have been debating) must be put. Use this if there seems to be a filibuster going on
- If the meeting chair proposes a straw poll (a non-binding vote) this usually means people have to declare themselves and it deters objectors. Insist on a proper debate and a binding vote
- If you disagree with a procedural ruling by the chair, you have the right to move a motion of dissent from his or her ruling – and if it wins, you go back to the previous one. Use this sparingly
- Minutes must be kept of all meetings, be agreed with at the next meeting, and the minute book should be available for your scrutiny
- You should keep copies of the minutes and take relevant or important ones with you to all subsequent meetings.

Referring to them can prevent reinventing the wheel, or someone from claiming that decisions have been agreed upon when they have not.

If you can't get your issues dealt with properly, attack from the flank. Sometimes you won't be able to get your policy up in the 'big' meeting. Look for other ways. If there are subcommittees that are working in association with your area of interest or policy development, get onto them – their decisions might carry greater weight than yours alone.

SLIPPING IN THE SIDE DOOR

Our committee was deciding on modifications to our premises. I pointed out that if we were spending, as we planned, a lot of money we should make sure they were accessible to people with disabilities, and, for that matter, parents with children in prams or strollers. The response from the overwhelmingly male group was to say, 'Surely that law doesn't apply to non-government bodies,' and the suggestion was simply dismissed.

So I nominated myself onto the subcommittee looking into new accommodation for our organisation. This time I didn't tell them that my purpose was to ensure that it would be accessible and that it had room for childcare facilities. When the chairman realised this – after I'd been confirmed onto that subcommittee – his face was a picture. The new premises were fully accessible: the committee's brief to the agents required it.

Moira

MAKING WOMEN FEEL INADEQUATE

One of the best ways to take women's power away in meetings is to give them too much to do and then not allow them the time or resources to do it properly. No matter how hard you try, things will sometimes go wrong. Women are really good at blaming themselves for this. They tend to have double loads –

work, children, partner and extended family – and the stress of feeling that you should be somewhere else can be crippling. Women may be accused, often implicitly, of being mothers first, workers second – or of being poor mothers because they have given work, or politics, priority in their lives. They have to put up with criticism whatever they choose to put first. When they choose both, they face dissatisfaction on all sides.

Many women do want to combine family life with working life (so do many men) and they have every right to say no to both home and work demands – especially work demands that require them to be at meetings out of hours. Men don't usually face this double bind. It is still more common for men to say yes to job demands and no in the home. This is unacceptable. Families, and their women members, are entitled to a decent working life *and* family life.

So, if the meeting is arranging its business in a way that wrong-foots you:

+ Signal to your colleagues that the fourth strategy is in place
+ Insist that meetings are timed to take into account the needs of people to have a life. No matter how pressing the issue, proper notice should be given so that you can attend
+ Choose your husband or partner very carefully, for they need to understand the burdens you will both have to share – not as a matter of kindness but because it is fair and right. Draw up 'an agreement' acknowledging your right to work and to be, if you choose, politically active, and agree on the sharing of home responsibilities
+ If you can, choose your employer carefully too. Have they family-friendly policies? Do they actually implement them, or is there a hint of disapproval if you can't come to meetings at 7 am, or have to take time off to be with the child with the measles?

✦ Expect your employer to accept your commitment as it is given, without assuming that you don't really want promotion or advancement opportunities.

When things do go wrong, don't cop too much blame. Women tend to flagellate themselves in public when they make a mistake. Men don't. Make sure too that other women take only their share of any blame, and no more.

If you personally should have done something and haven't, own up before the meeting and either set aside the time to do it, or arrange for someone else to take over. Admit your mistakes, but never throw yourself on the mercy of the men.

Moira was once called in to resolve a workplace dispute where the woman supervisor had problems managing non-productive staff. Her own (male) manager had encouraged her to take a firm, disciplinarian line: she had been calling the recalcitrant staff names, shouting at them and shaming them. By the time Moira spoke to her she was on the verge of tears and full of self-blame. Though her management had been poor, she had been doing what she was instructed to do and she hadn't been trained to do anything else. Moira had to intervene, and push the blame upstairs where it truly belonged. Her manager, of course, was looking holier than thou and saying it was entirely her responsibility. He wasn't, and it clearly wasn't, once the company had Moira's report.

Often when a woman complains about humiliating treatment or abuse or bullying – or even just that the meeting is not being run properly – the response is to blame her for making it difficult for her colleagues, as well as for herself. It may be said that she only has herself to blame, or that she more or less asked for it. Some kind of perverse sense of guilt for what has happened then builds up.

Women often *do* hesitate to complain, and such judgements can lead them to believe that their detractors are right. It is important to analyse the situation and form a realistic view of what has happened. Above all, realise that there is no call to feel guilty. And:

+ Never complain officially or formally until you have talked the matter over with someone who is a little more removed from the situation, and have considered their perspective
+ When the guilt trip is laid on you, call a close friend and analyse the situation together
+ Call up your support group and make sure that your friends defend you
+ Remember that guilt is a useless emotion. Get rid of it. Get it into perspective
+ Try to form a clear picture of the underlying pattern, your part in it and others' part in it
+ Get back to those who would wish to put all the blame on you: show them what actually happened
+ Defend other women who are victimised too: be responsible for one another.

COPING WITH RECRIMINATION

When I was Victorian Premier the state of the economy and the community mood was such that the Premier had to take the blame for everything. Opposition leader Jeff Kennett even blamed me when the West Coast Eagles became the first non-Victorian team to win the AFL premiership.

But one of the hardest things to bear was the politics of condemnation undertaken in the opposition's 'Guilty Party' ad campaign, which stamped me and other leading Ministers as guilty on issues from the sale of the State Bank to education and the state debt. I often wonder whether I should have taken the issue on legally, but I didn't and so I (and other Ministers and our families) had to face it personally.

I did so by:
+ Working through the claims in terms of shared responsibility and actual causes
+ Fixing what could be fixed
+ Taking a positive personal approach
+ Valuing the government's achievements
+ Acknowledging failures, rather than apologising for them
+ Refocusing on what could be achieved.

Joan

TRAINING JUDAS SHEEP

A Judas sheep is one who trots up the gangplank to the abattoir, or the ships that transport live sheep overseas for slaughter, leading the way so that others will follow, and is then rescued from the fate of its peers. A Judas sheep gets special privileges or protection in exchange for leading others to their doom. But they are 'special' for just as long as it suits the abattoir.

Co-opting women to the tasks of a male-dominated meeting is a dangerously effective way of marginalising women. It deprives women of their fellow-feeling and trust, turning them against one another – promising favour to one if she will only abandon her women colleagues and their cause. Some women fall for it, believing that compliance with others' agendas is politically astute and ethically acceptable. The best defence against it is solidarity. If you see it happening:

+ Signal that a traitor is in your midst, but not in such a way as to show up your colleague in a publicly humiliating way. No finger-pointing here
+ Do not be tempted to be used this way yourself. Be alert to the possibility – if you are being effective in your meeting, an offer may well be made. Keep your counsel, then caucus with your colleagues and work out a strategy for dealing with the offer together

✦ If you notice another woman being approached in this way outside a meeting, take her aside and speak to her in friendship, pointing out the effects on herself and on the rest of you

✦ If she falls, keep the door open for when she realises that she has not won what she wants, and wants to come back. If she doesn't rejoin the women, expose the strategy not the person

✦ Realise that the only way to be powerful is as part of a group with common interests and strategies. A strong and lasting decision is one that is thought through and owned by the whole group, not owned by a few and agreed to by others. Women's experience simply cannot be overlooked, if the group is to function at its best.

MERITING ATTENTION?

Our board was meeting to approve the appointment of a deputy, someone with management and administrative skills. The candidate was a male – in fact, all the management team were men.

The selection committee reported that it had looked for a woman, but unfortunately couldn't find one they could afford. One excellent female candidate wanted 'too much money' – about $25 000 more than they were planning to spend. The board agreed to the appointment of a man at the lower salary.

Then, without notice, one of the selection committee orally proposed that the CEO receive a pay rise – of $25 000! Several of the women board members protested. A recent restructure had resulted in virtually all senior women being retrenched or resigning, and the morale of the remaining women was extremely low. They said, What message would this send?

So what? replied the men, the CEO was underpaid. Indeed, one man said that to compare the status of the CEO with that of the failed woman candidate for the deputy position was like 'comparing apples with pears'.

The guillotine was applied to the debate, the vote was taken. Four of the 5 women voted against the rise, feeling guilty and disloyal to the CEO as they did; one abstained, and the vote was carried by the majority.

The issue – gender equity – was overlooked because the men did not understand that it was an important one.

Moira

Always debrief after meetings, over a drink or over the phone, on the success or failure of your strategies. Plan your next tactics, which might include broadening your number of allies or fronting up to your opponents between meetings. Don't give up on meetings. You will have disappointments, but a lot more success if you learn to manage them well.

horacek

chapter 6

The workplace

Beatrice Faust, founder of the Women's Electoral Lobby, once said that if the women's movement could be summed up in a phrase, it was 'the right to choose'.

Work is the key. It gives you the power to determine your own life – or it should. If you earn your own money, you make your own decisions about how to run your life. If you are in control of your finances, you are in control of your life, you have choices. Work should also be rewarding in itself – be worth doing, worth doing well, and be something where your worth is recognised. We are well aware that not everyone has a lot of choice about what work they do or how fulfilling it is, especially if they have limited qualifications and relatively little flexibility because of other responsibilities. Many women have to take whatever work they can get.

Our starting point is opening up your opportunities. Do whatever you can to give yourself more options. Don't just fall into a job – think about what you want to do and go for it. (Happiness follows.) To have choices, women need to have qualifications and skills that people want. We need bargaining power. We need the tools to unlock the system.

Make sure that if you're getting a qualification, it's applicable to what you want to do. Too many women are advised badly and don't go for the top. If you're interested in dentistry, aim to be a dentist, not a dental nurse. If you want to work with children, by all means take courses that will give you the skills, but don't expect to be financially rewarded for it. Like languages? Get skills that enable you to use those languages, rather than just reading them – become fluent in translating and you can work in other countries or with other nationalities.

There's no point in studying only the subjects that interest you if they will not give you saleable skills. You may love writing – by all means hone your skill, but don't expect to make much of a living writing novels. Lawyers who study feminist jurisprudence gain a tremendous insight into the limitations of the law and legal institutions, but that knowledge alone will not make you an attractive employee in the construction industry, if that's where you want to work. Want to help Aboriginal people? Learn not only about native title and international human rights, but study mining law, land law, get negotiation qualifications and experience, and become a whiz at drafting commercial contracts, understanding tax law and business practice. Let your values inform what you do and the way that you do it.

Don't fall into the trap of doing a half-baked technical course together with a pared-down business administration diploma. If your mentor tells you that a Master's in Business

Administration would be useful, aim for a doctorate. Employers want your technical skills and know-how, and don't necessarily value a polymath or someone with a dab of information.

Hardly anyone owns a job outright any more, or has a job for life. The whole emphasis of modern workplace laws is to individualise the contract between an employee and an employer. An individual has talents and skills and experience, and these

are her bargaining chips which she can use to strike a good deal with one employer or take to another. Acquire your skills and experience, build them, use them, and use your knowledge of other women's experience and your sensitivity to the rights of others, along with your personal values and ethics, to drive and if necessary change the policy and culture of the industry you work in.

Before you decide to take a job, get the information you need. What exactly is the job you will be expected to do? What opportunities will it give you, with either this employer or the next, and where might it lead? Do they have good equal-opportunity policies? What do they provide in terms of family-friendly work policies and programs? Do they have mentoring systems, career progression? What is their reputation? Ask yourself where you ultimately want to go, and whether this job or some aspect of it will get you there.

Insist on a proper job description and a duty statement before you're hired. A title won't do. One woman we know accepted a new position called the 'national recruitment co-ordinator' with no written statement of her duties. After her first week she was told that the organisation had reconsidered the duties of the position and she was now to be the company's training officer. It wasn't a good start.

You are entitled to a contract that spells out what is expected of you, and what your employer will provide in terms of wages or salary, leave, training and benefits. This can be in a letter, but it must be clear because your rights and protection depend on it. If you don't do this, you may encounter something very different from what you expected, and find that you have very little control over your employment conditions. So get it in writing and keep your copy at home. Refer back to it if there's a difference of opinion. It's a good idea to keep notes and memorandums of any subsequent decisions about your work duties.

If you are going into a kind of work traditionally done by men, one where you will be in a minority or seem different or novel, you need to be:

- ✦ Prepared. Make sure you are fit enough, skilled up and confident
- ✦ Balanced. Weigh up situations and see problems through. Rely on your commonsense to begin with. Don't fly off the handle. If you're feeling weepy, do it in private
- ✦ Thick-skinned. Expect problems. Don't be too easily bothered, offended, or thrown off balance
- ✦ Good-humoured. Be able to laugh any time and any-where. But never put down another woman or anyone else who's on the outer – gays, indigenous people, mi-grants, people with disabilities. Look for the funny side. It'll be there, even if it's against yourself
- ✦ Persistent. Know what you want to do, where you want to be, and why. Give it your best shot. Persistence wears others down while it builds you up
- ✦ Organised. If you want to make changes in the workplace, you need to organise with your immediate colleagues and/or your appropriate union or association
- ✦ Willing to grow. Work stays enjoyable most when your job expands and you grow with it. Make the most of any developmental opportunities, from golf days and computer training to overseas study tours. If your employer is an equal-opportunity employer, women should get equal access to these opportunities.

NEGOTIATING YOUR TERMS AND CONDITIONS

You may have to do many job interviews in your lifetime, so get used to doing them well. Many women don't interview well, and are less likely to feel comfortable trumpeting their achieve-ments. A good job interview depends on excellent preparation.

You need to have read everything you can about the job and its
challenges beforehand, and if possible to have talked with people
who work in the area; to have thought about why you want the
job, and to be very clear about how your skills, qualifications
and experience fit the selection criteria. Be prepared for some
questions about your personal life – hobbies, family and sporting
interests. If they seem gender-specific, you should ask them
sweetly whether they asked the men the same questions.

It is increasingly common for women to job-share. This is
consistent with the new emphasis on individualised employment
contracts rather than permanent employment under award
conditions. The keys to successful job-sharing are being very
clear about the tasks that are to be performed, keeping good
records for your job-share partner, handing over necessary information to maintain continuity, and being considerate about
your shared space and resources. Work these details out with
your employer first, so that there is no misunderstanding.

If there's a union covering your area of employment we
suggest that you join it, whether it's white-collar or blue-collar.
If you don't like what they're doing, or not doing, for you, let
them know. Unions are sensitive to criticism these days – union
membership is voluntary and they have to work to keep their
influence, and their financial basis, secure. In the past unions
have often failed to take women's concerns sufficiently into account, but now many women head unions, most women work,
and together with women members they can change that culture.
Unions speak on behalf of thousands of workers. They have
spent decades negotiating awards and agreements for groups of
workers with employers, from a position of strength. They have
relationships and power that you don't have, yet, as an individual.
Join them, contribute to them, use them and shape them so
that they service their members properly.

When it comes to negotiating your salary, our advice is to

know your worth, although this can be easier said than done. Most women find it very hard to negotiate with their employers. Many women, particularly those who have family responsibilities, feel they have to take any conditions, any wage that allows them to keep working. They are made to feel fortunate that they have a job, any job. Other, high-achieving women sell themselves short – they fail to negotiate appropriate salaries for themselves, because they like the responsibility and the rewards of the work. Too many women find themselves earning considerably less than men doing similar work, and without the perks that men get, such as cars and expense accounts and access to training. A lot of us haven't got a clear idea of our own worth. Money issues crystallise the lack of self-value that so many women have.

Some points to think about when setting your own price:

+ Though it might seem like a good idea in the short term to offer your services at a discount, bear in mind that once you charge less than the going rate you may be expected to charge low rates forever

+ Undervaluing your services is very destructive. Think of the effects of price wars in any industry. For a while the consumers rub their hands with glee as prices tumble, but eventually the industry ceases to be viable and at least one or two players go out of business. Think of the effect on your own future: you are setting a precedent for yourself and for other women in your line of work, and cheap labour means relatively under-appreciated labour

+ If you are really convinced that discounting is the only way to get new work, make it clear that the reduced price is a once-only, trial arrangement, and that any future work will need to be paid for at a proper rate

+ Charging low rates reinforces a belief in scarcity, not a belief in prosperity.

Even when we do decide on a salary we think is fair, we often find it hard actually to ask for the money. There are two ways to overcome this problem. Get someone else to negotiate for you, or get the confidence, skill and information to do it properly yourself. Each has its pros and cons.

The usefulness of getting someone else who is not personally involved to negotiate for you is that it gives you the moral courage to demand what you're worth. You might choose an agent, a lawyer, an accountant, or someone else with appropriate experience. Some points to consider:

+ It usually involves payment of some kind – either a fee or a percentage. You need to decide whether they're worth it
+ Make sure you find someone you trust – personal recommendation is the best, but you must also have a good rapport with them
+ Make sure they understand exactly what it is you do and what your skills are
+ Make sure they are acting on your behalf and that there are no conflicts of interest or double dipping. In the entertainment industry, for instance, an agent might take a fee from a venue to provide a performer and then charge the performer a percentage of her income as well
+ Ask for proof beforehand of their experience in negotiating successfully (they should be able to give you examples, or referees)
+ Make sure they are familiar with the industry you work in, or are willing to do some research to get themselves up to speed
+ Avoid giving your negotiator the legal authority to sign anything on your behalf.

If you decide to go it alone on your negotiations:

+ Compare what you do to what others in your line of work do, and ask them how much they charge
+ Research the usual rates of pay involved

+ Ask your union or professional association for details on minimum rates (even though you might want to negotiate for more). Such organisations often give free advice on contracts
+ Get some training in negotiation skills. If after that you are still not confident in your abilities, reconsider getting someone else to do it for you
+ Never sign anything without being absolutely sure that you understand it and are happy with it.

WORKPLACE AGREEMENTS

Awards, negotiated by unions, used to provide coverage for all workers and were enforceable in industrial tribunals if they were broken. But since the early 1990s, Australian workplaces have been encouraged to negotiate directly with employers about ways to improve productivity, wages and conditions, outside the award system. Now there are two kinds of workplace agreements that you and your co-workers can negotiate: certified agreements made between unions representing employees and employers, and enterprise flexibility agreements made between a company and a majority of its workers.

The needs and desires of many women employees get overlooked in this process. If the union representatives do not understand women's issues – and sometimes they don't, because the majority of their members or officers are male, or because the women work part-time, casual or shift rates and don't know how important it is to make the representatives aware – they can be overlooked. And sometimes women do not participate at all in the negotiations for enterprise flexibility agreements because they don't appreciate the significance it has for their conditions. It is up to you to get involved.

There are ten steps to negotiating an agreement and it is very important indeed that women take them. (Seek advice from the union, if there is one. They have decades of experience in negotiation.)

1 Get other women together informally. Talk about what you want – maternity leave, special leave for family reasons, consultation about changes in working arrangements, help with childcare, equal pay with men, recognition of skills or overseas qualifications, cultural and religious requirements (such as a place for prayers, or leave to attend funerals in the community or religious festivals), promotion opportunities, access to higher duties and special training. Meet regularly.

2 Make sure everyone has a say, and make special efforts to find out what women who work part-time or on late shifts want. Encourage them to take part too. It is in everyone's interests to make sure this happens.

3 Write down your goals. What do you want to change? Make sure you try to get improved conditions for everyone, not just for some. Write your objectives down and share them around.

4 Set up a group to represent you in negotiations, or, if a union is involved, insist that women be a significant part of the negotiation team so that it is fully informed about what women want. The group must present the issues of all employees, not just those of the largest number or the pushiest ones. It must include both union and non-union members.

5 Workers are entitled to meet in company time, on reasonable notice, to discuss what they want. Representatives are expected to consult with workers, and workers are entitled to be consulted. See if you can get training in how to negotiate. Make sure that the negotiators take into consideration anti-discrimination and equal-opportunity laws, the need to balance work and family

life, which workers are disadvantaged and how this could be remedied.

6 Negotiators must talk with management about the improvements they want, and what management wants in exchange. Usually this is better productivity – this is not the same thing as harder work for longer hours and the same pay.

7 Get advice on writing your agreement, before you vote to accept it.

8 Once the agreement is ratified by the group by voting, make sure everyone gets a copy and knows what it means.

9 No agreement lasts forever. It must be complied with and it must be reviewed, renewed, or renegotiated.

10 Keep up your women's meetings, whoever does the negotiating, so that women's issues are brought constantly to the attention of management, unions, and colleagues.

FAMILY-FRIENDLY WORKPLACES

Many women who take the brunt of family and household responsibilities find it difficult to choose different working hours or take up opportunities for training or development. Working mothers should not have to put up with being called 'the late Ms X' when they come in at nine, by arrangement, after dropping the children off at school or day-care, or with being sniffed at or forgotten about after missing a couple of after-work meetings.

Here are some strategies for dealing with this:

✦ Your employer should have an induction process and a manual that tells you what its policies on equal opportunity, promotion and work behaviour are. If not, seek them out

- ✦ If it doesn't already have one, ask the company/organisation to adopt a short, family-friendly policy statement (you write it out for them) so that when you ask for meetings to be held at appropriate times they have to consider it. Point out that men have families too
- ✦ Survey your fellow workers or members about their childcare needs and their preferences for meeting times. Pass the information on to management
- ✦ Build support for work-based childcare, if that is what is needed
- ✦ Find out and share information about how family-friendly policies lead to better productivity and retention of trained staff – this saves the company money
- ✦ When you get into a position of authority or power yourself, don't forget what you have been arguing for on family-friendly workplaces. Lead by example.

Joan Kirner noticed, when she was Minister of Conservation, Forests and Lands, that many of her best women operators were stressed out during school holidays; when she asked why, she was told it was because it was so hard to organise adequate childcare or ask for special leave. Joan and her staff organised a family-friendly school holidays policy, which included an acknowledgement of the need time off for and the setting up of work-based childcare, not only for members of her own department but for all Victorian government departments. The real bonus for Joan was that she could sometimes slip down to the childcare centre and play with the kids.

If you discover that, for example, important contacts or clients are to be entertained at men-only venues (such as some exclusive clubs) or sporting opportunities, ask them to change the venue. One woman employed in a senior position simply refused to attend the annual dinner held, according to hallowed tradition, in the Melbourne Club, which refuses to accept women members. She didn't change the club's policy, but she did change the venue for the next dinner.

Sport or recreation is often used to cut women out. Rosemary Neill, in her article 'Boardroom Backlash' (*Weekend Financial Review*, 19–20 April 1997), cites research done for the Karpin Report by Barbara Cail, founder of the Chief Executive Women's Network. Cail discovered an extraordinary obsession with sport in Australian business practice that filters right down to how business is done. She reported one instance where a female executive had worked very hard on a team to secure an important deal and then was cut out when key decisions were made on a golf course. (She also found cases where businessmen made policy decisions on toilet breaks, effectively cutting out women.)

It seems that golf has become so important in business networking that some women are taking lessons to play a sport they do not enjoy. We wish them luck. We think sport has other purposes.

WORKING WITH MALE MANAGERS

It is undoubtedly true that some men in management positions find it difficult to deal with women as colleagues or equals. Some find it easier to support and patronise up-and-coming young women, but are genuinely put off when they move into positions of relative equality. Others can manage to deal with a feminine manager of their own, up to a point. We recommend dealing with the uncomfortable male manager by:

- ✦ Expecting to be treated on your merits
- ✦ Treating him on his merits
- ✦ Being good at your job – of course. When you've done a particularly good job, report on it in writing and make sure that others get to see it too, just in case the awkward male manager forgets to pass it on, or he doesn't see it as noteworthy

+ Make sure you have a mentor
+ Make sure you have networks in the organisation, so
  you're not steamrollered by a culture that doesn't include
  you. Change the culture as you go
+ Refer back to our advice on meetings and apply those
  strategies to your work generally. You cannot afford to
  allow situations such as being left out of the information
  loop to persist
+ Ensure that women's issues in relation to working conditions are genuinely mainstreamed
+ If the company doesn't have an equal-opportunity policy,
  or clear career paths, or a mentoring strategy, or a clear
  promotions policy, get together with other women to
  make sure they do
+ Behave professionally. Don't even think of using your
  sexual attractiveness as a promotional strategy – among
  other things it will fade as you get older. Young women
  may not realise this, and it's not until their youth fades
  that they find themselves unaccountably missing out on
  promotion, appointment, or simply the warmth of the
  old days. Women who want to be powerful at work need
  fortitude and skills and a track record. Without them
  you've vulnerable when Cutie Mark II comes along
+ Never engage in sexist jokes or put-downs to other
  women – the men will only be encouraged to do it to
  you
+ Treat well those who work for you. If you're on the way
  up, treat others well; you'll need friends on the way down
  too.

Don't be afraid of asking for advice about work issues. Women
tend to hesitate in workplaces where this might be portrayed as
an admission of weakness. When you do seek advice, consider
the other person's workload in timing your request, and make

sure that you ask the right person – the one with the knowledge rather than someone you simply like.

Many women also find it hard to deal with performance reviews, or other one-to-one interviews that may have disciplinary or negative outcomes. It's useful to practise role-playing these with other women who have been through them, to ease your apprehension. Make sure before the meeting that you have a written agenda, so that you know exactly what will be talked through. Ensure firmly but politely that the agenda is adhered to: if the discussion roams to irrelevant matters, you are entitled to ask for a later appointment to respond. If it's a performance review, you need to know precisely what your performance measures are. If it's associated with perceived problems or weaknesses then you need to know exactly what these are, and if it's a disciplinary meeting it's best not to go alone: take a trusted colleague, or union or professional associate with you. In all cases, try not to be defensive, angry or weepy. These meetings are supposed to be objective, professional and work-related, but it takes two to keep them that way. Remember that your rights in such meetings are protected by your contract or your award; by the principles of natural justice (the right to know any case to be made against you, the right to respond, which means getting proper notice, and the right to have decisions made by an unprejudiced and unbiased decision-maker); and, should it come to that, by anti-discrimination and unfair-dismissal laws. You need to know this, but you don't need to threaten their use.

EQUAL-OPPORTUNITY LAWS

Gender is still an issue at most workplaces, though quite a few women don't want to believe this. Women are under-represented in management, board membership, and the heights of the major professions, and still earn a lot less than men. The reasons are complex: a mix of part-time work for women with family responsibilities; career interruptions; a very sex-segregated work-force, with women working in large numbers in poorly paid sectors; and just a touch of discrimination.

Most women have family responsibilities: the ABS found in 1995 that the main reason for unemployment nominated by half of all women not working or who were actively looking for work was 'family reasons', including not being able to find quality childcare. Moreover, women who work part-time or casually do not have the same opportunity to build up superannuation benefits for their retirement, even though they are likely to live longer than men.

Equal opportunity at work means being treated on your merits, without discrimination because of some irrelevant characteristic, such as your sex, or propensity to get pregnant from time to time. We have laws prohibiting discrimination. You need to know what they are and to be able to distinguish between being treated unjustly because you are a woman and simply feeling piqued, which is not proof that you have been discriminated against.

Anti-discrimination laws are better accepted in Australia than in any other Western country. We have nine statutory equal-opportunity or anti-discrimination institutions adminis-tering state, territory and Commonwealth anti-discrimination laws. Every level of government espouses equal-opportunity policies in its public-sector employment. We have had a Federal Affirmative Action Agency since 1986, which requires regular affirmative-action reporting from corporate employers to measure whether equal-employment opportunity is a fact or an aspiration. Federal industrial laws even seek to achieve anti-discriminatory objectives.

All this began with international politics. Australia signed treaties with other countries that identified discrimination as a fundamental breach of the human right to be treated with respect. These treaties oblige us to eliminate discrimination or face international criticism. The first international human rights instrument Australia signed was the United Nations' 1948 Universal Declaration of Human Rights. Since then we have made many other, more specific, international promises: to eliminate discrimination on race, sex and disabilities, for example. Under International Labor Organisation Conventions we have promised to eradicate discrimination at work and to protect the rights of workers with family responsibilities. We have promised to protect the rights of children.

As human beings we naturally discriminate about who we mix with and what we do in education and employment, in buying goods and services, or using public facilities, or providing and seeking accommodation. This is lawful and proper. Discrimination that is neither lawful nor right makes irrelevant distinctions among people that disadvantage some, for no acceptable reason. It is human to want to be surrounded with people just like ourselves, who make us feel comfortable. A group's rejection of those who do not conform with what is considered normal or acceptable binds that group together, but at some point this becomes anti-social and destructive to the long-term interests of the wider community, as well as to the individuals. So we have prohibited by law that kind of discrimination. It is not the unique experience of women.

Women who know how it feels to be subjected to prejudice or subtle exclusion should work to make sure it doesn't happen to anybody else. We can complain about discrimination, but it's far more effective to eliminate it by knowing the law and insisting that it doesn't happen.

The grounds and scope for discrimination complaints are similar in every state, but with many variations in exceptions or amendments. For example, Tasmania's anti-discrimination laws address sex discrimination and sexual harassment alone, whereas it is also unlawful in other states and territories to discriminate on the basis of race; disability (or impairment); political or industrial activity; religious, marital or parental status; family responsibilities and pregnancy; and, in most jurisdictions, age and sexuality too. Federal anti-discrimination laws cover some of the same ground.

But just because someone has been treated unfairly on one of the prohibited grounds, they do not necessarily have the right to make a formal complaint. The discrimination must have occurred in one of the areas of public life covered by anti-discrimination laws. These are:

+ Work
+ Education or training
+ Trade or occupational qualifications
+ Sport
+ Access to goods and services and facilities, such as public halls, public transport, service in shops or from government
+ Club memberships. However, it is legal to set up special clubs to preserve minority cultures, and there are still some private clubs that can discriminate – several that will not admit women members, for instance. These are becoming rare as their male-only membership dies off. Monoculturalism is boring.

It is important for women to know, and to act on their knowledge, that discrimination is unlawful and that there *is* something that they can do about it.

DEALING WITH DISCRIMINATION AND HARASSMENT

'Discrimination' means being excluded or treated less favourably than another person without your characteristics in similar circumstances. It includes assumptions about your being less able or less talented or less deserving. Some discrimination is direct. For example, if a school refused to accept Aboriginal children because it assumed they were less intelligent, or more likely to cause trouble, this would clearly be a breach of the Commonwealth's Race Discrimination Act. If there is a causal connection between a person's race, sex, or other ground covered by discrimination laws and their being given less favourable treatment, then the discrimination is again direct, even if it is not expressed or spelled out and may be difficult to prove.

But sometimes the reason someone is treated in a less favourable way is not because of obvious or conscious prejudices, but because people holding powerful positions have unconsciously developed biased rules and practices. Most organisations have rules, but if these rules have a very unfair effect on a group of people who cannot meet their requirements, they are discriminatory in an indirect way. Women often encounter work practices that have grown up over time – practices such as entertaining important customers after hours or at venues where women feel uncomfortable, such as tabletop-dancing clubs. This is indirectly discriminatory – it may be an implied condition of participating fully in your work that you fit in, when you in fact can't fit in.

Sexual harassment is unwelcome conduct of a sexual nature, be it in acts, words, gestures, pictures, calendars, screen-savers, emails, faxes, jokes, stroking, threats, unwanted and repeated invitations, direct requests for sexual favours, or personal remarks and teasing. Whether it was meant to or not, and whether it was aimed at you specifically or not, if the conduct is of a kind that makes you feel insulted, intimidated or offended – and if a reasonable person would, in the circumstances, expect you to feel that way – it's sexual harassment and it's illegal.

The difference between sexist remarks and sexual remarks is clear. A sexist remark is one that puts down the other person – either patronisingly ('girlie'), or rudely ('bloody feminist'), or unconsciously ('love'), and sometimes just plain insensitively. A sexual remark is one that focuses on sexual characteristics ('nice tits!') or sexual conduct ('You a dyke?' or 'Got a boyfriend, love?'). You should have a few remarks on hand to snap back at the smart-alecs, particularly if you're going into an all-male area. Think about the most likely remarks beforehand, so that you will feel that you can hold your own and not be a victim. Annie Cowling, who wrote *Breaking New Ground: A Manual for Survival for Women Entering Non-Traditional Jobs* for women working in the construction industry, offers the following retorts:

- ✦ Q: Why do you want to be a carpenter (or a mechanic or whatever)? A: Why did you? Or, My brother decided to be a nurse.
- ✦ Q: Do you get any hassles from the guys? A: No, do you? Or, No, you're the first.
- ✦ Q: Are you a girl? A: Last time I looked (never offer to show proof). Or, No, I'm a tree, book-end, walrus (etc.)
- ✦ Q: Do you live with your parents? A: Do you?
- ✦ Q: Have you got a boyfriend? A: Why? Do you need one?
- ✦ Q: Why are you taking a man's job? A: He didn't seem to mind.
- ✦ Q: What do you think you are doing here? A: I didn't realise you expected me to think.
- ✦ Q: What's a little thing like you doing here? A: Well, they say the meek will inherit the earth and I'm trying to figure out what I'm going to do with it.

This is based on the assumption that the questions are good-natured and there is a fundamental sense of goodwill. Annie also suggests working out a list of one-liners that might come in handy if you are being annoyed, even if you only think about saying them. (If you write them down, don't take the list to work, it might fall into the wrong hands.) It also does no harm

if, when you respond, you make it quite clear that you have a sense of humour but that you find the questions or comments unwelcome.

As Annie says, if you find yourself being particularly annoyed by ridiculous remarks or intrusive questions, remember that though you might get angry for a few minutes, they'll be stupid for the rest of their lives. But if you're really equal, they won't be offended if you ask them to stop.

CHEEKING THE NEW MINISTER

My first meeting with a trade union leader was marked by his put-down greeting: 'Good morning, Minister. New outfit? You didn't buy that at Target.'

Momentarily astounded, I replied, 'Thank you. I was going to say the same thing about your gear, but I thought better of it.'

The meeting continued on equal terms.

Joan

But when the remarks are not so harmless, the big question for women is, should they complain? Will they then be seen as a whinger? Won't they just be targeted as a troublemaker? The fear of being victimised or blacklisted may be a real one, based on previous experience. But if you don't stand up for your rights, nobody will know what happened to you, and it could happen to somebody else. It's hard, and you must not try to do it alone.

You need friends and advice. But do act: silence is often misinterpreted as consent, or acquiescence. Don't blame yourself: you have the right to be treated with respect and equality. Don't let it get you down, and don't be intimidated. You *don't* have to tolerate bullying. Never, ever, ever try to deal with sexual harassment on your own.

Though you may well try to ignore the offensive behaviour at first, if it's an ongoing problem you'll have to deal with it. You can't tolerate sleazebags making sexual remarks to you or touching you, anyway. It's unsafe. And you can't work for long in a hostile work environment, especially one that makes you feel sexually vulnerable, or embarrassed, or edgy. Sexual harassment is really bullying behaviour with sexual overtones. It can cripple your comfort at work, your effectiveness, your ability to satisfy your employer's demands; it can destroy your personal happiness and your health, and ultimately ruin your self-confidence.

Someone who complains about sexual, or sexist, remarks at work, especially if such behaviour has been tolerated for a long time, is like a branch suddenly popping out from under the surface of a smoothly flowing river. She sticks out, makes ripples, and suddenly it seems that the whole force of the torrent is trying to drag her back under, so that things can be as they were. But it is illegal to victimise or punish anyone who makes a harassment or discrimination complaint. It's legal to separate the people while the complaint is being investigated, even if the alleged perpetrator says it's unfair.

It's important to deal with sexual harassment because it has a way of building up. People start capping each other's dirty stories or jokes, and what started off as trivial and a bit vague and uncomfortable can end up very serious and very personal. And it's management's responsibility to head this off at the pass – not yours.

A CASE STUDY

THE CONSTITUTIONAL CONVENTION IN CANBERRA

When the convention began, many women delegates were hesitant to speak because of the way they were interrupted and even heckled by the mostly more experienced men. But they developed some strategies for dealing with this. Other women spoke up in defence of the women who were being heckled. The redoubtable Pat O'Shane, a magnificent Aboriginal woman magistrate and strong feminist, did this several times and was labelled Sister Sibilance by some of the sexists in the press gallery for her pains. But it gave other women, and some men, the incentive they needed to take the matter up with the chairman of the convention,

and induced him to speak out against the practice and to
clamp down when it resumed.

During one of the subcommittees' regular meetings
some of the politicians engaged in boisterous interruptions
and ridicule when women spoke. One blew kisses, and
became even more facetious and rude when objections were
made. After a quiet word with the chairman of that
committee about the hostile atmosphere it created, the
behaviour was damped down, even if only a little.

The hardest discrimination of all to deal with was
the subtle undermining acts – men with deep voices
talking over women and other people with softer or higher
voices; the cracking of in-jokes; the caucusing in all-male
groups before and after meetings. It happened during
the convention – it will happen anywhere where women
are in a minority. The important thing is to name the
conduct, identify its discriminatory effect, and not
accept it.

TIPS FOR DEALING WITH HARASSMENT

Remember our advice: never, ever try to deal with this on your
own. Talk to friends, but not at work – it causes instant gossip.
Get advice and support, even if you don't want to make a formal
complaint and want to talk to the guy on your own – the other
option is to get one of the offender's mates to do it. Talk about
it in confidence with the company's equal-opportunity or
harassment or grievance officer, or the personnel or human-
relations manager. Or call your union, or ring your local equal-
opportunity or anti-discrimination body for advice on whether
it's harassment and what can be done about it. You have the right
to make a formal harassment complaint within the organisation,
and the best option is to make the organisation itself fix the
problem as a matter of policy and good management. But if you

don't feel this is possible, you can make a complaint of sexual harassment to the statutory anti-discrimination or equal-opportunity body in your state.

There are some things you can do right away:

+ Tell the harasser that you didn't like what he (or she) said or did, and it wasn't welcome – if you can. If you are afraid to, get help to deal with it straight away
+ Most men don't intend to harass and are very surprised and often genuinely hurt to be told they have. Understand this, but do not be diverted by pity from getting it stopped
+ If it's ongoing, get help to rehearse what to do next time it happens. Try: Did you know harassment was illegal? Do you talk like that to boys too? Listen, I'm here to do my job, and you're not helping (this is sometimes very effective)
+ If it's really crude, *get away fast*
+ Some people advise being smart back – we don't think it's wise
+ If it's someone invading your physical space, take action not to be crowded. Move back, and don't get yourself in a corner at the office Christmas party. In a crowded lift take the corner closest to the buttons.

Suggestive 'girlie' or 'cheesecake' photos or posters or screen-savers can make many women feel uncomfortable. It's not a matter of being a prude, but of objecting to women being portrayed as sex objects. If this is happening in your workplace:

+ Quietly find out whose they are so you can work out how many people like them
+ Don't put up male pin-ups to retaliate – it only encourages competition
+ Don't just take them down or destroy them – there *will* be a backlash

+ If there's a sexual harassment policy in place, quietly ask management to enforce it
+ Remember that it's management's job to keep the workplace safe and secure for all workers, whether they like it or not
+ Remember that many men are as offended by suggestive pictures as women are. And many women say they're not, but that doesn't matter. If just one is, that's enough.

We recommend that you try to avoid getting into arguments with work colleagues over suggestive or outrightly filthy pictures, but if this should happen despite your best attempts:

+ Explain that you're no prude but you don't like feeling uncomfortable, and ask how they would like it if their sister/mother/wife saw the material
+ Appeal to their better nature. Explain that you cannot work properly and you're entitled to feel comfortable at work
+ Suggest that, if the men like the pictures so much, they should take them home and put them on the fridge
+ Ask who the material actually belongs to, and if no-one admits to it then suggest that nobody would mind if it came down, either
+ If they say they're 'just beautiful girls', suggest they be replaced with pictures everyone likes – a beautiful landscape, maybe
+ If they say it's on their own desk, in their own room, or on their own computer, so it's private and you don't have to look, explain to them that there is no private place in a workplace – every part of the office or floor or shop is your work environment and it affects you and other people
+ If someone tries to draw your attention to something really obscene on the wall, on a computer screen, or

anywhere, make a remark about something bland, like the weather, and walk away fast. (And complain formally. This is serious.)

You absolutely don't have to accept personal remarks in the workplace about your clothes, body, eyes, or anything that makes you feel uncomfortable. You may not be touched without your agreement. You don't have to overhear filthy jokes. The chaps may not have a stripper at a work party or talk at work about the stripper they had at home. If someone is putting the hard word on you to go out with them, persisting after you've made it clear you're not interested, that's not on either.

Sexual harassment has nothing to do with friendly, consensual relationships among equals. The law requires your employers to prevent it, and makes them responsible if they don't do everything possible to prevent it. Often, sexual harassment is founded on resentment towards women. Sexist remarks or put-downs are the first warning. They should be stopped by management.

We say again, don't try to deal with it on your own.

MAKING A FORMAL COMPLAINT

If it's really upsetting you, and it probably is, then see your doctor, tell her what the problem is, and get some counselling and relaxation advice and support *now*. Don't wait until you're having nightmares, or get shingles, or your self-confidence has gone.

You can complain of discrimination, discriminatory harassment, or of being victimised for having complained, to a statutory body, the name of which varies from state to state. Western Australia, South Australia and Victoria have Equal Opportunity Commissions; New South Wales has an Anti-Discrimination Board; Tasmania has a Sex Discrimination Commissioner; and the Commonwealth has the Human Rights and Equal Opportunity Commission. If you are dismissed for a discriminatory reason, you can also complain on the grounds of unfair dismissal to the Australian Industrial Relations Commission or to an equivalent state body everywhere except in Victoria, which no longer has a state industrial relations system.

Knowing that you can do this should give you the strength to try other alternatives first: a complaint may not necessarily get you what you want.

Complaining is not like prosecuting or suing somebody in the ordinary way. The process is much the same under state, territory or federal laws: a complaint has to be made in writing; it is then investigated by the relevant body, and if it seems to have substance to it, the primary remedy is conciliation.

Conciliation is a kind of mediation within a statutory framework, a process of talking through differences and coming to a resolution by agreement of the parties themselves, with the help of a conciliator. Commonly, the parties can be obliged to provide information, give statements and attend meetings, though they cannot be forced to agree. They may still choose to resolve or not settle their differences.

If that process fails the complaint can be referred to a specialist tribunal, or one of the traditional courts exercising a special statutory function, to be decided after a trial, with witnesses being called and cross-examined. The tribunal can make orders to put the wrong right, including damages, and these orders can be enforced.

There may be no enforceable remedy for the victims of discrimination on the grounds of age, social origin and sexuality, although people can still make complaints and the relevant body must try to conciliate those complaints. But there is no tribunal or court to which they can be sent should conciliation fail.

Before you proceed with a formal complaint it's a good idea to document the situation so that you have a proper record of what happened when. But do keep your notes at home. Write down exactly what happened, as it happened, and leave your feelings out of it. Write down why you think it was discrimination or harassment, and why you think a man wouldn't have been treated as you were. Note facts, dates and times of similar circumstances where men were treated differently. Get copies of documents you think support your stand – company or organisation policy, Affirmative Action Agency reports, memos, minutes, and don't forget emails.

The steps involved in making a written complaint to a statutory equal opportunity body are:

+ You write a letter or fill out a complaint form. In some states, such as Victoria, you have to go in and the staff take a statement and help you formulate the complaint

+ If your complaint is deemed to constitute discrimination under the law, it is assigned to an investigator. They may need to get more detail, after which they give notice to the person or the company named as responsible (the respondent), talk to the person who has complained (the complainant), and to witnesses to see what the issues are. Usually they will ask the respondent to reply in writing before they decide what to do next

+ The commissioner or president has the power to decide that the complaint lacks substance during this phase and not to take any further action. If the complaint proceeds, the conciliator arranges a conciliation conference, where both parties meet with the conciliator to try to work out a mutually satisfactory outcome: apologies, reinstatement, training, references, or even the payment of money

+ If the parties can agree, they usually sign a simple agreement and that is the end of the matter

+ If they cannot agree, then the complainant can choose to refer the complaint to a public hearing.

Most complaints are settled during investigation or conciliation, but that does not mean to say that you will necessarily find it easy at work. The cases that aren't settled usually go no further. The few that do go on to a hearing are likely to succeed – the strongest cases go on, of course. Overall, about half of all sex discrimination cases are decided in favour of the complainant: nearly all sexual harassment complaints are too. (Far fewer race complaints succeed.)

We do not recommend putting your faith entirely in the outcome of a complaint. It may take too long for an external body to deal with to be of much use to a woman who has to keep working in the organisation. Anti-discrimination laws are meant to provide an alternative for people whose choices are denied. They are meant to be informal, easily accessible, confidential, conciliatory, and empowering – all qualities that lawyers and courts don't often demonstrate. It takes courage, or desperation, to claim those rights and certainly to use legal remedies. You must be prepared to defend charges that you are incompetent, dishonest, potty or emotionally unstable. You might be told that you should feel guilt and accept blame for any detriment you have suffered. You might be challenged under cross-examination and have your private life and beliefs scrutinised; there could be challenges to your memory and character; there could be the pressure of financial loss, delays, humiliation, rebuffs, and long silent questioning looks from your family (especially your children) and friends, who might believe you have become obsessed. Don't destroy your happiness for the cause of all women. You need to decide whether it's the right choice for *you* to make. But those who do make that decision deserve our thanks. They are doing it for all of us.

The final point to consider when deciding whether to proceed with a formal complaint is whether or not you need a lawyer. The answer is: not to begin with. The anti-discrimination staff are supposed to help you write your complaint out. You will need a lawyer if the matter doesn't settle in conciliation. But you should be aware that:

+ It should be a lawyer who knows the area, not someone who's doing it for the first time
+ It may not be only you. The harassment might have been going on for a long time before you complained. Indirect discrimination affects a lot of people, and it is possible to make a joint complaint on behalf of a lot of complainants – that shares the load, gives you a support group, and minimises costs (though it complicates settlements when some want to settle and others don't)
+ You may not be eligible for legal aid, but there are lawyers who will act on a 'no-win, no-fee' basis – keep an eye out for their ads or ask around. There are Community Legal Centres that have experts who will help you. There are also lawyers who sometimes act pro bono – in the public interest – for no fee in appropriate cases. Contact your local Law Society, or in Victoria the Law Institute, for details.

Work is a crucially important part of all our lives. It gives us human contact, structure, and the means of supporting ourselves and choosing how to live our lives with dignity and comfort. Most women do both paid and unpaid work, yet there is still a fundamental view that the ordinary worker is a man. This is changing, but slowly. If you want to be in control of your own life and career, you need to know how the system works and how to make it work for you, as a woman, and all other women.

chapter 7

Getting the message across

Power requires good communication. Good communication means that more and more people understand what you want to achieve, come to share and expand the vision, and do something about it too. Some will feel obliged to attack your views. Provided you handle that well, even this will put you on the public map.

You can make complex issues understandable by breaking them down into digestible chunks, as long as you understand them fully yourself. You can make your issues a matter of public concern, and other people's issues too, but only if the public understands that the issue affects them, and wants action.

SPEAKING IN PUBLIC

The tremendous power of speaking knowledgeably, persuasively and with all your wit, humour and passion about what you believe in and what must be done should not be underestimated. Apply these six general strategies when making a public speech:

1 Know what you want to talk about, as thoroughly as you can.
2 Plan what you will say, and how you want it to end up.
3 Look for allies in the audience and among the organisers, and accept help where appropriate (advice on what they want to hear is a pretty good start).
4 Use your networks – some places are more useful to speak at than others.
5 Look for mentors – public speaking is an art you can learn by observation and practice.
6 Negotiate with your audience so that you arrive at the end of the meeting with a sense of goals achieved and consensus reached.

There is every logical reason to be afraid of public speaking. Whenever you stand up and address an audience you take a risk that you might bore them or offend them – which is worse? – or expose yourself as the not quite perfect (Joan Kirner's fear) or utterly worthless (Moira's phobia) human being that you secretly believe you are. But a little bit of fear improves your performance. If you are bored with public speaking, it will show. If you don't take each audience as a challenge, it will show.

Not a lot of people actually like public speaking, at least to begin with. Oddly, both Joan and Moira's first public speeches were from the pulpit of a Presbyterian church when they were sixteen – their first, and last, sermons.

PANIC ON THE PODIUM

When I started my professional life I was so afraid of public speaking that I almost fainted – I felt that everyone was looking at me, I was afraid of making a complete fool of myself, and I couldn't even use the telephone properly, let alone talk on a stage. Now I speak publicly all the time.

One of my greatest lessons – learned from jumping into 'mooting' competitions (mock trials) and debating – was that there is nothing like fear for making you effective. Fear and excitement are different words for the same experience: the rush of adrenaline. It makes you think fast and adapt to your circumstances really quickly. There is nothing quite as dreadful as your first experience of writing a speech only to discover that you have an entirely different audience from the one you expected, and realising that the speech you planned will go down like a lead balloon.

Moira

PERFORMANCE ANXIETY

People believe that I was born to be a public figure, and born confident. But it's something you learn, not something you're born with. From a little tot I've loved performing – in school dramas, saying thank you to visiting dignitaries, at calisthenics (though I wasn't much good), in school and interschool debating, and even as a young member of the Presbyterian Fellowship of Australia. But nothing prepared me for the public scrutiny of being Premier, when every speech, every interview was a total performance. These skills I had to learn. There was plenty of fear – and even more defamation.

Joan

THE FIVE Ps OF PUBLIC SPEAKING

1   passion   There's nothing like passion to win over an audience. If you're bored, or tentative, or insincere, why should they listen?

2   preparation   Some incredibly clever people know their subject matter so well that they don't have to prepare, they're always prepared. These people are few and far between, and you're unlikely to be one of them. Speech-making is a performance, and speech-writing is a matter of practice. When you write down what you want to say, focus on what you will feel comfortable saying. We speak very differently from how we write: remember that your task is to persuade people. Even if you don't write the speech out in full, do:

+ Asterisk the points that you want to make – three or five main issues

+ Write down the quotes you want to use, in full

+ Write your opening remarks and your closing remarks in full too. Try to make your end comments refer to your opening ones

+ Test how long it takes to deliver what you had in mind. Twenty minutes is about as long as most people can stand. Count the words: it should take about a minute to deliver a hundred of them. Twenty minutes will therefore need about 2000 words

+ Try not to cover too much. About three big ideas is as much as most people can take in. Lists of facts and statutes and dates are best summarised and attached to the written version of your speech.

If you make a really good speech to one audience on an issue, keep it to use again on other audiences, adapting it to the new context.

3   pauses   If there's a really important point you want to make, pause before you make it and look at your audience. If you've just made a particularly important or amusing point, stop and let people take it in. And if they're laughing, wait till they've finished or they'll miss your next point.

4 participation Let people respond to what you are saying. Ask questions and look for responses – movements, smiles, mutters – and respond to them. People don't want to be lectured or hectored: a good speech is a seduction. Smile back. Respond if it seems appropriate, but briefly.

Chat to your audience before you give the speech: that will help to give you an idea of their mood. Then when you're speaking, pick one person who looks friendly and on-side and address your talk to them. Pick another one who looks bored and keep an eye on them too. Both of these faces are important: they tell you how you're doing.

Ignore interjectors, or tell them they can have a go at question time. In general, encourage a question time. Audiences listen more attentively if they know they can ask you questions later. Some people actually speak better in response to questions than when giving a prepared speech. Answer questions confidently and openly. If you don't know the answer or the local context, say so, and offer other avenues for information. We recommend handling your own questions, unless the chair is very well aware of the troublemakers or dissenters in the audience. Make sure you give women and men, old and young, performers and the shy equal opportunity to ask questions.

5 presence You are the object of all attention. Don't be shy. Expect to be heard, and you will be. Don't shuffle up apologetically to the lectern and don't apologise for what you are about to say. Be authoritative: you have knowledge, an opinion and experience, and they are all valuable. If you're nervous, think of yourself as being excited, rather than afraid.

We suggest that you:

✦ Don't start with a joke. There aren't many people who

can tell one well anyway, and if you need to change your speech but you've only got a joke to kick it off with and now it's the wrong one, you're in strife

✦ Don't stick to your speech as if it were holy writ. You might have got it a bit wrong: a good public speaker embroiders their talk by feeding off the audience and their responses. But remember your main points, and make them

✦ Don't be the expert. It isn't often that you have to make an erudite speech. Most audiences want to hear something that resonates with truth and experience. Often they want something personal. Yes, you do have to know what you're talking about; no, you don't have to have carried out a formal literature search and regurgitate it. If you speak well, someone will go and search it out for themselves. You will have fired them up

✦ Don't look everyone in the eye. If your eyes are everywhere you might fail to engage the audience. On the other hand, you should scan the whole audience and catch someone's eye occasionally to see whether you're hitting the spot or not

✦ Don't read your speech, or learn it off by heart and recite it. Know what you want to say, of course. But you might have to modify the speech you had in mind, and you should be well enough prepared and flexible enough to do so without losing your thread. Read speeches are boring speeches: you might as well just publish an article. Recited speeches are boring, too. Practise delivering them – the greatest orators practise right down to the gestures

✦ Don't be rude to interjectors. Unless you are excellent at repartee that has no comeback (and most of us are variable), you'd do better to ignore them. The audience will deal with them, or the chair will.

Always have extra copies of your speech for any media that may be present, or for anyone else who wants it. Often journalists will ask for a copy of your speech first, so they don't have to come and listen to you. It's usually sensible to give it to them afterwards.

Getting your speech published somewhere, or at least distributed as widely as you can manage, will ensure that your effort is not wasted, that the speech will not be quickly forgotten or make no difference anywhere outside that meeting. Try to get an edited copy into the papers or your organisation's journal, or put it on-line.

If you give a particularly good speech that's a bit different from the one you wrote, write it up as you delivered it, straight afterwards.

TIPS FROM A PRACTISED SPEAKER

I never speak just off the cuff. I quite often read my speeches and re-embroider them orally; but I always:

+ Think who my audience is – I check this through the organisation and my networks
+ Work out my five major headings, my introduction and conclusion, the points I want people to remember, the facts I want to quote
+ Look at the audience
+ Move around the audience beforehand and work out their mood
+ Only have one ending in a speech: something that will move people and stay in their minds. To have three 'and finally's makes the audience restless
+ Modify my speech as I go, to keep the audience involved. I find it hard to make a very erudite speech – I'm better at making calls for action
+ Start with something that the audience can identify with,

something strong and personal. And the audience always
responds. The humour in my speech is usually my own, not
borrowed, except for the occasional apposite story that I've
committed to memory. I no longer tell Rottweiler jokes.

Joan

USING THE MEDIA

It's almost impossible, in Australia, to be an effective activist
unless you can communicate well through the media and gain
broad support. If you've already got a profile, just be aware that
media outlets and journalists often treat women differently
from men. Edith Cresson, who was Prime Minister of France from
1991 to 1992, once said, 'Cameras are not directed the same
way if you are a woman. For instance, when you get out of the
car the cameras are focused on your legs. It never happens to a
man.' But rather than seeing the media as a threat, you should
see it as an opportunity to influence people, change minds and
influence outcomes. To do this you need to understand three
essential things about the media:

+ What they are
+ How they work
+ What media strategies work for you.

Then you need to ask yourself the following questions regularly,
writing down the answers concisely and reminding yourself about
them often:

+ Who am I trying to inform or influence?
+ What am I trying to say to them?
+ What are the facts on the issue?
+ What results do I want to achieve?

Let's assume that you're just starting out, and not a star or
media personality yet. How are you going to get the media
interested in your issues in the first place? And why does it
matter anyway?

When Moira became the Victorian Commissioner for Equal Opportunity in 1990 there was virtually no media interest in discrimination apart from scandal and criticism. So she started writing letters to the editors of the Melbourne papers on topical issues – short ones, less than a hundred and fifty words, pithy, witty if she could, and to the point. Then, when journalists wanted statistics or information, she always spoke to them personally and gave them the information they wanted. It took a few months, but her letters were published more often than not, and radio and TV started to take an interest. The Equal Opportunity Office started to get mentioned in most papers and contacted regularly, and then, when it needed good publicity, it had relationships, credibility, and trust with the journalists. And it didn't cost a cent.

Media interest and reporting can give issues national attention and change government policy. All activists need media support.

Here are a few tips for getting the media's attention:

+ Suss out media outlets and reporters. Who is interested in what you are interested in? Remember that reporters have editors and sub-editors: sometimes they are directed to portray you in certain ways, so you need to know their line, as well as being clear about yours

+ Keep up with the news of the day. You have to be able to read the mood of the media if you want to grab their attention. News and views change quickly. Reporters have it on tap. They're not interested in old news, so you have to keep an ear out for current events and comments. Get into a routine: listen to the radio news or read a newspaper before you leave the house, make phone calls or do interviews. Ride someone else's wave to get on top of things

+ Be consistent. If you are getting some airplay or newspaper coverage, repeat your message to get it through,

and be clear, consistent and relevant. Consistency gives a
sense that you stand for something and you know what
you're talking about. Reporters love to catch out incon-
sistencies. If, after being a long-standing advocate of
affirmative action for women, you said something inconsistent with your stand, your headline would be
'Power Woman Does Backflip on Affirmative Action'.
Your inconsistency, not your message, becomes the story.
If you want to change your mind about something, say
so. Be upfront, not inconsistent

✦ Be creative. Sometimes the best way to get the message
across is with a picture. Who can forget the Tasmanian
conservation campaign's Save the Franklin poster? There
was one in half the houses of the nation during the 1983
federal election campaign (the Kirner family had one on
its front door). And in 1997, when Victorians rallied to
save Wilson's Promontory from commercial development
in a national park, the campaign became instantly more
effective when two thousand people hit the spectacular
beach, joined hands and beach towels and spelt out
'Hands off the Prom'. That night's TV shot and the
photographs in the papers the next day got the message
through to the Victorian government

✦ Organise backup. Your message is greatly enhanced if,
after you've made a statement or taken some newsworthy
action, other people or groups come in behind you,
apparently of their own free will. This takes good
organisation and networking, but it certainly pays off.
Always have a strategy. Always engage like-minded people
or organisations

✦ Take any opportunity. In 1997, the parents of children
at Croydon Primary School in Adelaide, threatened with
the closure of the school, followed the South Australian

Premier around to every major public appearance he made during the state election campaign. In 1994 the commissioners of the Victorian municipality of Olinda in the Dandenongs decided to close its pool after low attendance figures the previous summer. The locals started campaigns and protests – the pool had been built with public donations, not by council funds, and was used by the Country Fire Authority as an emergency water supply. Then, during a cold snap, snow fell on Olinda. The media trooped up the mountains to film snow-on-the-ground footage at Olinda Primary School, the highest point around. When they arrived nobody was there. 'Everybody's protesting at the pool,' they were told, so the cameras all headed for the pool, and on that night's news every service carried footage of the Olinda pool. That coverage was considered by many to be a major factor in changing the council's mind

✦ Document your outcomes. You need to review your performance and your achievements regularly if you are to be an effective media performer, and you might then need to revise your targets in light of your achievements, or non-achievements. When you have become a truly effective performer, the media will come to you for comment and you won't have to grab their attention.

THE FIVE GOLDEN RULES ON THE MEDIA
You must:
✦ have good content
✦ provide good pictures
✦ offer good grabs
✦ perform well and have an authoritative presence
✦ have great passion, and discipline in communicating it.
To summarise, you need to be able to provide informative

content with an authoritative presence, and with passion and discipline, and it doesn't hurt to offer great pictures and grabs while you're at it.

MAKING FRIENDS AND INFLUENCING PEOPLE

In 1971 I led a deputation of the Australian Council of State School Organisations to see Malcolm Fraser, the then federal Minister for Education. It was the first time we had met. Our agenda was to argue that he should end the practice of making per capita grants to private schools, and introduce federal grants to all schools, public and private, on the basis of need.

Mr Fraser was an impressive figure, but the ACSSO group had its facts marshalled and an essential social question to ask: why should schools like Scotch College and its peers get the same amount of government funds when they had far greater resources, far more luxurious grounds and more adequate facilities and staffing than other schools?

Mr Fraser responded coolly: 'But among state schools there are differences in wealth, too. Surely you're not asking me to give unequal amounts to Melbourne High, a well-off public school compared to Fitzroy Primary, where you say they have to run their classes from a broom cupboard under the stairs?'

'Yes,' I replied, 'we want all schools to have federal funds according to need.' Minister Fraser seemed staggered, and ended the meeting promptly.

The then head of the Commonwealth Department of Education said to me quietly as we left, 'Get to the media first.' I did.

I had already briefed the head of the *Age* education section about the time, place and content of the meeting. She was waiting outside. She had a real interest in the issue of needs-based funding for schools.

The next morning the *Age* ran the headline 'Parents Argue Needs Based Funding for All Schools'. I was delighted: at last, the parents of state school students were seen to be setting the education agenda. Minister Fraser had to respond to our policy position. His view that schools funding should be per capita, regardless of need, was no longer the accepted story. He could no longer argue that we were looking for needs-based funding only for private schools: we wanted it for all schools.

Thousands of parents responded to our policy line and our media and community campaign. By 1972 the new federal government decided to set up a Schools Commission, committed to funding all schools according to need. That view held sway in education politics for two decades. Twenty-five years later, with the current dominance of free-market policies in education budgeting, parents may again have to reset the needs-based funding agenda.

Joan

TALKBACK RADIO

Talkback programs are a very important way to get your message across. Government and industry monitor what is said, and they take it seriously. The National Women's Media Centre gives great advice on talkback radio, but here are the basics:

- ✦ Before you pick up the phone, work out the one or two points you want to make. You'll only have a minute or two, so note down some pithy ways of putting them
- ✦ First you have to get on air. The initial call probaby won't do it, you will have to persevere. It's a matter of luck as well. Keep hitting your redial button
- ✦ Once you've got through you have to persuade the producer that what you have to say is worth hearing. You won't get on unless you sound interesting. You're more likely to get on if you are a regular interesting caller, or if you're the official spokesperson for a group. The producer will ask you what comment you want to

make, which is where your notes come in handy. Don't
tell her how nervous you are, or start the whole spiel.
They want someone who will grab the audience's attention
or advance the discussion

✦ If what you say sounds worthwhile you'll be put on to
the presenter, and a quick description of what you'll say
goes on the screen in the presenter's studio. You can be
passionate, analytical, or controversial – but never dull
or longwinded

✦ Turn your own radio off, or you'll get feedback and be
put straight off the air

✦ Speak clearly into the phone

✦ Once you're on, you can be interrupted at any time by
the presenter, who's got a gadget that cuts in as soon as
they talk into the microphone, so that only their voice
can be heard. It doesn't matter what you say, the audience
won't hear you, so stop talking, listen to the presenter
and respond once they've stopped speaking

✦ You may not be able to interrupt, but you are still in
control. You don't have to answer questions you don't
want to. You can end the conversation, but if talkback is
part of your media strategy you will have arranged other
people to ring in too, to back you up.

MEDIA RELEASES

Another way to get media attention is to issue media releases,
but individuals needn't bother – this is a tactic for an organised
group or known performers. Media releases should focus on the
novel or unusual aspects of an issue, or emphasise the human
elements in a story – courage, compassion, cruelty, children and
animals. The media love this. Relate the release to current issues
where possible, and try to bring out the local interest. Media
releases which can create or add to a public debate are more

likely to grab attention, and the more people who are affected by your issue, the greater the media attention it will attract.

There are some definite dos and don'ts for preparing media releases:

+ State in the first three paragraphs what the release is about, who it is from, and why it is being released. Grab the reader's attention with the first paragraph

+ Use action words – 'Power women will blockade parliament today' instead of 'The power women have decided to take strong action to . . .'

+ Use short sentences

+ Write in the third person – 'The power women will blockade parliament', not 'We will blockade . . .' The personal touch is really only appropriate for revolutionary guerrillas issuing demands

+ Try to use a phrase that will give a journalist a good line to hang a story on, something that sticks in the memory: remember 'Well may he say "God Save the Queen", for nothing will save the Governor-General', for example

+ Use direct quotes – it gains attention. People like personal touches more than rhetoric

+ Check for errors in spelling, syntax, grammar and other irritating mistakes

+ Get a knowledgeable friend, one who is not afraid to be critical, to read your media release for its impact before you release it

+ Date and time the release

+ Make it look good – easy to read, one side of the paper – and never, ever do a release that's more than two pages long. A background or briefing statement can be provided separately or as an attachment

+ Get your timing right. Don't bother to release a statement if a major news story has already broken, or is about to break, and the media agenda is already crowded. Make sure your support people know you've issued it and are ready to follow up with their own comments or releases

✦ Address your release, clearly, to the person most likely to present the story. But send it to the chief of staff/producer as well

✦ Keep a log of all the outlets you've contacted, and whether they responded. This will help if you need to use them again

✦ Be clear about who and on what number the media should ring back if they want more information or an interview. Be there to answer, or have someone else there. They'll make *one* call, and if nobody answers or returns their call they'll be annoyed and they won't call back

✦ If, after a seriously negative experience, you decide that you are not going to deal with a particular journalist or media outlet, tell them so, and why

✦ If you've had no response to your release after a few hours, ring an appropriate journalist and ask them if they've seen it, and if they have whether they're using it, or would like some further comment

✦ You can send out a release marked 'Embargo' until a particular time or day so that your information will not be posted before that time. Note that when you are first trying to break into the media, Sunday is a good day for a release because it's usually a slow news day (so is Monday morning)

✦ If you want to catch the TV news, make sure that you issue your releases by 2.30 pm, so that they can be processed for the news bulletins between 5.00 and 7.00 that night

✦ Send your media release to Australian Associated Press. It is one of the best ways to get your message around quickly. All news outlets keep an eye on AAP news

◆ Establish good professional relations with journalists or editorial staff in your particular field. Keep a record of them and stay in touch. This will be useful to both you and them.

BLACKBALLING AN UNETHICAL JOURNALIST

I once blackballed a particular journalist because he fabricated a story about my believing that if schoolgirls could wear trousers to school, schoolboys could wear skirts. Of course, I believe nothing of the kind. When I rang and objected, the reporter bluffed that I had expressed such a view. So I asked the editor of his paper to correct the story, told my people that I wouldn't be talking to this young man again, and told the editor precisely why I had done it.

Anyone can make a mistake, but don't bother to deal with an unethical journalist.

Moira

There are some things you mustn't do when preparing media releases.

+ Don't send out a media release on what you know to be a busy news day, such as budget day. It won't get a run, and if you try to raise the issue later journalists will remember, feel that it's old news and leave it alone

+ Don't expect to get coverage for a story because you think it's worthy. It has to be seen by journalists as *news*worthy

+ Don't send it out, then go fishing. A good media release is one that encourages a desire for more information and interviews. Be there

+ Don't misquote people or get facts wrong. Your credibility, and thus your usefulness, will be shot for a very long time

+ Don't sign your name to a media release unless you have read and approved the final version

+ Don't attack your opponents personally

+ Don't rave on and forget to say what action you are calling for and by whom, or what action you will be taking.

You shouldn't be surprised by anything the media do. They're after a story. You'll give it to them, one way or the other, but don't be surprised when you're not given the same treatment as the men. Crying in public, for instance, is oddly enough considered to be okay for powerful blokes. Journalists tend to describe it as sensitive, redeeming or unexpected. When Bob Hawke wept over his daughter's drug problems, and when Marcus Einfield, the then President of the Human Rights and Equal Opportunity Commission, wept in 1989 over the living conditions of Aborigines in a remote township, they were widely and sympathetically reported on. But when women do it, it's not okay. Journalists tend to respond negatively, seeing them as over-sensitive, weak, or even manipulative and wily.

BIG GIRLS DON'T CRY

In February 1992 I was reduced to tears of frustration in a Cabinet meeting when some of my Ministers were fighting over irrelevancies – such as who got the executive loo! – while Victoria was in dire economic straits. I knew that the story would get out, and feared the possible headlines – 'Kirner Breaks Down', or even 'Kirner Cracks'. When the story did get out, I was giving a speech at the Radisson Hotel in Melbourne, and the media went into a feeding frenzy, though some of the women reporters seemed to be as worried as I was about the way my tears would be reported. There were photographers everywhere, perhaps hoping that I'd cry again. (I didn't.)

Imagine my surprise when the next morning the front page of the *Herald Sun* newspaper ran one of the anticipated headlines, together with a large photo of me at the after-lunch doorstop looking as though I were crying. I realised then why the *Herald Sun*'s photographer had had his camera stuck in my office at the doorstop and was constantly clicking his shutter: he, or his editor, wanted a shot of me with my eyes half closed, as if with suppressed tears. I unwittingly obliged: I blinked while closing the door. The editor got his photo – front page the next day.

This kind of thing probably won't happen to you until you have some real power and a media heavy wants to get you. But the good news about the episode was that, despite that front page, the rest of the media, and the public, understood and respected my reaction as legitimate at the time, and a sign of frustration rather than weakness.

Joan

NEWS CONFERENCES

Calling a news conference is only useful if the media are already interested and will definitely come. They may come to a conference called by a political candidate if there is a hot local issue, or if they want to ask some leading questions. For community or interest groups a news conference may work if there is a human, social or financial crisis affecting more than just you personally. One person losing their job isn't news unless it raises a major issue, such as sex discrimination. Major lay-offs are. So before going ahead and calling a conference, make sure your issue is newsworthy and that it couldn't have been dealt with by a media release. A conference can be held to announce a new study, a major endorsement, a scandalous story, or to pre-empt negative stories or answer a negative charge directly. Always have a few people there who can deal with these issues.

When you're planning a news conference, consider:

+ Who should participate. Make sure they know, and confirm their attendance
+ A convenient time – when media can get their stories or pictures in
+ A central location, visually obvious so that they can get there easily
+ A quiet location – too much noise messes up recording

- The weather, if you're outdoors. It might change. Situate speakers so that cameras are shooting away from the sun
- The number of and access to electrical outlets (camera crews need lights). Check personally
- Who will speak, when, and in what order
- When you will open up the conference for questions from journalists
- Where people will stand or sit. Check that the location isn't going to look empty – they'll focus on the empty chairs. (Remember when Bronwyn Bishop held a news conference, and nobody came?)
- That the mike isn't positioned so that someone can take a picture of you with a button on your nose looking like a clown
- Rounding up supporters to attend
- Faxing out an invitation announcing the conference
- Calling AAP to make sure it's listed
- Making a round of phone calls to your favourite journalists
- Preparing a release to be handed out at the conference (not before or they won't come).

At the conference make sure that you:

- Look good
- Start on time
- Provide background information on the spot
- Keep the speeches short
- Tape the conference, so there's no argument later about what was said and done
- Take down questions that are to be answered later (remember deadlines)
- Allow time to be available for separate interviews afterwards, if necessary.

After the conference make sure you:
+ Fax out your release to the media and journalists who didn't come
+ Make your tape available to radio stations
+ Make follow-up calls, but not until after the journalists' deadlines are over (they'll be too frantic)
+ Plan some follow-up activities, such as having friendly or like-minded organisations call the media to support your stand.

INTERVIEWS

If a journalist asks you for an interview, consider whether it's in your interests to give it; not all publicity is good publicity. Then confirm exactly who will be doing the interview and why they want to do it, and who else has been asked to comment and what they have said.

Don't panic if someone wants to do an interview on the spot but don't be bullied, either, if it's not the right time or place.

If you are asked to comment on something very early in the morning and you haven't caught up with the news yet, ask the journalist to quote what they want a comment on and offer to ring them back when you've checked it out. Don't be afraid to say to any journalist, 'Look, I'm busy at the moment and I'll ring you back in half an hour,' if you're not sure what you want to say, or need to check your facts or steady your nerves.

A CASE STUDY
WHO ELSE IS COMMENTING? HOW NOT TO DO IT

Moira was once asked to do an interview on a daytime TV chat show when she was Chairman of the West Australian Law Reform Commission. The interview was to be about one of the Commission's discussion papers that had stirred up a lot of controversy. The paper had been leaked to a local newspaper, which had misreported it, saying that the Commission had recommended lowering the age of consent to sexual relations to thirteen.

She agreed to the interview to help set the record straight. She discovered after she got to the TV station that another person was participating in the interview too – someone she had never met, whose views she didn't know, and who sat silently while she reasonably and charmingly explained what the report said and what the Commission was doing. That person then suddenly chimed in, right at the end, with a diatribe about Moira's supposed evil designs against vulnerable little girls and what he thought the paper had said. All the good work she had done was rapidly undone as he loudly asserted what he believed was in the paper he hadn't even read. All she could think to do was to interrupt, vigorously, and make sure he did not have the last word, knowing that the interview would come to an end soon.

If Moira had known he was to be there and what his views were, she would not have been taken by surprise. She would not have agreed to the interview in that format, and would have asked for an entirely different kind of opportunity to put the facts straight, and she would have advanced public understanding of the issues much better. The situation was only partly retrieved. It was a mistake, and she learned from it.

Never go into an interview as though you were going to have a nice chat. You are giving a performance and you will be judged by it. A reporter's job is to get or make news out of you. If you don't give them what *you* want, well prepared and well presented, either they will get what they want out of you, which mightn't be anything like what you wanted, or they might decide you are not newsworthy and your contribution is not a good grab. And they will remember this in the future.

Be disciplined: know what messages you want to get across and be prepared, if they don't seem to be getting across, to change your tack. Take control of the interview, or you will not be able to deliver the messages you want to.

The following tactics will be useful:

+ Practise. You will need practice to perfect your personal reactions in interviews. You may be hurt, frightened or embarrassed, but you must not show this. You may find yourself wanting to help your interviewer by giving them the answers they seem to want: don't do it, unless it progresses your cause. Practise diverting questions so that you can get your message out. But also practise giving the straight answer – say 'I don't know', if you don't. It takes experience to project a particular image while delivering a message and answering difficult questions. It's worth working with a more experienced interviewee on this

+ Keep clippings. As a media performer, especially in the early days, it is important to build up your own files of media clippings on the issues and people you deal with. Media outlets have extensive files. They will build one up on you, so return the favour. Journalists are impressed if they know that you know what their game is, as well as their own, and if you have information that they don't

+ Negotiate the format and content of the interview before you give it. Don't assume that you know what journalists want or that they do

+ In preparing for an interview ask yourself or others what questions might be asked, and if you've given similar interviews before ask people how well they think you answered those questions

+ Ask yourself what the likely angle will be. Is there likely to be any bias in their approach? How can this be addressed by what you say or do?

+ If the interview is going to be recorded, remember that it may be edited, or presented in part only. If you make *one* mistaken or emotional remark under pressure, be assured that that will be the one they use, and they may package it in such a way that you look like a twit, or appear to be saying something entirely different

+ If you're feeling a bit down or tired, either snap out of it or don't do the interview at all

+ Be brief. The media look for grabs (for radio and TV) or quotes (for print media). Don't waffle. Keep your radio grabs to about twenty seconds – a couple of sentences – and TV grabs to five or ten words

+ Use examples, analogies and anecdotes. Examples illustrate your point, clarify it and make it concrete. Comparisons with everyday images help others understand your message more easily: if they can understand what you are talking about in terms of it being 'a bit like' something else, you're home. Think of a label, or a catchword ('banana republic' said it all a few years ago) that people will remember and might reuse

+ Use everyday language, and use your own. Don't be pompous – and speak positively. Tell them how it is, not how it isn't, so that you don't sound like you're whingeing or on the defensive. Don't answer any question 'yes, but' or 'no, but', because the qualification can be edited out. Don't repeat anything you don't agree with – that could be edited too, to make it look like your view

+ Don't be evasive or rude. Never say 'no comment'. Don't show you're irritated with the question – the journalist will only dig deeper. Be firm, courteous, unflappable and in charge

+ You don't have to be skinny, svelte, or wear power clothes to be successful but you do have to look good and be confident in your image. There's no need to conform to what other people want, but make sure that your appearance and presentation do not distract from your message
+ Make sure the journalist knows when you are off the record. You can always brief people off the record and then put some good grabs on the record
+ You can sometimes change a journalist's mind with new facts, an alternative angle for the story to what they started off with, some personal insights, or a background briefing
+ If you are in criticism mode, be prepared for the obvious question: 'What would you do about it?' (Well?)
+ Don't laugh uproariously, cry, or be distracted by personal questions or the reporter's agenda. Stick to your message
+ Never, ever lie. Journalists have good archives and so should you. It takes a brilliant person to tell the same lie consistently, and nobody's that brilliant
+ Never lose your temper. Keep your perspective and your sense of humour
+ Don't answer hypothetical questions, and don't say you won't answer them and then answer them. If there's an expectant silence from your interviewer, don't feel impelled to fill the gap: that's the interviewer's responsibility
+ Avoid hyperbole. If something's a common practice, don't say it happens thousands of times. Never say 'never', or 'always': that simply sets reporters off, chasing the one example that will prove you wrong (and how very clever they are).

ANSWERING THE QUESTION THEY DIDN'T ASK

If I am discussing a sexual harassment case and my message is to emphasise that it is management's responsibility to prevent workplace bullying, not the victims', but the journalist asks whether I am a feminist, I simply answer the real question. Whether or not I describe myself as a feminist is a red herring, calculated to make a commentator look like a ratbag with a politically correct attitude rather than an expert with professional experience and an informed opinion.

I would say something like 'All women, and all decent men, would agree that no bullying is acceptable in the workplace, whether it's sexual bullying, whether it's perpetrated on women or men, whether it's practical jokes played on vulnerable people, or teasing a man who has a disability. Eliminating bullying is good management, based on equal respect for women and men. And of course I believe that.'

You haven't refused to answer the question, and you haven't been defensive.

Moira

NEVER WEAR FLORAL ON TELLY

I always liked a particular Australian designer's clothes and felt really good wearing them, when I could afford to buy them. They were floral, patterned and brightly coloured, often with mixed bright colours. When I started appearing regularly on television as Minister for Conservation I would often wear these favourite clothes.

One day, after an appearance on 'The 7.30 Report', I met a friend in the street who remarked, 'That was a really good interview you did last night.' Of course I said thanks, but then he added, 'It would have gone a whole lot better if I hadn't been distracted by your dress, then I could have concentrated on what you said.'

I learned from that, and when I got money I used it to buy clothes in single bright colours, without fussy bits – often blazers. You only see the top half in TV interviews.

The other thing I used to do was wear green eyeshadow. I really liked it until Vicki, Minister Kay Setches' daughter, told her to tell me, with a fifteen-year-old's brutal frankness, that I looked like a leper and should stop wearing it. I did.

In my early political days my TV image was a bit of a problem. I felt pretty good on radio, but on television I thought I was coming over as tough, a cardboard cut-out of myself. It began to dawn on me that I had to change when casual acquaintances met me and said, 'You look so much better than you do on television.' And they weren't talking about my weight. I learned that I had to talk past the camera and the interviewer to the people in their kitchens and lounge rooms. When I mistressed that art I became human, in their eyes, again.

Joan

YOUR MEDIA RIGHTS

Recognise that you are not a media victim. You have rights, too. Good interviews are based on mutual respect – yours for the journalist's professionalism and talent, and theirs for your role and for who you are. Your rights include:

+ The right to be informed about the reason for the interview
+ The right to some privacy
+ The right to be consulted about the time and place
+ The right to negotiate where and how you are presented on camera
+ The right to have your position respected about what is on and what is off the record. As a rule of thumb, you are always on the record, unless you say otherwise
+ The right to be quoted accurately. You can check that a journalist has correctly heard what you said, but don't

insult their integrity by suggesting they're incompetent or dishonest. Reporters are professionals, and most of them are doing their job well. Remember, too, that this means they are not your friends

✦ The right to have your family left alone. You don't have to expose your family to the media even if you are a public person and on call: your family are not.

BE GRACIOUS WHEN NECESSARY

Once, I was confronted in my own office by a wired journalist from a TV station who insisted on asking questions, there and then, without an appointment, about a complaint that a government Minister had discriminated against one of his own staff. There had been totally outrageous, false claims that I had consulted with the Premier – Joan Kirner – about the political implications of the complaint and how to settle the complaint politically.

I had to make a line call: talk to him now and get my message about confidentiality, integrity and the statutory process on record, or refuse and end up looking and sounding defensive and evasive. So I took him into my office and gave him a very short, sweet and to-the-point interview, and turned a potential disaster into a minor victory. He believed me, or realised that I would be believed, and I didn't get negative publicity.

Moira

TRICKS OF THE MEDIA TRADE

✦ Practise deep breathing before an interview to help you relax

✦ Don't raise the pitch of your voice, especially at the end of a sentence. Lower-register voices are more authoritative, carry better and gain attention. You can speak *louder* without squeaking

- Remember that you're performing for the public, not being interviewed for the approval of your peers
- Be in the studio, if possible, for radio interviews. On the phone the interviewer has all the power: they can talk over you (and so can callers), hang up, or put you on hold while they rabbit on
- Make yourself valuable to journalists but don't get too close: familiarity breeds carelessness
- If you are concerned about the treatment you got during an interview, take it up with the journalist, politely, afterwards – or with their editor or manager, more firmly, later
- Construct a clear picture of yourself and the picture you want transmitted: your personality, your values, your knowledge, your process. Be aware that on TV you have to project your personality as much as your words: you can't do the one without the other. Smile with your eyes, as well as your mouth. Overact a bit, don't be too concerned to get the thing perfect. When you want to stress a point, you can slow down, lean forward, lower your pitch and yet raise the volume a little. Remember that you are talking not just to the interviewer but to the people watching you
- Remember that most reporters, photographers, technicians and camera people are decent human beings. Unless they are under editorial orders, or personally dislike you, your politics, or your message, if you respect them they will respect you.

BECOMING A MEDIA PERFORMER

After a bit of constructive criticism following my TV appearances, I did three things:

- I changed my focus from the questioning journalist to the listener in the lounge room

- I overacted so that the passion would come through
- When I was tired I took the advice of Paul Lyneham and swigged two cans of Coke before an interview, which helped to keep up the energy for at least as long as the interview.

Joan

HAVE AN ANSWER FOR THE HARD ONES

I have been asked in live-to-air radio interviews, 'Are you now, or have you ever been, a member of the Labor Party?' The first time I was asked this, I just spluttered with anger. Then I learned to reply that the McCarthy era was long gone and my political independence was so well known that there was no need to answer such a question, even if it was relevant, which it wasn't.

Moira

In this tough world, your ability to communicate is crucial to taking control of your own destiny and gathering support for your causes. Power means working with others and getting support for your causes, because they are theirs too. Communication builds community.

chapter 8

Community activism

Being a political woman is, according to Eleanor Roosevelt, a bit like being a missionary. As she put it:

+ You cannot take anything personally
+ You cannot bear grudges
+ You must finish the day's work when the day's work is done
+ You cannot get discouraged too easily
+ You have to take a defeat over and over again, and pick up and go on
+ Argue the other side with a friend until you have found the answer to every point which might be brought up against you

✦ Be sure of your facts
✦ Women who are willing to be leaders must stand out
   and be shot at.

Eleanor Roosevelt was never elected to any political office, but this activist wife of Franklin Delano Roosevelt, the Democrat who was President of the USA before and during the Second World War, was most certainly a political woman.

Personally, she paid a high price. She insisted that, above all, the political woman needs 'to develop a skin as tough as rhinoceros hide'. Yet in her last book, published posthumously in 1963, Eleanor Roosevelt wrote: 'There is no more liberating, no more exhilarating experience than to determine one's position, state it bravely and then act boldly.' Action created its own courage, she believed, and courage was as contagious as fear.

Political life is demanding, but, as Joan Kirner says, 'You make space in your life for what you really care about: how you do it is up to you.'

When we talk about politics we mean a range of political activity:

✦ Personal politics
✦ Community activism
✦ Party politics
✦ Local government politics
✦ Campaigning for change anywhere.

Making a difference for yourself and others is what politics is about. Working with and on others is the political process. There's no point in holding a parliamentary or media debate unless the community is going to be convinced, and respond.

Politics is about the art of the possible. There are a lot of possibilities. All the hot air, posturing and speech-making, all the passion and fire at the Constitutional Convention in 1998 would have been of no value at all if the people of Australia had not responded. And they did, on that last day. When the delegates stood up and held their ballots in the air to show that the convention supported, in principle, Australia becoming a republic, the people in the public gallery and in King's Hall stood up and cheered as well. It was an astonishing and moving moment.

COMMUNITY CAMPAIGNING

Community advocacy and activism have never been more important than they are now. Our government is run on managerial principles; most economic and policy-making power is in the hands of a small number of people at the top in both government and the private sector. Ordinary people know this, and resent it.

Letting communities stew over feeling left out and powerless is downright dangerous – it fosters the kind of thinking that grows right-wing racist groupings like One Nation, and turns citizen against citizen in the politics of blame. We believe in community advocacy – using power to reveal, influence, participate in and make decisions. We believe in being agents of change, not complainants or victims. Community advocacy is critical to making government listen and making democracy work.

A lot of advocacy simply reinforces existing power structures. Community-based advocacy is distinguishable: it includes those who have been left out. Unless community development principles underpin the process, advocacy can just as easily create dependence on a professional advocate rather than getting the people involved.

Community development has at its heart two basic principles. It assumes that the community has the expertise to participate in developing solutions to its problems, and it insists that unless the community participates in the decision-making process it won't own the outcome. In the long term, the 'solution' to the problem won't work.

Participation in a democracy does not mean the one-off experience of voting in an election. It does not mean handing over all the decision-making power to whoever wins an election, leaving them to make all the decisions. Participation and democracy are part and parcel of the same thing. Both are rights, and both are ongoing processes. Advocacy and networking is an essential part of both.

A community development approach to advocacy and networking is critical to the success of the community sector because it fundamentally shifts the focus to community perceptions. It shifts a victim from an embattled stand to a position of power – a change of mind and a change of viewpoint. It shifts the humble asking for favours into an insistence on entitlements. Community-based advocacy tries to create a more inclusive society, one made up of structures and procedures that are less alienating, less divisive, more collaborative, to which all contribute and in which all share the rewards. It defines social justice in a political context, though this is a somewhat unfashionable phrase these days. Community advocacy moves us from being a simple consumer or dissenter, subject to manipulation by media owners and other powerful people, to a citizen saying, 'I have rights and I want to express my views, and I intend to shape the decision.'

You don't lose your individuality when you become part of the community: in fact, as an individual you are empowered. You don't lose power if you share it: in fact, your power is strengthened. Working with the community means accepting that better decisions are made when they are made by those who will be affected by them, and that people learn to make responsible decisions once they have the opportunity to be part of the decision-making process.

Working with the community must be based on:

+ Openness and mutual trust

+ Acceptance that difference is an asset rather than a problem
+ Respect for each person's contribution
+ Respect for individual rights
+ Critical analysis
+ Dialogue, not dictation
+ Collective responsibility
+ Encouragement of innovation
+ Building on experience
+ Progress – for everyone who participates, and at their own pace.

It's important that those asking for their interests and experience to be considered are not portrayed as somehow asking for special favours. This has become common in recent years.

Joan Kirner recalls hearing a few years ago a country caller on talkback radio challenging a decision to shut down her town's hospital. The radio host said to her, 'I agree with your concerns, but can the economy afford it?' She snapped back, 'We live in a society, not an economy.' That is the central tenet of citizens' power.

NETWORKING THE COMMUNITY

As a young mother in the 1970s I quickly learned that the process for developing advocacy networks was critical to their effectiveness in empowering or disempowering the people involved, and ensuring long-term successful outcomes. I took a community development approach in my early activist days. At least, in retrospect, that's what I would call it. But I didn't then: I hadn't done the appropriate university course at the time.

Joan

When a community wants to influence a decision, whether it is to be made by governments, their bureaucracies, big business or unions, it has to lobby. It needs to make its wishes known, provide information, educate the decision-makers, and promote a particular cause or interest so that it gains popular support and the support of influential people and organisations. (Josephine Conway and Robyn Cotterell-Jones have produced an excellent lobby kit for the Women's Electoral Lobby which is well worth reading.)

To lobby successfully, you need to:

- Know who's responsible for the issue, what you're talking about, and when and where to go public
- Set your target
- Understand your opponent
- Involve your allies
- Use the right tools. These include letters and submissions (often very successful), petitions (not often very influential), leaflets (as part of an information campaign), telephones, faxes, emails, meetings, delegations to powerful people, public rallies and marches, street theatre, and the media.

You also need to be organised, informed, efficient and determined. Success depends on your becoming more than personally concerned, you must become politically active.

GENERAL RULES FOR POLITICAL ACTION

Politics is about power: power to set directions, power to make or not make decisions, and power to choose and use resources. Citizens are entitled to a share of the power to make decisions about their own lives and their communities' future. If you are not interested in politics this means either you are happy with the situation as it is or you are prepared to give away your entitlement to power as a citizen. Those who do not act give away their power. Not to be interested in politics is as political an act as to insist on your share of power.

To be politically effective you first need to identify why you want to exercise power and who already has it, and then talk to them to find out how they are going to use it and whether you can insist on sharing it. Organise potential allies:

+ People already involved in the fight
+ Family, friends and fellow workers
+ Local community groups and members
+ Like-minded groups – teachers and unions, for example
+ Members of Parliament, government and opposition
+ Ministerial advisers
+ Local council
+ Local, state and national media
+ Bureaucracy. In every government administration there are three groups: government-servers, time-servers and community-servers. You will find people useful to your cause in the third category: people who are willing to give you information, internal networks and opportunities to influence and shape government policy and action.

Work out who your potential opponents might be too, and how you might win them over or defeat them. Before you meet with people in power, research who they are and what they have said in policies, in the media and to other organisations on the issues that concern you. Set an agenda and forward it to them and, preferably, get agreement on it before the meeting. But leave it flexible enough to be added to. Never go to a meeting by yourself unless you are as powerful as the person you are meeting. Always take notes of the decisions of the meeting, and agree on them either at the meeting or by written submission after the meeting. Have an action sheet attached to your minutes and distribute this as soon as possible after the meeting. If you can bring a note-taker, that's the best of all. If you want to tape a meeting, ask ahead of time. If they agree, there's a price; taping inhibits frank discussion and prevents off-the-record discussion. Do not be flattered or overwhelmed by a meeting with a Minister, department head or politician – remember that they are accountable to you when they make decisions on your behalf. A cup of tea is not an outcome.

Sometimes you win on the justice of your case or the cogency of your argument, but you are more likely to win if you have the numbers as well, so identify the people who understand and support your issue, and get them together. Talk through the issue and allocate clear tasks for the group, including recruitment targets. This group, and their networks, will become your core group with whom you will be constantly in discussion and from whom you will draw your drive and support.

Build, maintain and update contact lists (phone, fax, email, address) for your support and action network, and the people you need to influence. Make sure you address them correctly. There are no brownie points for addressing a Ms as Dear Sir. One of the lighter moments in Joan Kirner's time as Premier was receiving an advertising brochure and invitation from Myer's Personal Service addressed to 'Mr J. Kirner, Premier of Victoria' and offering a special service for a beautiful grey or navy business suit and matching ties, shirt, shoes. Joan's reply to Myer was a gem – but not for publication.

Make sure you cover all important meetings. If the decision is going to be made at a meeting or series of meetings, make sure you plan the strategies and organise the members for each meeting, whether you will be there in person or not.

Remember to enjoy yourself. If the cause is just, you can have fun doing it and get companionship and lifelong friendship from working together. Keep, and practise using, your sense of humour.

Keep an eye on the finances. Any campaign requires some resources. Work out the costs of your campaign, stick to your budget, and review it regularly. The success of your campaign will depend on acting effectively and responding to new demands. Work out cheap, effective ways of getting information out and mustering support. The good old-fashioned telephone tree, described in Chapter 2, is a terrific way. It really works.

Here are some tips for organising a specifically political lobbying telephone tree:

- ◆ Set up the telephone-tree contact list
- ◆ Set up timelines for the contact list to ring the target – a Minister, or department head, or a local MP
- ◆ Arrange for two or three calls from each person on the tree to the target person
- ◆ Callers should keep written records of responses, and should ring through to the captain if a major change takes place, or to report on the attitude of those called
- ◆ If it is a very large telephone tree, groups can be set up, with group captains linked with the overall captain by teleconference or single call
- ◆ Stop the action if it is not producing useful results, but keep the telephone-tree list for future action
- ◆ You can do something similar by fax, but you'll need more people so that the target's fax machine is kept constantly engaged. They hate it!
- ◆ Rehearse your message with all the members of the telephone tree before they start calling. Write it down. Make sure the message is simple and personal: you need to be seen to be ringing as a legitimately concerned citizen, not as part of an organised group
- ◆ On the phone be persuasive, well-informed, polite and persistent. Don't be argumentative or angry or abusive
- ◆ Maintain your integrity and sense of humour.

LOCAL GOVERNMENT

Many women start their activities at a local level, and so local government becomes a good testing ground for women who are thinking of going into the wider political sphere. Linelle Gibson is a former councillor for the city of Hobson's Bay, one of Melbourne's amalgamated municipalities. Linelle was a local teacher and had been a community activist for more than ten years, but was a newcomer to formal politics when she ran for the council. We asked her what advice she would give to a would-be councillor, and she listed the following:

- ✦ Understand that you don't know everything: you need networks for feedback and advice, networks that can communicate and act – schools, pensioners, teachers, political parties, conservationists should all be part of your network. Work out who you can trust – who will advise and support you
- ✦ Build alliances inside and outside council. Remember that you can't effect change by yourself. Make sure agreements are open, not closed: not nod-and-wink deals. Alliances may shift according to issues: you have to work on them continually
- ✦ Don't make assumptions about people: check them out and work issues through with them first
- ✦ Build a team. New councillors and senior staff need to spend time with an independent facilitator to develop an overview and build the team
- ✦ Be insistent about your intention that elected councillors, not officers, are the decision-makers. Officers are the advisers and implementers. Set up processes to make sure this happens, especially on budget and planning matters. Be aware of officers' ability to both support and undermine council and community control
- ✦ Beware the managerial approach. It can cut across the

need to engage the community in decisions and meet community needs

+ Put responsibility for funding where it belongs: with government
+ When controversial issues have to be dealt with, explain them clearly to the community; involve interested community leaders and groups in round-table discussions; make the decision-making process clear and accessible; make complex issues easier to understand by breaking them into manageable components; listen to and use the community grapevine to keep up with the latest information and spread it; be accountable for your decisions
+ Always follow up, making sure you do what you said you'd do
+ Balance your work, family and community life and accept help from friends where it's offered; have an exercise regime; make time for the family and for yourself; employ someone to help clean the house; maintain your friends, and simplify your life
+ Make the best use of the media. Build good, respectful relationships with professional journalists: encapsulate complex issues in simple messages and keep in regular communication – not just when you want to impress them or are in trouble (they'll come to *you* then)
+ Be clear about your values. If you believe in something, you might have to stick your neck out sometimes. Say where you stand. Those who don't are more likely to be pressured and trapped in deals. People respect councillors with integrity
+ Admit mistakes and learn from them
+ Give yourself space to think. You don't have to own the silence and you don't have to wear the pressure. You don't have to decide straight away

- Learn from others' experience. You are not on your own. Analyse problems and agree on how to move on and cope with criticism
- Value staff and treat them well: they are your team. They keep councillors and the community going
- Say thanks. People matter. It's nice to be important, but it's important to be nice. Remember the Christmas card, personal phone call and thank-you note
- Remember that the written word is powerful. If you write the policy document, you're calling the play
- Identify apprentices and mentors. You won't last forever. Get people lined up in advance to take over from you when you're ready to move up. Too many people stay too long. Plan to do a job one, two or three terms and then pass it on. Passing on knowledge does not mean losing your power. Sharing knowledge is for your own and everyone else's benefit. Finding apprentices means you can all exert more influence together.

Postscript: As an effective and well-organised community activist and councillor, Linelle Gibson decided to take the next step, running for pre-selection for a safe seat in the Victorian parliament. She ran a great campaign, but didn't have the numbers: another effective young woman with a solid union background won pre-selection. But Linelle considered community activism to be just as politically important as being in parliament, and didn't take her bat and ball and go home. She decided to maintain her interest and activity. She might try again. Women rarely win pre-selection on their first try, no matter how good they are.

POLITICAL MENTORING

Because not nearly enough women are standing, or succeeding in being pre-selected, as political candidates, we need to take active steps to encourage and support women candidates, in all the parties. Joan Kirner is, of course, a Labor politician and former Member of Parliament and has taken steps to improve the chances of women in her party through, among other things, the development of a political mentoring system for women, by women, called EMILY's List, which was set up in Australia in 1996 (EMILY is the acronym for Early Money Is Like Yeast). Based on similar American and British models, it provides funding, moral and strategic support for Labor women candidates who are pro-choice and pro-equity, pro-childcare and pro-diversity. In its first years of operation the List has found that whilst the financial assistance is appreciated, especially if given early in the campaign, it is the personal mentoring which is most valued by the candidates.

Helen Shardey, a Liberal MP, credited her own success to networking, mentoring and 'doing her time' (she was electorate officer for Michael Wooldridge, Minister for Health, for six years), as well as luck. Helen also acknowledged the importance of the Liberal Women's Forum, set up in 1993 after Dame Beryl Beaurepaire and other leading Liberal women challenged their party's performance in relation to women after that year's federal election defeat. The Forum was set up by the party's Federal Council specifically to recruit more women. It has focused on training and mentoring women to develop their skills, plan their future, stand for pre-selection and win their seats. In the 1996 federal election this really paid off. Liberal women were elected into the federal parliament in unprecedented numbers.

EMILY's List mentors have been effective Members of Parliament, or women who have skills in media and communication, or who have recently successfully run for parliament. The mentor needs to have:

- A sound knowledge of the political trends in the state and the electorate

- ✦ A rapport with the candidate and an ability to build their confidence and self-image
- ✦ A timetable for regular contact (say, every two weeks) by phone or in person or both
- ✦ A sixth sense of when a spur-of-the-moment call might be needed to the candidate – for example, when a good, or bad, newspoll has been published or the candidate has made a public gaffe
- ✦ An ability to help the candidate determine her campaign strategies and priorities
- ✦ A good network of people and information that the candidate can use and build on
- ✦ An ability to anticipate or detect changes in the candidate's mood and needs throughout the campaign and into parliament
- ✦ A willingness to say what is needed in a way that will take the candidate and the campaign forward.

A mentor must be highly sensitive to her candidate's need for support, ringing and keeping in contact often. They must listen to their heart on this. One of Joan Kirner's clearest memories in EMILY's List is mentoring Frances Bedford, a candidate in the 1997 South Australian election and now the Member for Florey. Frances needed a 14% swing to win the seat and was determined to get it. One day, in the middle of the campaign, Joan just felt it was important to ring and check her progress. The answering machine clicked on and she left a message: 'Just checking, how are you going?' That night a worried Frances rang back. She had a problem with the questions she was getting about the One Nation candidates, and wasn't getting much help from the party machine in dealing with them positively. She and Joan then workshopped some ideas on the phone, particularly on how to turn questions back to the constituents so that they would look for answers, not slogans. Frances was relieved, and resumed door-knocking with renewed confidence. This was political mentoring at its most basic, and important, level.

BECOMING A CANDIDATE

Becoming a candidate for an elected office, whether it's in local government or for a state, territory or federal seat in parliament, is quite a challenge – and women have more challenges than most males aspiring to be politicians. Perhaps the greatest challenge is how to get and share political power without becoming a chap.

Marilyn Waring, a former New Zealand National Party politician, wrote in *Women, Politics and Power*:

> Some women seek power as an achievement in itself; some do not want or need it; some boast that they have more by manipulating behind the scenes (and fool only themselves). Some women seek it because it shuts out another patriarch, infiltrates like a good spy or guerrilla, confuses the male world and stops it from bounding on in the unquestioned macho course, and can be used to mobilise the female world. All the above routes are more valid than remaining contentedly powerless. Yet all of these routes are also insufficient . . . To change the nature of power requires enormous personal integrity and resilience, but even to attempt the change is threatening to the establishment.

The challenges to women candidates – whether for pre-selection or election – are very much the same whatever their political affiliations. Dame Beryl Beaurepaire, Liberal Party matriarch, gave these 'battle' rules for aspiring female politicians, which Susan Mitchell recorded in her book *The Scent of Power*:

◆ Get in
◆ Always know your subject

- ✦ Don't open your mouth unless you have something worthwhile to say
- ✦ Don't try to take a rise out of the men. They hate to be ridiculed
- ✦ Don't try to be a pseudo-male
- ✦ Think clearly. Do not suck up to them
- ✦ Be sensible, not silly
- ✦ Learn how to network
- ✦ If you lose the vote and still believe you are right, have a dissenting vote registered
- ✦ Don't take things personally
- ✦ Use every opportunity to lobby
- ✦ If you can't get support for something you believe in, choose someone you think is likely to be the most sympathetic. Explain your views carefully, and then, when you have that person on side, move on to the next one. It takes time, but it's worthwhile.

Women have different experiences, in political life, from men. Most political structures are designed to be comfortable for men. It will take a lot of women to change that culture. Women will not succeed by simply becoming second-rate clones of male politicians.

The day that Mary Robinson was elected as President of Ireland she said, 'This is a great day for Irish women. The women of Ireland, instead of rocking the cradle, rocked the system.' When Nancy Astor was elected in 1919 as the first woman MP in the House of Commons of the British Parliament, she was greeted by a pompous MP with the words 'Welcome to the most exclusive men's club in Europe.'

'It won't be exclusive for long,' she smiled in reply. 'When I came in, I left the door open.'

But there is still just a trickle of women coming in. By the year 2000 there will be ten million women and girls in Australia, but unless the structures and processes of politics are changed, parliamentary office will remain an elusive goal for them. In 1999, ninety-seven years after Australian women (excluding indigenous women) won the right to vote and sit in federal parliament:

+ Our national parliament is still overwhelmingly male
+ The voice of government is still a male voice
+ Women remain governed, rather than participating in government
+ The norms and processes of government are male, not female
+ The alienation of women from the current political system is marked, and growing.

This raises serious issues about the legitimacy of our democratic condition and the basis of two-party politics. More women must participate, if it is to survive. It took forty years from Federation before the first women made it into a federal Cabinet, and eighty-eight years for the first two women to become state premiers. And the rule remains that the higher the status, the fewer the women; the safer the seat, the fewer the women.

Why is this so? We hesitate to suggest that it is because existing politicians have not perceived the merit in women candidates. Women have been slow to put themselves forward, or they have failed to be selected when they should have been. Whatever the cause, the result is just unacceptable. If we go on at this rate it will take fifty years to have equal representation of women and men in parliament, and a thousand years for women to have equivalent economic clout. We can't wait that long. Unless the full pool of talent is used, we will have a weakened, illegitimate democratic system, mediocre parliamentarians, and a second- or third-rate system of government.

HALF BY 2000

I am passionate about achieving 'half by 2000' – that is, a 50% representation of women in government – for two main reasons. First, as a political 'elder stateswoman' who has scaled the heights (and occasionally plumbed the depths) of politics, I believe that women in parliament have an obligation to ensure that other women are coming behind us, in large numbers. Currently they are not, and our party and the society will be the poorer for it. Second, as a feminist Labor politician, my view of politics and fairness is the same as that of the former President of Ireland, Mary Robinson: 'I believe that equality for women enhances humanity.'

Women must decide that that is what they want to do, then they have to organise to make it happen. My view is confirmed by EMILY's List research, which shows that women voters expect women candidates standing for parliament and winning office to make a difference in:

+ Ensuring that decision-making processes are more democratic and inclusive of women and community
+ Accepting and expecting greater accountability, in that they ensure other women benefit from their being in power
+ Effecting change and making government work for ordinary people – a powerful force in today's political environment
+ Understanding women's needs better than men.

Women are seen not as part of the problem, but as part of the solution to the politics of alienation.

Joan

This reality is recognised by intelligent political observers. In 1992 Andrew Robb, then Federal Director of the Liberal Party, told a parliamentary inquiry into equal opportunity and equal status for women in Australia that 'Women are less identified with the sources of strong political disillusionment that are around. They are seen as honest, not captive, and better placed to understand the problems of ordinary people living through a recession.' He noted, however, that 'At the same time, voters and preselectors see politics as a very tough business and they wonder whether women will be tough and effective enough for the profession of politics. Prospective candidates face an unusually difficult challenge to establish their competency.'

Joan Kirner has been approached by more women than she can count who say, 'I'm interested in being more active in politics and one day, perhaps, getting into parliament. How do you start?' Her answers vary according to the circumstances, but these pointers may help:

+ First, get information and experience. You need to know about yourself, the issues, and your opportunities. Analyse your skills and where you can make a difference. Write a short biography for public use

+ Start small. Go to meetings of your party's local branch (even though these may be boring), or to a student or political briefing, or get involved with a local or national organisation which is seeking change in an area of public policy that interests you

+ Find a mentor you can talk to about your hopes, dreams and experiences and who will give you wise advice

+ When you find your feet, *then* join a party and participate in the party's structures – branches, committees or whatever else is reasonably available to you

+ Gain some work experience in a Member of Parliament's office

+ Volunteer to help in an election campaign

+ Try local government as a further step in your political experience

+ Expand your knowledge of political issues through books, newspapers and community experience

✦ Find out what the pre-selection requirements and procedures for your party are, and start working your
   numbers

✦ At all times, no matter what else, remain yourself, be
   prepared, and be accountable.

The question of whether or not you should join a political party
will no doubt arise. These days independent members are more
common than ever. Be warned, though, that to stand as an independent candidate means that you will not have a party
machine behind you to provide you with information, policy
advice, a sounding board for your ideas, and with the organisation, experience and people to spread the word, set up meetings,
distribute leaflets and respond to your supporters and critics.
You will have to do everything yourself – with the support of
friends, family, and well-intentioned strangers, and no money
at all. Or, worse, you may have to take support from other
groups who then take your agenda over and may compromise
your values.

The decision to join a party or not can be no-one's but
your own. However, the advice we give about deciding whether
to stand, campaigning and dealing with the media applies to all
aspects of political campaigning, and to staying in office. It is
certainly not limited to a particular party philosophy. No sec-
tional or special-interest group will deliver your votes. Everyone
votes: you need to appeal to the majority of people in your
particular electorate.

Before you decide to run for parliament, ask yourself, your
family and your friends these questions – and be ruthlessly
honest with yourself about the answers:

✦ Why do you want to run for parliament?
✦ What do you have to offer?
✦ What difference would you make for your electorate or
   the issues you believe in?

- Are you in for the long haul – for as long as it takes to win?
- Is the seat winnable? First time, or second (or third or fourth) time? You'll need to look at voting trends, demographics, local issues and the qualities of the other contenders
- Will your personal and family life withstand public and media scrutiny? Don't run if it won't, or if you don't want yourself or your family to be exposed to it. If there are things the public should know, tell them. Angela Eagle, the British Environment Minister, announced that she was gay and intended to live with her partner. After the first headlines, interest just faded away
- If you are looking for a party's support, who else is running for pre-selection, what are the rules, and what are the numbers? Who controls them? Seek out a friendly person in the electorate and find out. Work out how you can win the pre-selection contest and keep working on your plan, to the last day
- Who comprises, and who could comprise, your support base and networks at local, state and national level?
- If you are pre-selected (or decide to run as an independent), can you build a strong and effective campaign team, office, plan and financial base?
- Do you have the energy, determination, discipline and vision needed to win the seat *and* be effective in parliament?
- Do you know how to make the most of the media? Do you know how to listen and communicate? If not, how will you learn?
- Have you sorted out the impact that running for parliament and winning or losing will have on your personal and professional life? Do you have support? What will you do to keep it, or if you lose it?

Sorting out the personal effects of your decision, negotiating and keeping your personal support base is often harder than making the political decision. If you don't do this, and keep doing it, the difficulties may build up and determine your personal and political future – nasty, brutish and short!

CAMPAIGNING FOR BEGINNERS

Having made your fateful decision and won the first campaign of getting pre-selection, you then have to start on the 'real' campaign trail to win your seat. How you develop this campaign depends on your answers to another set of hard questions. The answers, worked through with your campaign group, will frame your campaign plan and message:

+ Why should people vote for me?
+ What values do I advocate?
+ What do I want to change?
+ What are my future constituents' values, needs and experiences? How are they different from, or similar to, mine? How do I connect their values, needs, experiences and desire for action with mine?
+ What do my future constituents want to keep and what do they want to change? How do I find these things out?
+ How can I make, and demonstrate I can make, an ongoing difference in constituents' lives, in ways which they need and appreciate?
+ What will be the central message of my campaign, a message that describes the aspirations, and wins the vote, of the community I want to represent? How will I build my campaign around this message so that the message informs the campaign, and the campaign is the message?
+ How will my local campaign fit in with the state or national campaign of the party I've hitched my wagon to?

✦ How will my campaign contrast with those of my opposition?

✦ What am I going to do with my preferences?

✦ What resources have I got, and what more do I need, in funding and in-kind support?

These answers will then help you write your strategy plan, which must include the following:

✦ Target the base vote for your party, plus 'soft' votes, identified by telephone canvassing. Your task is to keep your base and convert some of the softies

✦ Be clear about what you stand for: contrast this with your opponents' stand

✦ Passionately follow though on each special case. This will enhance the community perception of you as an active candidate

✦ Build up new support bases among your constituents

✦ Get endorsed by local people of good standing in the community

✦ Be positive – be seen as a real person

✦ Criticise any lack of commitment to the electorate by the sitting member and their party

✦ Build a top-class campaign team. Be the candidate, not the campaign manager

✦ Get an adequate funding base

✦ As Fred Daley, long-term Speaker of the House of Representatives, said, 'Believe that you can win, but campaign as though you might lose'

✦ Have a clear campaign message that links you to the community's values, experiences and needs

✦ Write down the people responsible for day-to-day administration, overview of the campaign, finance, purchasing, media, policy and research, timetables, volunteers, postal

voting, polling booths, food and fun. Keep saying thank
you!
Many people believe that a good campaign is one that converts
voters to the big picture of your party. But once the local
campaign is off and running the big picture recedes and the real
work is reaching and persuading voters to vote for you, and
there the local issues matter. Teamwork and attention to detail
will determine whether you succeed. Here are some helpful tips:

+ Announce your candidacy as early as possible
+ Devise TV and photo opportunities, street walks, shop
  and factory visits, so that people get to know your face
+ Keep a file on your opponents. Get to the local paper
  before they do if you have something sensible to say on
  emerging issues and community needs
+ Don't attack your opposition personally. Attack their performance in parliament or the electorate, and their policies
  or lack of them
+ Be aware of the local issues and mood, and develop a
  well-informed, easily understood position – one which
  reflects party policies if you're a party candidate and
  which reflects the electorate's needs
+ Begin community consultations by inviting local people
  to meetings, or sending them written surveys to find out
  their opinions, then door-knock personally
+ Advise people of what you or your party will do, or have
  done, to respond to their views. Tony Blair and his
  women's policy colleagues had great success in attracting
  the women's vote in the 1997 UK elections by conducting
  community consultations to define the five issues most
  important to women, feeding that into policy, then ad-
  vising in writing all those who took part in the consultation what a Blair government would do about their
  community concerns

✦ Get the big brass to visit and really meet the people, and make sure that they're seen to do so (brief them first).

RAISING MONEY

In Australia, federal election campaigns of all parties receive public funding according to the number of votes won. Political parties also provide funding for national or statewide campaigns, TV advertising and basic campaign material. Nevertheless, all candidates for federal, state and local election campaigns need additional funds. A very basic campaign requires at least $10 000 to be raised by the local candidate and their campaign committee. The average federal campaign in Australia costs between $60 000 and $70 000 per electorate. A tough campaign in a marginal seat may need $150 000 or more, if regional TV or saturation mail is proposed, or if top-quality, electorate-specific polling needs to be done. When it comes to raising money:

✦ Set your target
✦ Appoint a fund-raising committee
✦ Determine which individuals and groups you will raise money with and get money from
✦ Set up a campaign account with a requirement of two signatories on any cheques. Keep careful records of income and expenditure for the Australian Electoral Commission
✦ Remember the motto of EMILY's List, Early Money Is Like Yeast. Money makes the dough rise and gets the campaign moving
✦ Start off with a personal request for an upfront amount from close friends and supporters (whatever they can afford)
✦ Keep records of who donates and who doesn't, for future requests and the law, and always write thank-you notes
✦ Solicit donations by mail or phone
✦ Have different fund-raising events for different levels of

income – from a family pie day to a sit-down, paying
dinner with top speakers and entertainment

✦ Don't fund-raise in ways that cut across your message. If
you're anti-gambling, lottery tickets aren't a good idea

✦ Make sure your campaign plan and campaign budget are
in sync.

YOUR RELATIONSHIP WITH THE ELECTORATE

First impressions are lasting impressions, so make sure that your
first pamphlet, appearances, interviews and published letters or
articles are attractive, authoritative and relevant to your electorate.
You may wish to have an early pamphlet endorsed by one or
more leading community figures who support you. Australian
political history reveals that people will vote for you (and your
party) if they believe you understand their life experience and
will fight for their needs to be met. In these days of insecurity,
you must be able to listen to and identify with community demands and act on them. People want to be clear about your
values, and about your (and your party's) solutions – present
and future.

Listen carefully to the community and use your experience,
insight and policies to develop your message: for example, 'Joy
Mathews: Working for Our Community', or 'Maggie Deahm:
Caring and Active'. If you can, test the campaign message with
some local polling of constituents, as well as with your campaign
committee and your party headquarters.

Review previous election data, voting booth by voting booth,
according to totals and trends. Work out where you should put
your energies: winning back voters who have strayed; targeting
the soft voters in the middle, specific age groups, those worried
about a government policy, or those who are just plain angry.

Build a network of key people in the electorate whom you
need to know, and others who can be called on for support in
funding and for endorsement. Meet, and stay in contact with,

as many of these people as possible. Your networks should be many and varied but all with one purpose – enabling you to become and remain an effective MP. Apart from family, friends, old acquaintances and professional associates, your network may include like-minded people in local, state or national organisations, people who want to defeat the current government on ideological or current-issue grounds, and people who think you may win office, or that your party may win government, and be useful to them. Work with your network to:

+ Find out about local needs
+ Harness local media, business, organisations and local government to your cause
+ Develop solutions
+ Raise resources – money and in-kind support
+ Speak at as many local engagements as possible
+ Door-knock and letterbox
+ Conduct telephone polls
+ Staff your campaign office.

CAMPAIGN COMMITTEE

No matter how good a candidate you are, you can't run a campaign and win by yourself. The law requires that all election material be authorised by a person acting for you, and endorsed with their name and address. There are no exceptions to this.

On your campaign team you will also need:

+ A campaign manager, preferably someone with earlier campaign experience and someone you get on well with. The campaign manager needs good political analysis and management skills
+ A secretary or personal assistant
+ A media liaison person
+ A treasurer
+ A postal-vote manager
+ Fund-raisers

+ A lawyer – on call
+ Someone with computer skills (for research, web site, email, and database management)
+ Someone to maintain a good local and national media file on yourself and your opposition
+ Volunteers roster for door-knocks, the campaign office, and other tasks.

CAMPAIGNING

Jenny Beacham is a top community-based campaigner. She is terrific at assessing what can be done, what works and what doesn't work in campaigns. She had been a Victorian ALP candidate and ALP Secretary, and we asked her for advice on how to run a campaign as a woman candidate and help other women candidates to get elected.

A CASE STUDY
JENNY BEACHAM: CAMPAIGNING AS A WOMAN

Find a woman who will be a mate. She might be your campaign manager, or someone who will just agree to go everywhere with you. I had a great mate who was prepared to put her life on hold while we went from one end of the electorate to the other, who got to know the personalities, who said, 'Did you hear what that bastard said?' when we climbed back in the car. The boys in our campaign never understood the importance of our relationship and thought we spent our time arguing, but she was the only person I could depend on for a gut reaction from a feminist perspective. She was the only person I could be sure would understand the need to look after the volunteers, and who took some responsibility for the dynamic of the campaign office. She was the only person with whom I could be sure of at least one laugh for the day.

Where do women meet? The usual place people think

of is the school, so let's look at that first. I would find someone who collected her kids after school and ask if she belonged to the school council or parent organisation, then ask her to introduce me to her friends, the lollipop lady and the teachers. At the end of the day the teachers are often keen to have a chat. And of course there are always the school functions – the fêtes and fairs and boot sales. Now that schools are being forced to raise more and more money in their own communities, there have to be more and more of these events. You must try to go to these (again, with some friendly parent) and do things like giving prizes for the chocolate wheel. You will find these events advertised in the local paper. Don't depend on other people to tell you – they don't always realise which events are important. No-one told me that over five hundred people go to the Christmas Carols at Mount Clear, yet there were lots of party members there, quite pleased to see me too, though none of them had thought of suggesting that it was the place to go.

But women meet at many other places too, like the local baby and child welfare centre when they go for the baby's immunisation shots. I got a list of these sessions from the local medical officer and those mums were quite surprised to see me because they didn't think they were important enough to warrant the attention of politicians. So if you can cope with tearful babies and bring something that is of interest, like safe toys for under-fives, this is a good meeting point.

Be prepared to be flexible about being around – you don't have to be on stage. We had a stall at a Trash and Treasure regularly, a great way of getting to talk to people in a relaxed setting.

Take the initiative and organise some events – chances for your supporters to meet well-known women. Over three hundred women came to meet Carmen Lawrence on a freezing night in Ballarat, but it doesn't have to be just political women; you can use women who are leaders in their field, writers, sportswomen, and so on, to add their expertise or fund-raising resources to your campaign.

Some candidates think campaigning is about making speeches, but this is only a very small part of the overall job. Being a good woman candidate means holding and attending events that are inclusive, that are child-friendly and don't cost too much. It means revealing a bit about yourself, whether you are a grandmother, a single parent, an aunt, whether you are coping with an ageing parent yourself – in other words, whether there is enough in your experience to enable you to represent their interests in the parliament.

Value yourself, your knowledge, your networks. Think about what you personally have to offer women in terms of values and experience and networks. Write them down, then use them. If you choose public life, you have to go in boots and all. You can't be afraid of scrutiny. Your aim is to be recognised. Even now, years after the election in which I was the failed candidate, what surprises me is that people still know me. It is a great privilege to be a political candidate. You get to see dimensions of a community that you would never otherwise see. Go out and enjoy it.

Remember that women have particular skills and qualities to offer the electorate; build on them. Remember too that women feel very strongly that politicians do not focus on issues that are relevant to them. These issues include:

+ Improving the standard of living for their families (including having some free time)
+ The state of the health system

+ The quality and cost of education for their children and themselves
+ Job prospects for young people
+ Problems affecting elderly parents.

Research done by EMILY's List shows that women feel that politicians 'don't have the faintest idea' what their lives are like: they're 'not on the same planet'. Women also feel very strongly that things would be much better if there were a lot more women in parliament. Their reasons are:

+ Women are seen as less likely to be in it for themselves, less ego-based, less likely to engage in petty point-scoring
+ Women have more commonsense and are able to sit down and work out a solution more co-operatively
+ Women have experienced the problems more directly. They know more about the issues associated with children, education, the elderly, and dealing with the health-care system.

Women feel it is important that women parliamentarians retain these qualities and not become sucked into the game of self-interest and party-political point-scoring.

Women contesting seats need to demonstrate these qualities in the way they present themselves, the issues they address, and the language they use. They should realise that being down-to-earth, honest and direct are important qualities, as is the capacity to transcend one-eyed party allegiance in favour of seeking solutions to the larger issues. And they need to use concrete examples to explain complex issues. A woman candidate wishing to focus on an issue should articulate values, aspirations and personal conviction, and use simple and direct discussion. She should tie into a local issue where possible, speak in terms that resonate with people's experience and concerns, and, when she criticises the opposition, she should focus on important and relevant issues and include a positive statement of alternative direction.

The main issues are similar for women and men, but the emphasis and orientation are very different. Men like to talk about the big picture (though no-one uses that term any more) and translate issues into their overall impact on the economy. Women want to hear how the big picture will translate into the concrete details of their lives.

ORGANISING EVENTS

There are four reasons for running events – to raise your profile, extend your networks, raise your money, and have fun. Well-run and financially successful events require careful planning and selling. There are some basic steps to follow:

- Select a small committee whose members will work and run the event by themselves, or bring in others, including sponsors, where needed
- Determine the true price your prospective attendees can afford
- Project the income and profit that you will make, taking into account all costs and income
- Prepare a budget, a timeline and an allocation of tasks. Allow at least two months to organise and sell the event
- Decide the hooks that will attract the audience you are targeting – performers, format, auction, raffle, speakers, and so on
- Where possible, go for prepayment of tickets. People who've paid are more likely to show up too. Monitor ticket sales and back up original invitations with telephone-tree reminders
- If the event is a sit-down affair, put yourself and one event worker in charge of appropriate seating arrangements. Give trusted hosts responsibility for a table each. Be sure to talk, however briefly, to all the guests. They will understand if you have to move on quickly. If they have a burning issue, ask them to make an appointment

to see you. Make sure your door and greeting arrangements are organised and welcoming

+ Put one person in charge of media, if you are having media, and be clear about your involvement and the picture you want. Collect the media reports on the event
+ Plan the program so that people have time to chat, listen and enjoy.

A low-key way of raising funds is selling your name and message on goods that people can afford, and will want to buy, such as campaign buttons, car stickers, T-shirts, caps, mugs, bottles of wine (but don't sell them without a licence, or from your Ministerial office, as Jeff Kennett did in 1993). Cost the merchandising so that you will make a profit on each sale and a good profit on the whole.

STRATEGY DESIGN QUESTIONS

+ Have you built up an accurate picture of the electorate in each polling-booth area?
+ Have you polled or worked out what they want from a local MP? (Most people are realistic about this.) Does your campaign material reflect this?
+ Is the campaign budget sufficient?
+ Is the media and advertising campaign appropriate and effective?
+ Do you have a door-knocking strategy for the campaign? Preferably you should poll before you door-knock. It gives you a better feel for the electorate
+ Have you lined up friends, supporters, family and campaign workers to volunteer to letterbox, hold community morning or afternoon teas, pre-poll, blow up balloons, hand out material at markets and shopping centres and railway stations, take the kids off your hands for a break, and organise postal votes?
+ Have you done an analysis of the polling booths for the

last three elections, analysed swings in the vote, and
worked out how you can get them to change their vote?
Research shows that a good local candidate can get a
2–3% swing in her favour, but a personal swing will
rarely stand up to an even national swing of 5% plus
+ Have you been briefed on key issues in the electorate?
+ Have you brainstormed ideas with your campaign committee and others?
+ Will you manage a regular audit procedure to see how
the campaign is going?

SETTING UP YOUR OFFICE

This advice is just as relevant to setting up your electorate office
(when you win) as your campaign office – only the length of
the lease is different. A well-set-up campaign base will easily
transform into your permanent base for your constituents.

+ Have your office *in* the electorate. Make it visible, welcoming, and on street level, so your constituents will feel that
the office is theirs (within reason)
+ Get a good filing and personal record system. Build up
a good data base
+ Pick the right people to work in it. Staff confidentiality
and loyalty are essential. Your electorate office staff are
your public face much of the time
+ Build your team: this means team practice and having a
meal or coffee together once a week
+ Always answer correspondence; keep records of every
letter, reply and outcome. Address people correctly on
your letters, read what you sign, and check personally
any material that goes out of your office
+ Build your networks and stay in touch with them. You'll
be surprised how many you have. If you demonstrate
that you deliver to constituents and groups your networks will expand.

VOLUNTEERS

Volunteers are essential in any campaign. For their enjoyment, and yours, they need to be co-ordinated, given clear tasks and timelines, and thanked often, from the heart. To attract the maximum number of volunteers you might send out an invitation form to all party members and friends – in unions, professional groups, business and community. Ask if they would be interested in helping the campaign; what special skills they have in letter-writing, street stalls and markets, polling booths, events, envelope-stuffing and photocopying, phones and administration. Suggest days and hours that they can choose from. Then sign them up.

DOOR-KNOCKING

Though some candidates hate it and some just don't do it, door-knocking is the best way of getting known in the electorate. It has three stages. The first is direct mail, to say that the candidate will be in an area on a particular date. The second is volunteers or the candidate knocking on the door and talking, offering material directly to the constituent. The third is writing back and saying what you have done or what your party will do to address the constituent's and the community's concerns.

To make door-knocking work you need to:
+ Target on the basis of pre-polling, if you can
+ Choose your team and divide up the streets
+ Get a calling card printed
+ Leave a written message – with your photo, your address and your phone contact – for the people who aren't home, to say you'd still love to hear from them at their convenience
+ Keep a tally board on the people who've been spoken to and their voting intentions – your party, an opposition party, or unsure
+ Keep an eye on the issues revealed during door-knocking

◆ If you promise to get back to someone, keep your promise. If the door-knocking seems be going against you, discuss and rethink or confirm your strengths and weaknesses and the campaign strategy. Here are some additional tips:

- ◆ Look out for toilets. You'll need them. Go before you start, and go regularly
- ◆ Beware of dogs. Take a dog whistle
- ◆ Don't go alone
- ◆ Take a watch with you, have a timetable and stick to it
- ◆ Take a clipboard and keep notes
- ◆ Wear an outfit with pockets, comfortable shoes that look okay, and take a fold-up umbrella and a hat
- ◆ Don't go inside anyone's home
- ◆ Don't get yourself trapped into talking too long to the already converted, or to opposition supporters (because you won't win that argument)
- ◆ Comment on the good points of the home you're calling on
- ◆ Find something in the community that they're interested in to talk about
- ◆ Know your local issues and local government personalities
- ◆ Be prepared – have an introduction ready
- ◆ If you think you might need someone to interpret, have them available or arrange to come back with them at a convenient time.

AUDITING YOUR CAMPAIGN

To keep your campaign on track you need to review it constantly. You can do it yourself or get an outsider to do it. The questions to ask include:

- ◆ Has the candidate identified community networks and key issues?
- ◆ Is the campaign budget adequate? If not, how will you bridge the gap?

- ◆ Is the campaign team clear about their values and roles, and about your role?
- ◆ Is telephone canvassing to identify swinging voters in place? This can be done by trained volunteers
- ◆ Is there an adequate door-knocking strategy in place?
- ◆ Is there an adequate community-meeting strategy in place?
- ◆ Does your advertising strategy adequately explain your good qualities, your ability to make a difference, and your community connections?
- ◆ Have you got your pre-polling or absentee votes covered? In a close contest this can make the difference
- ◆ Are there enough volunteers? Do they know what to do? Is there a volunteer network?
- ◆ Have you picked the eyes out of others' campaigns to ensure that you have the best campaign profile?
- ◆ Have you built up a good relationship with your party office, particularly on conducting Ministerial or Shadow Ministers' visits?
- ◆ Can you get some confidential polling done to assist your campaign strategy?

THE DAY AFTER THE ELECTION

Congratulations. You've won. Don't celebrate (well, just a little bit): work! Your first media appearance after your election is crucial. You should manage to look confident, but not arrogant, and as though you are not exhausted (even if you are), but elated. Remember to thank those who voted for you, and promise to work for all your constituents and to stay close to their needs, working in partnership with them to strengthen your community. Restate how you will make a difference, and be gracious to your defeated opponents.

You also need to send thank-you letters, or put up thank-you notices on your billboards; finalise your election accounts;

and set in place plans to locate your office and establish your files, communication system and media contact list.

IN PARLIAMENT

Find a mentor, in or out of parliament, to whom you can confess your fears and who can help you build up your confidence and expertise. Be yourself: calm, confident, and as well informed as possible. Review your wardrobe. Make sure you have a basic wardrobe that won't crush, doesn't need dry-cleaning (except for special outfits), and will take you from weekday work through to dinner at Government House. Find people in parliament you can trust, in your faction or group, the Clerk of the Parliament, and other MPs. Use them, and only them, as sounding boards or confidantes and partners in action. Learn the basic rules of the House. Remember, the Speaker or President is the boss, and the House rules make them supreme so, good or bad, observe the courtesies:

- You stand when they enter the House and stay standing as they say the Lord's Prayer
- During debate you sit down when the Speaker stands in their chair to speak, even if you are mid-sentence
- You bow to the chair (just a little nod) when you enter and leave the House, or when you cross in front of the table to go to the other side of the House
- You can enter and exit by either door, but each time you must bow/nod to the Speaker.

The Clerk of the Parliament will advise you on:

- How to word a question
- How to get into question time or onto the adjournment list
- How to word and present a petition
- The rules and forms of the House
- Legal matters and precedents.

Here are some other basic procedural rules:

- ✦ If the House divides on a vote, members go to the appropriate side of the House for a yes or a no vote. The Speaker appoints tellers to count the vote from among the MPs. Once you have taken your seat during a division, don't move until the count is over or you won't be counted as a vote. You can sit anywhere so long as it is in the designated yes or no side
- ✦ Make sure you don't leave important pieces of paper on your seat, wherever you are. Take them across the floor with you if you are working on them

+ You can't speak in the House – not even to interject – until you have made your first speech. It's good to have some supporters in the gallery when you do it, so try to get ample notice

+ To ask a question or speak on the adjournment (question time begins the afternoon session and the adjournment is at the end of the day), you will need to sort out your place on the queue with the Speaker's list run by the leader of your party in the parliament. Stand up to ask your question as soon as the Minister has answered the question before your question. Ask the question when the Speaker calls you as 'the member for [your seat]'

+ As well as questions in the House, you can ask questions on notice. These are more detailed questions, usually, and get more detailed answers

+ Refer to honourable members by the seats they represent, not by their names

+ Ask the Clerk for a list of names, then consult the parliamentary handbook and do yourself a map of names, constituencies and where they sit. Study it during the boring bits

+ Don't refer to people sitting in the gallery by name or with gestures – it's out of order

+ Be careful with interjections. Unless they are very clever they can rebound on you

+ If you make a mistake in the House on a point of fact or information, correct it as soon as you can. You might need to make a personal explanation. Ask the Clerk how to do this

+ Attend the House first thing in the morning. Check the orders of the day on the green running sheet, which will be in your room, to see what debates are listed for the day and what debates are coming up that you might like

to contribute to. You will need to negotiate with the
Clerk for your turn in the debate, and stand in your seat
when it is time to speak

+ Always attend for question time, the beginning of the
day, and the adjournment
+ You don't need to be in the House all the time. There is
a speaker box in your room that you should leave switched
on. You may have a compelling need to get back in, on
short notice
+ The division bells must be obeyed instantly. After three
minutes' ringing the doors are locked and you can't get
in to vote, so start moving in when they begin
+ You might put tea- or coffee-making facilities in your
room, plus a supply of dry biscuits and dried fruit, and
a couch, pillow and rugs for a very occasional late night
+ Mind out for the media hanging around the House. They
will catch you off-guard if they can, and they will watch
for any unguarded moment in the House
+ Try to get a quick walk around the parliamentary gardens
at least once a day
+ Do your networking on the phone, walking, at dinner or
on coffee breaks, not in the bar.

Finally, remember that there is nothing required of an MP or
councillor that a woman cannot do.

horacek

Chapter 9

An A to Z of power

The greatest obstacles to power for women are the myths and stereotypes about our capacities and potential: socially, at work, in politics, and in the home. The language used in our society reflects these, and a history in which women have had a very limited role. We would have liked to write a dictionary for women, as John Ralston Saul did for democrats (*The Doubter's Companion: A Dictionary of Aggressive Common Sense*). Instead, we have written an A to Z of power, a micro–reference list of some of what we have learned through our experiences. It is not particularly erudite or reverent. We had fun writing it. Try writing you own: it is a defining experience.

A is for:

achievement   Women seek power to achieve for themselves and for others. Know the achievements of the past, understand how they were won, protect them, and build on them. Expect it of yourself and expect it from others, and you'll get what you aim for.

assert   Assert your right as a citizen to have a say, especially on issues that affect you and your community.

audacity   People with power are often jealous of it, and very defensive or aggressive if you challenge their precious possession. You have to risk being put down, labelled as cheeky, impertinent, insubordinate, or out of line, in order to claim power. Audacity means daring, taking risks for good reason. Go for it.

B is for:

backbencher   This is a term used for non-Cabinet members of parliament, who do not hold positions as Ministers or office holders. Some of the more cynical political power-brokers think that backbenchers are parliament-fodder whose only purpose is to use their vote to carry a government or opposition motion. But a backbencher is your servant, and holds a very important political trust: to represent your needs and interests in the parliament. They are part of government, for your and your community's benefit. Good backbenchers don't need to be reminded of that. Remind them anyway, regularly, not just at election times.

balls   Some boys like to show off their 'balls' as political-speak for strength. Some also like to judge you against their display. A quick way to dispense with this nonsense is to substitute the word 'breasts'. For example, 'That's a tough decision, that took balls' turns into 'That's a tough one, that took breasts'. Joan Kirner got tired of the macho language of some of the men in John Cain's Cabinet and started using the second: decisions were never described as ball-breaking again.

blacklist Strong women may find themselves blacklisted by a new government, business or professional groups, or employers. This is usually temporary but can sometimes be long-term. It can be survived if you understand it as a compliment, not a sentence. Respond by finding other ways to use your values and skills, and earn more compliments.

bullying Make no mistake, the world is full of bullies. If your ideas are unfamiliar or unpopular, there are many powerful men – and a few women – in every power situation or political movement who will use ridicule, threats and standover tactics to try to shut you up or marginalise you. Never accept bullying. Have strategies ready to deal with it: a strong sense of purpose, allies, supporters, and a few techniques for self-protection. Bullies usually back off when you stand up to them. They thrive on fear and avoidance.

C is for:

cabinet Cabinet is the group of Ministers elected, if it's a Labor government, by caucus; or appointed, if it's a coalition government, by the Premier or Prime Minister. It meets regularly (usually weekly) to make government decisions, or in some cases to rubber-stamp yet another leadership group's decisions – a 'kitchen cabinet', in this case. The kitchen cabinet of the first Labor administration in Victoria, for instance, was the Premier, Deputy Premier, Treasurer, leader of both Houses, and one Minister. Ministers are forever grateful if lobbyists and citizens help them persuade Cabinet to their cause (just kidding).

caucus This is the total group of members of parliament of the Labor party. They are important people to influence, collectively and individually. Form your own caucus of women, to influence your group's decision-making.

citizen   Democracy wouldn't work at all if citizens didn't participate in their government. Government would be just another form of tyranny if it were not accountable to citizens. It is in everyone's interests for citizens to value their position and make government take its obligations seriously. These days there are many government attempts to turn voters from being citizens with a right to participate in government business, to customers or clients with the right only to choose between decisions already made by someone else. An individual is a citizen, first and foremost, but if they do not use their position and assert their rights then they may lose their status, and their rights and obligations will wither away. Citizens are much more than consumers; their relationships are much more important than financial exchanges in some open market. And citizenship is not a user-pays commodity.

common good   This quaintly old-fashioned phrase indicates what politics is meant to protect and promote. We all have an interest in working co-operatively for a better society. All of our individual interests are protected by a process of compromise and consensus called the democratic process. The antitheses to this include self-interest and consumerism.

commonsense   As the English philosopher William of Occam said hundreds of years ago, sometimes the simplest answer is the right one. There is much accumulated wisdom in organisations and communities. Listen to it, seek it out and add to it. Commonsense is often referred to as the wisdom of the people. When wisdom is applied for the benefit of all people it is called the common good. Commonsense is not sufficient for political effectiveness, but when in doubt it's a good basis for making an initial judgement.

communication   Effective politics is based on good communication: clear, simple, consistent and, above all, two-way.

D is for:

decoration   Women are often welcomed into political parties, onto boards, committees and working groups for ornamental purposes. They make the inviters appear women- and community-friendly. If the woman is already a star she adds status to the male leaders. The challenge for the woman is to join with other women to make a difference for herself and other women. The challenge for the men is to get used to that idea.

democracy   This is an old-fashioned notion much talked of but being undermined in Australia today. Democracy isn't particularly efficient, cheap, profitable or jingoistic, but it is the only system of government capable of balancing the interests of individuals and the community. Societies are only productive and effective when democracy is working properly, and it only works if citizens believe in themselves, participate in their community, and practise democratic virtues daily.

detail   There's an old saying, 'the devil is in the detail', that is very true in politics. Many an idea fails because the details are not attended to. Successful campaigners must understand and care about the fine print, or have someone behind them who is taking care of it.

diary   You need an appointments diary, and to keep a daily diary too with notes of any important meetings or decisions, and you need to keep a list of things to be done and who is to do them. Keep your appointment diary at work and your personal diary at home. Don't show your diary to anyone until you have to. Diaries are very useful when someone is trying to discredit you. Diaries can also be subpoenaed or stolen and become embarrassing. Keep them accurately, and locked up.

E is for:

equality   It's a traditional notion that everyone is equal before the law, there being no special privileges for elite groups or privileged individuals. Equality as a principle requires respect for other individuals, whether they are like you or not, and a willingness to acknowledge their essential freedoms, dignity and right to speak whether they are men, women or children.

equity   This has long been the central idea of Australian political life – a fair go for all – and it's a constant struggle to achieve it, and keep it.

ex-office-holder   Don't grieve or become bitter over what you've lost. Celebrate achievements and get on with your next challenge. You learn as much, if not more, from defeat and loss as you do from winning – it just doesn't feel as good.

experience   It's unique and it should be valued by you and by your government, employer and community. Others can learn from yours, and you from theirs.

F is for:

faction   Factions are interest groups who work within a group to extend their influence and control, and they exist in every walk of life. Most political parties have factions – in the ALP they are called left and right; the conservatives call them wet and dry. Factions are often informal and very influential. It is important to know what faction the politician you want to influence belongs to. There are many ways to influence individual actions, and sometimes a group or network approach is the best. Factions are only destructive when they are exclusive and exercise power for power's sake, rather than for the party or the cause. This is a standing temptation to any powerful group.

facts   You must collect them, check them, know them, have access to them, and insist on being told them. Any source will do, so long as you check it – clippings, Hansard, remarks on radio or television, websites and Internet newsgroups. Use facts wisely and well. Every fact has an attendant horde of interpreters and obfuscators (people whose purpose in life is to conceal their significance). Without the facts you can be fooled and foolish.

freedom of information A relatively new idea, this has become a bulwark of democratic government, keeping it accountable to the people through elections and changes of government. In the 1970s and 1980s the Commonwealth government and most state governments introduced laws that let people have access to information, which, though often embarrassing to governments, you have the right to know about. Within a very short time governments started winding it back, making citizens pay, deferring, denying that the information existed, claiming 'commercial confidentiality' or that its release would make government impossible. You have the right to know what government thinks it knows about you: use that right freely.

F is also for **freedom from information**, or the right to privacy. It may be very convenient for governments to go through your house, to value it or to search for information, but a citizen is entitled to close the door on the public gaze and have a private life. The Commonwealth, and some states, have laws protecting individuals from invasions of their privacy by government bodies – use them. And the 'off' switch on your television.

G is for:

ginger group A democratic necessity. As Don Dunstan said in his last ABC interview, 'You will never have change without a ginger group.'

guru   Everyone needs one for inspiration and encouragement, and to challenge and guide our thoughts and actions. They can be intellectuals, teachers, writers, or commentators in newspapers, radio or television. They needn't be still living. One of Moira Rayner's gurus is Thomas Jefferson, a founding father of the US constitution. One of Joan Kirner's is Dr Jean Blackburn, a leading Australian educator who taught her how to combine economic and social imperatives in public-policy making, and how to write analytically as well as passionately.

H is for:

head of department   The heads of public service departments are government appointees, responsible for implementing government policy and briefing the Minister on all issues that go to Cabinet or which are causing public concern. Often they are as powerful as the Minister, and sometimes more so. Department heads can be potential allies or formidable foes, but either way they're important.

heart   Remember you have one. Work at keeping it alive, always listen to it before applying the head. Often your sense of humour is what keeps both together. Your family and friends help.

humility   This can be either destructive, keeping you from asserting your point of view or standing up against injustice, or very necessary, if you have a certain amount of clout or real power, to keep you from pride and error. In the latter case, humility is the sense that, though you might have power, you are also ordinary. You have to take your clothes off at night, do undignified things in the bathroom, make mistakes and be corrected and supported sometimes.

humour   A powerful tool for warming up meetings, breaking tension and forming friendships. If you dish it out, you have to be able to take it too. When a rude Labor senator called the Liberal senator Amanda Vanstone a 'fatty' during a debate, she responded that it was better to be broad in the beam than to have bullshit for brains (see also *zoo*). Don't make sexist jokes about other women, or laugh at them, if you don't want to be the butt yourself. Humour keeps us alive and human.

I is for:

independence   This is necessary if you are to claim power. You'll need independence of thought; independent means of financial support; control over your own body, especially your reproductive capacity and health; and the freedom to choose your emotional, social and community support base. Value independence highly. It requires your thoughtfulness and good judgement.

independents   Increasingly, members of parliament whom we call independents but who are often members of smaller parties, such as the Democrats or the Greens, One Nation or the Festival of Light, are holding the balance of power. It is important you get to know them, understand where they are coming from, and either influence them yourself or ask them to influence others. If their views are dramatically different from yours, don't waste your time trying to persuade them to change their minds: instead, work at defeating or neutralising their influence by making sure that others understand their real agenda.

instinct   Acknowledge it, trust it, but never act until you have checked the facts and sought advice. A lot of 'instinct' is old programming, emotional manipulation, or button-pushing.

integrity   Contrary to the received wisdom, no politician – no leader of any kind – is worth supporting unless they have a highly developed sense of public interest and the common good, and a fundamental sense of integrity. If you are in

politics, protect your integrity with your life. If it is compro-
mised, get out and find another avenue for using power
properly.

J is for:

jack of it all   Most activists get this feeling. When you do,
either push on and get over the hurdle, or take a real break
and come back refreshed and with a new agenda. Or get
another life, because **J** is also for **joy**, and a life without it
isn't worth having. Remember, if it's too hard, you're probably
doing it the wrong way.

K is for:

kindness   There is always reason to give it, but in power
relationships – especially in politics – expect it rarely. Joan
Kirner says it was the small kindnesses from friends and
strangers she never met, as well as the ever-present generosity
of her husband, that helped her to keep going through those
difficult years at the top.

knowing your enemy   Sometimes, to understand is to lose
an enemy and gain an ally (but pretty rarely). Knowing what
the enemy thinks, being able to walk around in their shoes,
means that you can predict what they will do. It's one of the
first tactics of the urban guerrilla: to think as the enemy do
means you can outmanoeuvre them.

kudos   If this is why you want power, forget it. There can
be kudos, but you are much more likely to get criticism, and
you have to learn to take it, laugh at it, or ignore it. Anyway,
public figures who act only for kudos or out of fear of criticism
are ineffective on the big issues in the long term.

L is for:

letter writing   The received wisdom is that if a Minister is sent one letter on an issue, staff reply; if they get ten, the Minister notices it; if twenty arrive, she gets advice; and if the staff receives forty, she acts. The same thing goes for letters to the editor. If there are one or two, they are of interest. If there are ten, the issue is checked out. If there are more than twenty, the papers know there is an issue and maybe a campaign. Editors are also cynical beasts: if the letters are exactly the same or look like a form letter, they disregard them.

Letters are also a great way of saying thank you, or well done. When someone does you a kindness, thank them – colleagues, public servants, politicians and Ministers included. It helps to prevent their becoming cynical.

lies   Don't tell any. They come back to haunt you, and you need too good a memory not to get caught out on them. You may not be able to tell the whole truth at a particular time, but it is important not to mislead deliberately. When Joan Kirner was preparing to sell the State Bank, no-one could be told, though rumours were rife and journalists were asking. She fixed on answering media questions by saying that the matter of its future was under ongoing consideration. True enough.

litmus test   The litmus test for an *effective* activist is whether, and how, you made any difference. The litmus test of a *good* activist is whether, when you no longer have power or influence, people will still respect you and your actions.

local government   Your council is your most direct experience of representative democracy there is. It is easier to get elected to local government (and learn about campaigning, debating and strategising), than it is to be elected to any other level. Local government is also the focus of government funding, business activity, and not-for-profit and non-government activity. It is a national network of community interests. If it isn't working as you want, get involved in a local group, vote, persuade others to vote, learn to campaign. Start local, and go global.

M is for:

making a difference This is why you deserve, need and will get power – to make a difference for you and other women.

media Television, radio, newspapers and magazines, and the journalists who report for them, make or break news, create and influence opinion, and have rightly been called the fourth estate – a part of our political system. This means they are very powerful. Learn to love the media and use them wisely. You know you're in trouble when the papers start printing bad photos of you, but it's even worse when they don't bother to print anything at all. The most powerful medium, in terms of public opinion, is television, followed by talkback radio and, least of all, newspapers (though they haven't worked this out yet). If you can't get a hearing with a Minister, your member of parliament, or the head of a department, learn how to get your issue into the media, then stand back and watch the government twitch.

member of parliament They are your representatives, and you have the right to expect them to read your letters, listen to your concerns, tell you what they are doing, and raise your issues. They are accountable to you, whether you voted for them or not. Their first responsibility is to the people, and their party membership is intended to facilitate that purpose too. A letter from your MP to a Minister or other official is taken seriously. And remember that politicians need support too.

men's room This is any space with politicians in it. Many important decisions are made in the men's rooms fitted with big white ceramic pedestals that flush. We hope to change this.

mobile phone Never use one in public. Always remember that anyone could eavesdrop on what you are saying on a mobile phone, that every call is logged and can be traced. Weigh up its convenience against the possible risks. Joan says, own one but use it wisely. Moira uses other people's.

N is for:

networks Networks are an essential part of all power and especially politics. More deals are done and achieved because people know and trust one another, and can call on one other to influence a decision, than because of the truth or justice of a cause, a passionate speech, a learned book, or a law suit (though these at least get you some attention.)

nice Good women are. Good leaders sometimes can't be. Remember this at all times.

note-taking This is a discipline and one you must acquire early: she who keeps the minutes and records the decisions writes the history. Memories fade fast and are easily reconstructed. The winners write the history (with themselves as heroes). Keep accurate notes of any discussion, listening carefully for the key points and who made them: write them up later, date them, and distribute them promptly. Keep your own copy as well as the one in files.

O is for:

ombudsman This office is meant to expose government maladministration – lies, rule-breaking, inefficiency or unethical conduct – but the ombudsman does not have the power to order the government to do anything. This doesn't matter. The ombudsman is a whistleblower to parliament. The major usefulness of a complaint to the ombudsman is its nuisance value (departments have to respond to an investigation and give access to their records), and the fact that someone higher up the food chain in the department you are complaining about gets to review the file. Don't hesitate to use it. Many other institutions have 'ombudsmen' nowadays – utilities like electricity, gas, banks, telephones. These people provide informal, impartial avenues for consumer complaints. Use them too.

organisation   Without organisation you are not a movement but a protest. Nobody can be effective unless they are in control of their own life and managing their time. If you are seriously pursuing power, you will need to have a very efficient secretary or assistant to help you with this. The biggest fools are those who double-book appointments or miss meetings.

ownership   Lao Tzu wrote, 'When the best leader's work is done, the people say we did it ourselves.' The most effective use of power is to persuade others to own what you seek to achieve. There is not much room for a big ego with this kind of power.

P is for:

party   Your MP almost certainly got into parliament because she was selected as a candidate by a political party, which then threw its resources into making sure of her election. A member's approach to parliament is guided by her party's platform, but she is responsible to you for how the party interprets it.

The other sort of party is the one you have to relax, unwind, network, or be seen at to support a friend or a good cause. We tend to lower our guard at parties. Never drink much at one. It lowers your political sensitivities (and heightens others). Someone will always remember what you said and did when you would rather they didn't.

personal   The personal is political. Never take a personal attack without remembering that it is political in purpose. This puts it into perspective.

privacy   If you are using power, remember you need down time and private relationships. Everyone does.

process   Process shapes the result. If you know what you want to achieve, you can set out a path to it. Meeting procedures are intended to come to an outcome, but the process that led to the meeting is just as important. There's an old saying, kings never meet unless they have already agreed. Queens should not meet until they have plotted their ememies' downfall.

Q is for:

quorum   Make sure you have one, and that it contains the votes you need.

R is for:

repeat   If you want people to get your message it has to be clear, consistent, and repeated – repeated, repeated, repeated and repeated.

republic   A republic means more than just having an Australian as our head of state. A republic is a form of government based on the political theory that the power to govern comes from the people being governed, not from being born into a privileged family, or from God. Australia will be a republic soon.

risk-taking   Do it. Be aware of the possible consequences, and accept whatever happens. It was a brave woman who first ate an oyster.

S is for:

sex   This is not the same as gender. A powerful force for good and evil, sex misapplied in jokes or put-downs or compromising relationships has no place in any kind of workplace. (And never video yourself doing it.)

sue   Don't be frightened out of doing what you think is right and necessary by the threat of a law suit. Get proper advice at once. Never threaten to sue, yourself, unless you are really prepared to do it. The best lawyers tell you to stay out of court. A judge takes away all power – he (it's still usually a he) decides what you could have worked out between you, and neither of you might like the result.

support   This is essential for anyone wanting or exercising power. Support groups of like-minded people kept both Moira Rayner and Joan Kirner sane when the world seemed quite mad. There is no greater misery-guts than an idealist who feels lonely and misunderstood.

symbols   The Queen is a symbol of government – she does not actually wield political power, just as her man in Australia, the Governor-General, doesn't, or shouldn't. Parliament House is a symbol of democracy, and getting yourself cartooned for the first time is a symbol that you are a political presence – even if it shows you as fat and frumpy, with pink hair and a grumpy expression.

T is for:

targets   This is not the same thing as quotas. You need to aim for success and be able to measure whether you have achieved it. Always check your progress against some fixed target. You are less likely to kid yourself.

tension   Politics is all about creating, enduring and using tension in order to get particular results. That's why we have debates about differences. Power creates stress. You'll get used to living with this, and there are even some who genuinely enjoy it. The trick is not to be fazed into doing something to break the tension in a situation if this will not result in something you want. Many women, for instance, respond to an argument with a male colleague who appears to be tearful or anxious or under stress by backing off. Don't. He wouldn't do it for you. Change your strategy, but not your intent.

toilets There are never enough toilets for women, and men hold important meetings in theirs (see *men's room*). Joan Kirner seems to have spent half her life demanding and getting enough toilets for women in educational institutions, in theatres, at the football, even in Parliament House. There were no toilets for women in the Legislative Council chambers when she and four other women were elected. The nearest ones were three minutes away and another three back – and the time allowed for division bells was three minutes.

truth Your own power depends on your being true to yourself and what you value (see also *integrity* and *lies*).

U is for:

underground Sometimes the best results are achieved through networks, and covert acts rather than overt ones. Sometimes you need to go underground to escape from the heat. EMILY's List, the movement to support women candidates in the ALP, worked quietly away for twelve months without seeking the party's executive approval, because its founders wanted to ensure that it was organised along feminist principles, including equity and controlling the money raised for women candidates. It succeeded in setting up a strong organisation, though it has not yet been accepted as an ALP entity.

unions If you can, join one and participate in its activities. Despite their history of male dominance, unions have great potential to empower women at work, and many are now doing just that.

u-turn If you take a U-turn in your beliefs then your change of heart, and not your policies, becomes the media story.

Political parties who take U-turns on policy after they have been elected to government alienate people from the political process.

V is for:

values Core values are, whatever the received wisdom, essential to the exercise of all power. Without them, all the lobbying, deals and number-crunching, planning and strategising could drag you into a vortex of cynicism and manipulation. Remember that you went into activism for a purpose, and never lose sight of it. Joan Kirner often says, 'People may not agree with what I say but they know what I stand for.'

vortex The feeling of spinning round and round in ever decreasing circles until you are sucked down and drown. Just remember that you are more likely to be sucked down if you fight against the current instead of finding a life-line and swimming across it. Even if you are pulled under, you can hold your breath and strike out for the shore. The average duration of a political or media scandal is between two and eight days. You can wait it out, so long as you have acted honestly and according to your own values. Or you can admit you made a mistake, and if it is a one-off you may be forgiven.

W is for:

woman Hear me roar.

X is for:

x-files The truth is out there – you have to search it out. Seek and you shall find.

Y is for:

you Only you can decide to claim your power. When you do, remember why you wanted to; your experiences before you did; who supported you when you were on the way up; that your views were valid then and are valid now; and that you are accountable to all your community, not just the ones who supported or voted for you.

Z is for:

zoo This is what the public sees when they look in at question time in parliament. Carmen Lawrence, the first woman Premier of Western Australia, said that the behaviour and management of parliament could embrace sanity but still retain the drama. Christine Milne, leader of the Tasmanian Greens, conducted political business by consensus. Why can't all parliaments follow their lead? Must they remain bear-pits?

A zoo is also where public figures feel they live when public appearances and media take over their lives. If you become a public figure, you must create and maintain an escape hatch and retreat for the sake of yourself, your family and your sanity.

AND A FINAL WORD

We began writing this book to share with other women our experiences of getting, using and losing power. We wrote in reference to constant questions about our experiences, and in the hope that women seeking power would not have to reinvent the wheel – that they could use our knowledge.

Women can share power with men if they have the tools, and the skills to use them. We hope this book has been as useful as the toolbox Moira's father gave her all those years ago. We also hope that you will add to it. We learned even more by writing this book together, sharing our experiences and our beliefs in the essential goodness of people, our trust in women, our faith in our fellow citizens, and our similar senses of humour. We had fun writing the book, and we hope that you will have fun claiming your power, and raising other women with you as you climb.

horacek

Chart of Australian women's achievements

The first column of the chart represents a rollcall of Australian women of achievement; the second documents the collective achievements of Australian women and changes within their society.

24 000 BC	A woman from Lake Mungo provides the earliest evidence of ritual cremation in the world, her body having been prepared with ochre before cremation.
1792	Mary Haydock (later Reibey) arrives in Australia, transported for horse theft. She eventually builds an extensive business based on hotels, grain, shipping and real estate.
1807	Wool merchant Elizabeth Macarthur ships first consignment of wool to London (approx. 245 lbs), six years after her husband John first took samples across. This is the beginning of a huge wool empire and the New South Wales wool industry.
1822	John Macarthur receives the Society of Arts Gold Medal for the quality of his wool. Elizabeth is not mentioned, despite having run the farm and business entirely alone in the years 1801–1805 and 1809–1818.
1826	Industrial School for Girls founded in Sydney by Fanny Macleay and Lady Eliza Darling.

1830	Aboriginal freedom fighter Walyer uses guerrilla war tactics to defend her people but is eventually captured. She dies the following year while still detained.	
1834	Fanny Cochrane (later Smith) born at Wybalenna Aboriginal Settlement, Flinders Island. She is moved to Oyster Cove with other inmates (including Truganini) when Wybalenna is closed in 1847, and in 1884 the Tasmanian government grants her title to 300 acres of land, some of which she donates to build a Methodist Church.	
1838		Introduction of pre-paid postage lowers previously exorbitant cost of mail, allowing greater communication among the women of New South Wales who can read and write (about 40%).
1839	Englishwoman Maria Ann Smith comes to Australia; she later becomes famous for the development of the Granny Smith apple.	Children's Visitation Act means that divorced or separated women – so long as they are the 'innocent' party – can get limited access to their children; and in exceptional cases may be granted custody of children under the age of seven.
1840		The colony of New South Wales passes legislation which imposes direct liability on a parent for the support of their child, allowing Justices of the Peace to order maintenance for

a wife or children 'in such
moderate sum' as they
considered expedient.

1841 Female Immigrants Home in
Sydney established by Caroline
Chisholm; in the first year, jobs
are found for 1400 women and
600 men.

Artist Georgiana McCrae arrives in
Port Phillip with her husband.

Charlotte Barton (Atkinson)
writes the first Australian
children's book – *A Mother's
Offering to Her Children* –
published in Sydney.

1844 Mary Penfold arrives from
England with her husband, Dr
Christopher Penfold. She starts a
winery near Adelaide to provide
wine for his patients.

1849 Family Colonization Loan Society
founded by Caroline Chisholm,
with the backing of Angela
Burdett-Coutts, to bring women
to Australia.

1853 Artist Eliza Thurston arrives in
Sydney and opens a school and
drawing academy.

1854 Catherine Helen Spence publishes
*Clara Morison: A Tale of South
Australia During the Gold Fever.*

1857 A novel by Caroline Louisa
Atkinson, *Gertrude the Immigrant*,
is published anonymously in

Sydney; it is the first novel published in the Antipodes by an Australian-born woman.

1858

Governor Denison (New South Wales) gives thirty-nine laws to the citizens of Norfolk Island (descendants of the *Bounty* mutineers), including adult suffrage, thereby inadvertently giving women the vote.

1861

First Australian divorce legislation sets out requirements for divorce. Women have to prove repeated adultery, together with cruelty and desertion, by the husband. (Men only have to prove one act of adultery by the wife.)

1868 Sister Lucy Osburn and her Nightingale nurses arrive at Sydney Hospital and reform the vermin-infested institution, leading to hostility from some doctors.

1869 Henrietta Dugdale writes a letter to the Melbourne *Argus* advocating full citizenship, probably the first recorded movement towards women's suffrage within Australia.

Contagious Diseases Act is passed in Britain and also enacted in various Australian states. This law ensures that prostitutes in garrison towns are forced to attend inspections at the Lock Hospital; if they are found carrying venereal disease, they are locked up in the hospital for nine months.

1871

Young Women's Christian Association started in Geelong.

1873	Brettena Smyth sells imported contraceptives to women in her North Melbourne general store and from a travelling cart, thereby causing a public outcry.	First Victorian Factory Act passed, setting out minimum hours and conditions for women and juveniles, but with no provisions for policing these conditions.
1876	Tasmania's Truganini dies.	
1878	Opening of the Brisbane Children's Hospital, founded by Mary McConnel, who pays the salary of the first matron and supervises engagement of staff.	
1880		Australian schools for girls begin providing serious education based on the same standards as boys' education.
1881		University of Melbourne becomes the first Australian university to admit women students.
1882		Melbourne Tailoresses' Union strikes against the practice of 'sweating' – forcing women to take work home to complete after hours.
1883	Julia Bella Guerin, BA, becomes the first woman to graduate from an Australian University (University of Melbourne). Henrietta Dugdale publishes *A Few Hours in a Far-Off Age*, Australia's first feminist tract – a biting satire on discrimination, male ignorance and the denial of women's intelligence and potential.	South Australia becomes the first state to give married women the same legal position regarding property as unmarried women, through the Married Women's Property Act. (The last state to enact such legislation was Tasmania, in 1935.)

		Public Service Act (Victoria) sets out regulations preventing women's promotion.
1884	Dagmar Berne enrols as the first female medical student in Australia, at Sydney University. She completes her degree in London following hostility from male students. Henrietta Dugdale and Annie Lowe form the Victorian Women's Suffrage Society.	
1886		Aboriginal Protection Act (Victoria) amendment excludes all part-Aboriginal persons under the age of thirty-four from Aboriginal reserves, resulting in the removal of children from their families and culture.
1887	Debut of Nellie Melba (later Dame Nellie).	Despite fierce opposition from some professors, Melbourne University officially opens medicine to women students, the first university in Australia to do so. Women's Christian Temperance Society formed. Fundamentally a feminist society, it opposed alcohol and sought woman suffrage and equal moral standards for both sexes.
1888		Women's Suffrage League founded in Sydney.

1889	Feminist Louisa Lawson begins seventeen years of editing the *Dawn*, a periodical produced solely by women.	
1890	Constance Stone becomes the first registered woman doctor in Australia, having studied overseas after she was refused entry into Melbourne University at the beginning of her studies.	Australian Women's Franchise Society formed to gain parliamentary franchise for women; it has connections to the Labour Movement.
1891	Womanhood Suffrage League founded by Rose Scott and others, with Lady Mary Windeyer as its first president, in New South Wales. Clara Stone and Margaret Whyte are the first women medical graduates from the University of Melbourne.	Women's Christian Temperance Union, Victorian Temperance Alliance, and the three Suffrage Societies present the Women's Suffrage Petition, with 30 000 signatures, to the Victorian Parliament.
1893	Miss L. J. Little, BSc, is the first woman science graduate, from the University of Melbourne.	
1894	Margaret G. Cuthbertson becomes the first female factory inspector, in Victoria.	South Australia introduces adult suffrage (including indigenous women) at the state level. Women win the right to sit in parliament in South Australia. Karrakatta Club established in Western Australia – probably the first women's political discussion group in Australia – with Edith Cowan as its first secretary. Women's Suffrage League gathers 11 000 signatures on a suffrage petition.

		Australian Labour Party includes woman suffrage in its party platform.
1895	Lady Mary Windeyer helps found the Women's Hospital in Sydney, and becomes its first president.	
1896	Dr Constance Stone starts the Victoria Hospital for Women in a small church hall in Melbourne.	First free kindergarten in Australia established in Woolloomooloo, Sydney.

Factory Workrooms and Shops Act sets minimum conditions and introduces registration of outworkers. Also appoints inspectors and sets up Special (wages) Board.

Children's Protection Society founded.

New South Wales feminists establish the first National Council of Women. |
| **1897** | Catherine Helen Spence becomes the first Australian woman to stand for public office when she stands (unsuccessfully) in South Australia as a candidate for the forthcoming Australasian Federal Convention. | |
| **1898** | Maybanke Wolstenholme establishes the Women's Federal League in Sydney to discuss and campaign for federation and constitutional issues. | |

1899   Vida Goldstein begins publishing a monthly newspaper, the *Australian Women's Sphere.*

Western Australia introduces adult female suffrage (but not for indigenous, Asian, African or Pacific Islander women) at state level.

Queen Victoria Hospital opened in Little Lonsdale Street, Melbourne – the first hospital in Australia run by women for women.

1900

Women's Progressive League founded to secure civil and political rights for women, equal to those of men. By December there were thirty-two societies making up the League, with strong connections to the Labour Movement and the socialists.

1901   Publication of Miles Franklin's novel *My Brilliant Career.*

1902   Ada Emily Evans becomes first Australian woman to receive a law degree (Sydney University), but is unable to practise law until 1918 (see below).

Adult suffrage – all white women can vote for the Commonwealth Parliament, and can stand as candidates for the Senate or the House of Representatives. New South Wales introduces adult suffrage (including indigenous women) at state level.

1903   Vida Goldstein stands as an independent candidate for the Senate, receiving 51 497 votes and coming fifteenth out of eighteen candidates. She is the first woman to stand for parliamentary election in the British Empire.

Tasmania introduces adult suffrage (including indigenous women) at state level.

Victorian Legal Profession Practices Act enables women to practise law in Victoria.

1905	Grata Flos Matilda Greig becomes the first Australian woman to be admitted to the Bar.	Queensland introduces adult female suffrage (but not for indigenous, Asian, African or Pacific Islander women) at state level.
1907	Rose Scott becomes president of the Peace Society. Australian long-distance swimmer Annette Kellerman is arrested in Boston for indecent exposure: wearing a one-piece skirtless bathing suit.	Harvester Decision is first national wage decision based on the needs of the employee rather than the needs of the employer. Mr Justice Higgins sets seven shillings per day as a fair and reasonable basic wage to enable a man to support himself, a wife and three children.
1908	Henry Handel Richardson (pen-name of Ethel Robertson) publishes *Maurice Guest*, a landmark in the treatment of homosexuality in English fiction.	Victoria introduces adult suffrage (including indigenous women) at state level. Invalid and Old Age Pensioner Act provides social security (but not for Aboriginal women or men).
1909	Vida Goldstein begins publishing the *Woman Voter*. Women's Socialist League founded by Lizzie Ahern.	
1912	Australian women enter their first Olympic competition. Swimmer Fanny Durack wins a gold medal in freestyle.	Maternity Allowance Act provides for a grant of £5 on the birth of a child (but not for indigenous women). Marriage Act (Victoria) guarantees the right of a wife to guardianship of her children on the death of her husband – previously, the husband could

		appoint a guardian other than the mother by his will.
		Equal pay granted only to women working in direct competition with men (Rural Workers Case).
1915		Women's Peace Army formed – a militantly pacifist organisation working to empower women and enable self-help.
1916		Testator's Maintenance and Guardianship of Infants Act (NSW) guarantees guardianship of children to the mother on the death of the father.
1917		First two women police officers appointed in Victoria.
1918	Soprano Nellie Melba is made Dame Commander of the British Empire. Women's Legal Status Act passed after strong lobbying by Ada Emily Evans, enabling women to practise law in New South Wales.	Women win the right to sit in parliament in New South Wales and Queensland.
1919		Mr Justice Higgins, required to set a female minimum wage for clothing workers, sets it at approximately 57% of the male wage.
1920		Women win the right to sit in parliament in Western Australia.

1921	Edith Cowan becomes the first woman in Australia elected to parliament, standing for the Nationalist Party in the seat of West Perth in the Western Australian state elections. The *Woman's Clarion* is the first Australian women's journal. It is published by the Female Confectioners' Union. Margaret Wearne is the union's general secretary and the journal's editor.	Child endowment introduced, but limited to Commonwealth Public Service employees. Women win the right to sit in parliament in Tasmania.
1922		Country Women's Association founded.
1923	Australian Federation of Housewives founded by Eleanor Greencross.	Women win the right to sit in parliament in Victoria. First jury service for women introduced in Queensland.
1925		Business and Professional Women's Club founded and asserts the right of women to work; also makes submissions to the Arbitration Commission on Equal Pay.
1928		First International Women's Day rally in Australia, organised by the Militant Women's Movement of the Communist Party of Australia, held in the Domain, Sydney.
1932	Soprano Marjorie Lawrence makes her debut at Monte Carlo.	

1933		First birth-control clinic set up in Sydney by the Racial Hygiene Association; later becomes the Family Planning Association.
1937	Poet Mary Gilmore (later Dame Mary) awarded an OBE. Campaign of Action for Equal Pay formed by Muriel Heagney, leading to the first International Conference on Equal Pay held in Sydney in 1938.	
1941		Child Endowment Act provides for payment of five shillings a week direct to the mother, as an allowance for each child after the first, under the age of sixteen years (but not available to nomadic or dependent indigenous women). ACTU Congress adopts Equal Pay Principle.
1942		Women's Employment Board set up to draft women into essential wartime work at higher rates of pay and to monitor the replacement of men by women; female wages range from 70 to 100% of male wage. Commonwealth introduces means-tested Widows' Pension. Restrictions placed on the movements of Aboriginal people, especially women, after

the bombing of Darwin by the Japanese sees many Aboriginal people relocated into 'control camps'.

1945 Dame Enid Lyons becomes the first woman elected to the Federal House of Representatives (Darwin, UAP). Dorothy Tangney becomes the first woman elected to the Senate (Western Australia, ALP).

First World Congress of Women held in Paris – forms the Women's International Democratic Federation; the Union of Australian Women is affiliated.

1947 Florence Cardell-Oliver (later Dame Florence) becomes the first woman Cabinet Minister in an Australian parliament (Western Australia).

Annabelle Rankin (later Dame Annabelle) becomes Opposition Whip.

1948

General Assembly of the United Nations adopts the Universal Declaration of Human Rights.

1949 Dame Enid Lyons becomes the first Australian woman Cabinet Minister in federal Cabinet.

Nationality and Citizenship Act gives married women the choice of retaining their Australian citizenship or taking their husband's nationality.

Commonwealth Electoral Act extends the right to vote to Aboriginal ex-servicemen.

1950

Union of Australian Women founded in Victoria, promoting women's rights, equal pay, economic justice and peace.

1952	Myxomatosis is introduced to control the rabbit population – virologist Dame Jean MacNamara had helped to obtain it from South America, and is credited with saving the wool industry over £15 million.	
1954		International Labour Organisation Equal Remuneration Convention No. 100 (Equal Pay) ratified by Victoria.
1956		National Conference on Equal Pay (ACTU).
		Victoria passes legislation granting permanency to women teachers; married women retain positions, seniority and rights but are excluded from superannuation.
1957		First ACTU deputation to the Commonwealth Government presents a petition with 61 000 signatures asking for equal pay.
		Confinement leave, without pay, up to eighteen months gained by the Victoria teaching service.
1958		Acts Interpretation Act formalises the male bias in parliamentary language – it reads in part 'words importing the masculine gender shall be deemed to include females unless the contrary is expressly provided'.

		Teaching Service Act (Married Women) establishes the Married Women Teachers' Pension Fund.
		Equal Pay legislation introduced in New South Wales, giving progressive equal pay to teachers and phased in over three years.
		Victorian Crimes Act, Section 65, proclaims abortion illegal.
1959		Federal Matrimonial Causes Act 1959 (which comes into effect in 1961) abolishes the double standard on adultery, making separation alone (at least five years) a ground for divorce, and enabling courts to make orders in divorce proceedings for the support of the children of the marriage.
1960	Judith Anderson becomes the first Australian-born actress to be named Dame Commander of the British Empire.	
1962	Roma Mitchell (later Dame Roma) becomes Australia's first woman Queen's Counsel.	Suffrage for indigenous women (and men) is achieved in the remaining states, though still restricted by enrolment provisions.
1963		The Women's Bureau created in the Department of Labour and National Service (now in DETYA).

1964	Oodgeroo Noonuccal publishes her first book of poems, *We Are Going*.	Victorian Health (Child Minding) Act provides regulations for private centres, after a fire kills seven infants.
1965		Save Our Sons movement formed by women to oppose the conscription of young men to the Vietnam War.

Federal Government adopts a policy of integration of Aboriginal and Torres Strait Islander people.

Aboriginal people in Queensland finally get the right to vote in state elections. |
| 1966 | Senator Annabelle Rankin becomes Minister for Housing, the first woman Minister to administer a Commonwealth department. | Lifting of the marriage bar in the Australian Public Service, giving married women access to permanent positions.

Stockmen and -women from the Gurundji and other groups walk off Lord Vestey's property at Wave Hill in protest at appalling working conditions and inadequate wages; the strike lasts nine years and finally results in the return of some of the Gurundji's lands by the Prime Minister in 1975.

Council of Aboriginal Women founded in South Australia. |
| 1967 | Caroline Chisholm is the first woman (other than Queen Elizabeth) to appear on Australian currency. | Referendum held to change clauses in the Federal Constitution which discriminate against Aboriginal people. With |

the changes in the Constitution, Aboriginal and Torres Strait Islander women and men are fully recognised as Australian citizens, with equal rights to participate.

1968

Victorian women teachers achieve equal pay, phased in over three years.

Reform of abortion laws in South Australia.

Bilingual welfare workers employed by the Department of Immigration to assist young women, predominantly from southern Europe – out of concern for male migrants needing partners.

1969

Commonwealth Conciliation and Arbitration Commission introduces equal pay for equal work – except for work which is 'essentially or normally performed by females'.

Criminal Law Consolidation Act Amendment Bill in South Australia legalises abortion in that state.

Mr Justice Menhennit presides in Victoria at a trial relating to Section 65 of the Crimes Act (i.e. abortion); his ruling sets a precedent which considers abortion lawful if there is reasonable concern for the woman's physical or mental

		health, followed in courts throughout Australia.
1970s		The Pill becomes easily available in Australia, giving women access to control over their own reproduction for the first time.
		First women's liberation meetings in Canberra.
		National Council of Aboriginal and Islander Women established.
1970	Tennis pro Margaret Smith Court wins the grand slam of women's tennis competition. Germaine Greer's *The Female Eunuch* published.	
1971	Dame Annabelle Rankin becomes Australia's first female ambassador, serving as High Commissioner to New Zealand until 1975.	Bank of New South Wales becomes the first bank in Australia to grant loans to women without a male guarantor.
1972	Australian publisher Carmen Callil founds Virago Press in London. Women's Electoral Lobby founded in Melbourne by Beatrice Faust and others – a non-party organisation focused on the political system and its impact on women.	Commonwealth Conciliation and Arbitration Commission formally adopts the principle of equal pay for work of equal value; however, many industries that used to be traditionally female still carry undervalued rates of pay because of industrial history. First International Women's Day march.

Sales tax on contraceptives removed when they are taken off the luxury-tax schedule, where they had been included as 'entertainment'.

Federal Child Care Act 1972 provides federal involvement and funding for childcare.

Policy of self-determination for Aboriginal and Torres Strait Islander people brought in by the Whitlam Government.

1973 Elizabeth Reid appointed first adviser on women's affairs (to the Whitlam government).

Elizabeth Evatt appointed as first woman to be Deputy President of the Conciliation and Arbitration Commission.

Maternity Leave (Australian Government Employees) Act 1973 is the first recognition of the needs of working women having children.

Whitlam Government adopts multiculturalism as a policy.

First women's health centre opens, in Sydney.

Flinders University teaches first course in Australia on women's studies.

1974

First refuge for women – The Elsie Women's Refuge – established in Sydney.

First Rape Crisis Centres set up in Australian capital cities.

First Australian survey on migrant working women is conducted by Datrina Brown and Des Storer.

Royal Commission on Human Relationships deals with issues such as education, sexuality, fertility, discrimination, rape, incest, health and the family, and makes over five hundred recommendations; chaired by Elizabeth Evatt.

Inner West Regional Council establishes a migrant committee in New South Wales which develops into the Ethnic Communities Council.

Establishment of a section of government which becomes the Office for the Status of Women in the Department of Prime Minister and Cabinet.

1975 Joyce Barry becomes Melbourne's first woman tramdriver.

Family Law Act 1975 – irretrievable breakdown of a marriage becomes the only ground for divorce (previously various states' laws and the 1958 Matrimonial Causes Act imposed significant delays and required evidence of cruelty, adultery, desertion or combinations of the above).

International Women's Year.

Working Women's Centre founded in Melbourne.

South Australian Parliament passes first sex discrimination Act in Australia (Sex Discrimination Act 1975).

Amendments to the Jury Act 1967 put women on an equal footing with men for jury duty.

Girls Own (a Sydney feminist journal) devotes an issue to racism and migrant women's issues.

1976	Elizabeth Evatt becomes the first Chief Judge of the Family Court.	First Migrant Resource Centres trialled in Parramatta, New South Wales and Richmond, Victoria.
1977		ACTU Congress adopts a Working Women's Charter.
		Victoria and New South Wales enact sex discrimination laws.
		WICH (Women in Industry and Community Health) begins in Victoria.
1978		Establishment of National Women's Advisory Council to advise the Minister for Home Affairs and Environment.
		First Women and Labour Conference co-sponsored by Macquarie University and the Society for the Study of Labour History, Canberra.
1979	Deborah Wardley wins the right to be employed as a pilot with Ansett in a case heard by the still-new Victorian Equal Opportunity Board; she had been passed over despite having far better qualifications than her male counterparts.	Unions achieve Maternity Leave in the private sector; ACTU Maternity Leave test case results in provisions being inserted in most awards, guaranteeing continuity of employment.
		Reclaim the Night march organised by Women Against Rape.
		United Nations International Year of the Child.
		Elizabeth Hoffman House established as an Aboriginal Women's Refuge in Victoria.

1980	Roberta Sykes begins postgraduate studies at Harvard, the first Black Australian woman to do so.	Crimes (Sexual Offences) Act 1980 provides for prosecution of rape committed by a husband on his wife while separated or living apart.
		Formation of Ngaanyatjarra Pitjantjatjara Yankunytjatjara Women's Council.
1981	Mary Gaudron becomes the first woman Solicitor-General (for New South Wales).	Formation of Immigrant Women's Caucus.
	Pat O'Shane becomes the first Aboriginal woman to head a government department, as Permanent Head of Aboriginal Affairs in New South Wales.	
1982		Right to Choose Coalition formed by various organisations to campaign for women's right to control their own reproduction.
		Migrant Women's Issues Group formed in Sydney.
		First Migrant Women's Speak Out conference (Australian Council of Churches).
1983	Dame Roma Mitchell appointed first woman University Chancellor, at the University of Adelaide.	First of the Accords between the ACTU and federal government – during the period 1983–1995 the pay gap between men and women is reduced by between one-half and one-third.
	Dr Roberta Sykes completes her postgraduate studies (in Aboriginal education) at Harvard.	Australia ratifies United Nations Convention on the Elimination of All Forms of Discrimination Against Women.

National wage case attempts to lift wages in traditionally female work areas to match those of men; the attempt is rejected by the Australian Conciliation and Arbitration Commission, which effectively acknowledges the undervaluing of women's work but also acknowledges that the economy cannot afford to pay women's work at commensurate rates.

Family Law Amendment Act gives Family Court of Australia jurisdiction in marital property disputes prior to divorce.

1984 Marcia Langton graduates as an anthropologist and begins work on land claims.

Sister Elizabeth Nghia awarded Order of Australia medal for work with Indo-Chinese Australian Women's Association (the first Vietnamese woman to be honoured).

Sex Discrimination Act 1984 passed by federal parliament.

Women's Ethnic Network established in Victoria.

Women's Information Referral Exchange (WIRE) established with bilingual workers.

1985 Helen Williams appointed as Secretary of the Department of Education, the first woman to head a government department.

The Hon. Joan Child, MHR, becomes the first woman Speaker of the House of Representatives.

Adoptive Leave introduced for workers wishing to adopt.

Ethnic Women's Working Party established in Victoria (ministerial advisory committee for Premier and Minister for Ethnic Affairs).

Australian Conciliation and Arbitration Commission affirms the equal pay principles of the 1972 Equal Pay case, but

		rejects the comparative worth concept.
		Crimes (Amendment) Act 1985 gives legal protection from rape in marriage in Victoria.
		Ethnic Affairs Commission employs a women's officer to work exclusively on ethnic women's issues in Victoria.
		Access and Equity program launched federally.
		First National Immigrant Women's Conference held.
		Immigrant Women's Resource Centre established in New South Wales.
		Multicultural Women's Health Centre established in Western Australia.
1986	Janine Haines becomes the first woman leader of a political party in the federal parliament (Australian Democrats).	Affirmative Action (Equal Employment Opportunity for Women) Act 1986 passed by the Federal Parliament; the Affirmative Action Agency is set up to administer the Act. Commonwealth Human Rights and Equal Opportunity Act passed 10 December.
		National Working Group on Immigrant Women's Issues launched.

Association of Non-English-Speaking-Background Women of Australia established in New South Wales (national office established in 1990).

1987 Di Yerbury becomes the first woman appointed as a University Vice-Chancellor, at Macquarie University.

Mary Gaudron becomes the first woman to be appointed to the High Court of Australia.

Joan Winch is the first Australian woman to receive a World Health Organization Prize, for her work in establishing the Aboriginal Health Worker Program.

Nurses successfully pursue higher award pay by demonstrating sex bias in the setting of their old wage rates.

Clothing trade outworkers officially included in industrial awards, giving them rights in line with other clothing trade workers.

Victorian Crimes (Family Violence) Act becomes law; aims to protect victims of family violence through the use of restraining orders.

1988 The first female pilots in the Royal Australian Air Force graduate (Flight Lieutenant R. D. Williams and Flying Officer Hicks).

Marcia Langton heads the Aboriginal Issues Unit (Northern Territory) in the Royal Commission into Aboriginal Deaths in Custody.

Introduction of Child Support Scheme enables separated or divorced parents to register maintenance arrangements for support of their children and have the payments collected by the Child Support Agency, which has wide powers of enforcement.

National Agenda for Women (Office for Status of Women). A stated objective: for migrant women to have the same status in Australian society as other Australian women, including equal share in community resources and equal access to programs and services.

1989

Diana Patterson (Mawson) and Alison Clifton (Macquarie Island) become the first female station leaders of Australian National Antarctic Research Expeditions.

Rosemary Follett becomes Australia's first female head of government (Australian Capital Territory).

Women are permitted to join in Australian National Antarctic Research Expeditions for the first time.

Unions convince the Australian Industrial Relations Commission to make Maternity Leave standard in all awards.

National Agenda for a Multicultural Australia released.

Collective of Filipinas for Empowerment and Development formed.

Greek Women Against Oppression established in Victoria.

1990

Two women become state Premiers – Joan Kirner in Victoria, and Carmen Lawrence in Western Australia. The first in Australia.

Cathy Freeman becomes the first Aboriginal person to win a gold medal at a Commonwealth Games, in Auckland, New Zealand.

Aboriginal and Torres Strait Islander Commission established with Lowitja (Lois) O'Donoghue as first chair.

Deirdre O'Connor becomes the first female Federal Court Judge and president of the

The report 'A Fair Chance for All: National and Institutional Planning for Equity in Higher Education' is released, setting targets for the participation of women in non-traditional fields of study.

Unions obtain entitlements for fathers to be recognised as primary care-givers through the Parental Leave Test Case.

Non-English-Speaking-Background Women's Health Strategy released federally.

Griffith University, Queensland, establishes the first Australian chair in women's studies.

Administrative Appeals Tribunal.

The Liberal Party in Victoria elects Fran Bailey as its first woman member of the House of Representatives.

1991   Dame Roma Mitchell appointed Governor of South Australia and becomes Australia's first female vice-regal representative.

Gail Owen is appointed first female president in the 132-year history of the Victorian Law Institute.

In a significant move for women and men of Aboriginal and Torres Strait Islander heritage, the Council for Aboriginal Reconciliation is established, with Pat Dodson as chair.

Islamic Women's Welfare Council of Victoria established.

1992   Justice Elizabeth Evatt, President of the Australian Law Reform Commission, becomes the first Australian elected to the United Nations Human Rights Committee.

The provisions of the Sex Discrimination Act 1984 relating to sexual harassment are strengthened and the Act is extended to industrial awards.

The Anglican Church in Perth ordains the first Australian women priests.

Traditional women's sites near Alice Springs are protected from a threatened dam, with the support of the Minister for Aboriginal Affairs, who invokes the Aboriginal and Torres Strait Islander Heritage Act.

Mimosa House opened in New South Wales – a refuge for Indochinese survivors of domestic violence.

1993 Jane Campion wins an Oscar for Best Screenplay for *The Piano*.

Professor Trang Thomas appointed Chairperson of Ethnic Affairs Commission in Victoria.

National strategy on Violence Against Women released.

Older Women's Network established.

1994 Dr Heather Munro becomes the first female president of the Royal Australian College of Obstetricians and Gynaecologists.

Cathy Freeman links indigenous and non-indigenous cultures by wearing both flags in her victory lap after winning gold at the Commonwealth Games.

Irene Kwong Moss becomes the first woman of Asian background to be appointed a magistrate in New South Wales.

Dur-é Dara becomes the first female president of the Restaurant and Caterers Association of Victoria.

ALP Annual Conference in Tasmania makes a commitment to a minimum 35% of winnable seats being contested by women by the year 2002.

Australian Industrial Relations Commission hands down a decision to begin the introduction of Family Care Leave for *all* workers who need to care for sick family members or dependants.

Maternity Leave made available to all women, including those not covered by federal awards.

Working Women's Centres established in New South Wales, Queensland, Northern Territory and Tasmania.

Indigenous Women's Network established.

1995 Dr Wendy Craik becomes the first female director of the National Farmers Federation.

Jennie George becomes the first female President of the Australian Council of Trade Unions.

1996	Nova Peris-Kneebone becomes the first Aboriginal woman to win an Olympic gold medal (for hockey).	At the Reconciliation Council Conference in Melbourne, all speakers (except Prime Minister Howard) say sorry to Aboriginal women and men.
	Senator the Hon. Margaret Reid becomes the first female President of the Senate.	
1997	Pat Dixon becomes the first Aboriginal woman to win Labor Party pre-selection in the federal seat of New England.	Major changes to industrial relations, aged care, childcare and child support laws – which all impact on women.
	Evelyn Scott is appointed Chair of the Council for Aboriginal Reconciliation.	
1998	Rachel Perkins directs *Radiance*, the first Australian commercial film directed by an Aboriginal woman, and starring three Aboriginal women in the lead roles.	National Sorry Day allows all Australians the opportunity to make a personal apology to Aboriginal women and men for the events of the past.
	Jacki Katona leads the fight to stop uranium mining in Jabiluka, Northern Territory.	National Hotline established for outworkers in the textile and clothing industry, mainly Chinese, Vietnamese, Laotian, Macedonian and Turkish migrant women.
	Tan Le honoured as Young Australian of the Year.	
	Cathy Freeman honoured as Australian of the Year.	

Bibliography

These are the sources of the information given in the text, including the 'Where We Are Now' section in Chapter 1 and our 'Chart of Australian Women's Achievements'.

REFERENCES

Australian Bureau of Statistics. *Child Care, Australia*. AGPS, Canberra, 1996.

—— *Community Services, Australia, Preliminary, 1995–96*. AGPS, Canberra, 1997.

Australian Bureau of Statistics and Office of the Status of Women. *Australian Women's Year Book 1997*. AGPS, Canberra, 1997.

Australian Council of Trade Unions. *Advances in Equal Pay Under the Accord*. Melbourne, 1993.

—— *Equal Pay*. (In Enterprising Ideas series.) Melbourne, 1995.

—— *Family Leave Care*. (In Enterprising Ideas series.) Melbourne, 1995.

—— *Maternity Leave*. (In Enterprising Ideas series.) Melbourne, 1995.

—— *Parental Leave*. (In Enterprising Ideas series.) Melbourne, 1995.

—— *Women Workers: Our Priorities for 1997*. (Labour Information Network 1997 update.) Melbourne, 1997.

Australian Education Union. *Australian Education Union Submission to the Senate Inquiry into the Status of Teachers*. Melbourne, 1997.

Australian Human Rights and Equal Opportunity Commission. *Enterprise Bargaining: Manual for Women in the Workplace*. Sydney, 1996.

—— *Sexual Harassment: A Code of Practice*. Sydney, 1996.

Australian Law Reform Commission. *Equality Before the Law: Justice for Women*. Report no. 69, pt 1. Sydney, 1994.

Beacham, Jenny. Written communication to authors, 1998.

Behrendt, Larissa. In *Cultural Survival Quarterly*, Spring 1998, p. 46. (Available from 96 Mount Auburne Street, Cambridge, Massachusetts 02138, USA.)

Bellear, Lisa (Goernpil). Recorded interview and personal communication with authors, 1998.

Bowen, Jan, with Child Support Agency. *Child Support: The Essential Guide.* Jacaranda Wiley, Brisbane, 1992.

Burton, Clare. *Gender Equity in Australian University Staffing.* Ed. assistance of Linda Cook and Susan Wilson. Department of Employment, Education, Training and Youth Affairs, Canberra, 1997.

CCH Australia. *Australian Family Law Guide.* Sydney, 1998.

Charlesworth, Sara. *Stretching Flexibility: Enterprise Bargaining, Women Workers and Changes to Working Hours.* Human Rights and Equal Opportunity Commission, Sydney, 1996.

Child Support Evaluation Advisory Group. *Child Support in Australia: Final Report of the Evaluation of the Child Support Scheme.* Vol. 1, main report. AGPS, Canberra, 1992.

Commonwealth of Australia. *Affirmative Action Agency Annual Report.* 1995–96, 1996–97. AGPS, Canberra, 1996, 1997.

Cowling, Annie. *Breaking New Ground: A Manual for Survival for Women Entering Non-Traditional Jobs.* Building Workers Industrial Union, Victorian Branch, Melbourne, 1991.

Cox, Eva. *Leading Women: Tactics for Making a Difference.* Random House, Sydney, 1996.

—— *A Truly Civil Society: 1995 Boyer Lectures.* Australian Broadcasting Corporation, Sydney, 1995.

de Vries-Evans, Susanna. *Strength of Spirit: Pioneering Women of Achievement from First Fleet to Federation,* Millennium Books, Sydney, 1995.

Dominguez, Joe, and Robin, Vicki. *Your Money or Your Life: Transforming Your Relationship with Money and Achieving Financial Independence,* Penguin, New York, 1993.

Dyer, Wayne W. *You'll See It When You Believe It.* Arrow, London, 1990.

Else-Mitchell, R., and Flutter, N. (eds). *Talking Up: Young Women's Take on Feminism.* Spinifex, Melbourne, 1998.

EMILY's List (Australia). *Gender Gap Research: Trends, Issues and Attitudes.* Melbourne, 1998.

Gaudron, Mary. 'Speech to Launch Australian Women Lawyers'. High Court of Australia web site. http://www.hcourt.gov.au/wlasp.htm

Gibson, Linelle. Recorded interview and personal communication with authors, 1998.

Greenspan, Karen. *The Timetables of Women's History: A Chronology of the Most Important People and Events in Women's History*. Simon & Schuster, New York, 1994.

Hartley, Anne. *Financially Free: Think Rich to be Rich: A Woman's Guide to Creating Wealth*. Doubleday, Sydney, 1990.

—— *The Psychology of Money*, Hart Publishing, Sydney, 1995.

Healey, Kaye (ed.) *Child Care*. (Vol. 69 in Issues for the Nineties series.) Spinney Press, Balmain, NSW, 1997.

Hede, Andrew, and O'Brien, Elizabeth. Empirical Analysis of Women's Managerial Representation in the Private Sector. Paper presented at Australian and New Zealand Academy of Management annual conference, Wollongong, 4–7 December 1996.

Holt, Lillian. Oral communication, recorded by Joan Kirner, to the Centenary of Federation Advisory Committee, 1994.

House of Representatives Standing Committee on Legal and Constitutional Affairs. *Half Way to Equal: Report of the Inquiry into Equal Opportunity and Equal Status for Women in Australia*. AGPS, Canberra, 1992.

Irving, Helen (ed.). *A Woman's Constitution?: Gender & History in the Australian Commonwealth*. Hale & Iremonger, Sydney, 1996.

James, Vivienne. *The Woman's Money Book*. Anne O'Donovan, Melbourne, 1996.

Johnson, Eva. 'Right to be'. In Gilbert, Kevin (ed.), *Inside Black Australia: An Anthology of Aboriginal Poetry*. Penguin, Ringwood, 1988.

Jonas, Bill, and Langton, Marcia, with Australian Institute of Aboriginal and Torres Strait Islander Studies. *The Little Red, Yellow & Black (and Green and Blue and White) Book: A Short Guide to Indigenous Australia*. AIATSIS, on behalf of Council for Aboriginal Reconciliation, 1994. (Ch. 'The Cultural History of Australia' adapted from *Land Rights News*, vol. 2, no. 6, January 1988, courtesy Central and Northern Land Councils.)

Kaplan, Gisela. *The Meagre Harvest: The Australian Women's Movement 1950s–1990s*, Allen & Unwin, Sydney, 1996.

Kennedy, G., Benson, J. and McMillan, J. *Managing Negotiations: How to Get a Better Deal*. 3rd edn. Hutchinson Business Books, Sydney, 1987.

King, Poppy. Unpublished speech to the Lighthouse Foundation, 3 June 1997.

Korn–Ferry International. *Boards of Directors in Australia: Fifteenth Study 1996*, Sydney, 1996.

Lundy, Kate. 'Talking Back'. In Else-Mitchell, R. and Flutter, N. (eds), *Talking Up: Young Women's Take on Feminism*. Spinifex, Melbourne, 1998.

Magner, Eilis S. *Joske's Law and Procedure at Meetings in Australia*. 8th edn. Law Book Company, Sydney, 1994.

Maclean, Sarah. *The Pan Book of Etiquette and Good Manners*. Pan Books, London, 1962.

Maggio, Rosalie. *The Nonsexist Word Finder: A Dictionary of Gender-Free Usage*. Beacon Press, Boston, 1988.

Mant, Alistair. *Intelligent Leadership*. Allen & Unwin, Sydney, 1997.

Marles, Fay. Recorded interview and personal communication with authors, 1999.

Mitchell, Susan. *The Matriarchs: Twelve Australian Women Talk About Their Lives*. Penguin, Ringwood, 1987.

—— *The Scent of Power*. Angus & Robertson, Melbourne, 1996.

National Health and Medical Research Council. *An Information Paper on Termination of Pregnancy in Australia*. NHMRC, Canberra, 1996.

Neill, Rosemary. 'Boardroom Backlash'. *Weekend Financial Review*, 19–20 April 1997.

Newell, Malcolm. *Ten Steps to Financial Health*, Stirling Press, Old Noarlunga, South Australia, 1995.

Office of the Status of Women. *Community Attitudes to Violence Against Women: Executive Summary*. AGPS, Canberra, 1995.

Oldfield, Audrey. *Woman Suffrage in Australia: A Gift or a Struggle?*. Cambridge University Press, Melbourne, 1992. (Includes the quotation from Louisa Lawson given on p. 141.)

O'Leary, Olivia, and Burke, Helen. *Mary Robinson: The Authorised Biography*. Hodder & Stoughton, UK, 1998.

Olsen, Kirstin. *Chronology of Women's History*. Greenwood Press, USA, 1994.

Owen, Mary, Dinner Committee (eds). *A Decade of Mary Owen Dinners*. Shortrun Books, Melbourne, 1995.

Parliament of Victoria. *Parliamentary Debates, Legislative Assembly*. Melbourne, 1989.

—— *Parliament of Victoria Information Kit.* Melbourne, 1996.

Petersen, Donald E., and Hillkirk, John. *A Better Idea: Redefining the Way Americans Work.* Houghton-Mifflin, New York, 1991.

Poiner, Gretchen, and Wills, Sue. *The Gifthorse: A Critical Look at Equal Employment Opportunity in Australia*, Allen & Unwin, Sydney, 1991.

Robbins, S. P., Waters-Marsh, T., Cacioppe, R., and Millett, R. *Organisational Behaviour.* Prentice-Hall, Sydney, 1994.

Ronalds, Chris. *Affirmative Action and Sex Discrimination: A Handbook on Legal Rights for Women.* Pluto Press, Sydney, 1987.

—— *Discrimination: Law and Practice.* Federation Press, Sydney, 1998.

Roosevelt, Eleanor. *Tomorrow is Now.* Harper & Row, New York, 1963.

Saul, John Ralston. *The Doubter's Companion: A Dictionary of Aggressive Common Sense.* Penguin Books, Canada, 1995.

Sawer, Marian, and Simms, Marian. *A Woman's Place: Women and Politics in Australia.* 2nd edn. Allen & Unwin, Sydney, 1993.

Scutt, Jocelynne (ed.). *Breaking Through: Women, Work and Careers.* Artemis Publishing, Melbourne, 1992.

Schubert, Misha. 'Strategic Politics of Organizations'. In R. Else-Mitchell and N. Flutter (eds), *Talking Up: Young Women's Take on Feminism.* Spinifex, Melbourne, 1998.

Shardey, Helen. 'Report of a Forum, La Trobe Forum'. *Magazine of the La Trobe University Politics Society*, vol. 13, December 1998.

Summers, Anne. *Damned Whores and God's Police: The Colonization of Women in Australia.* Penguin, Ringwood, 1975, 1994.

Sun News-Pictorial, 13 October 1942.

Sveriges Socialdemokratiska Kvinnofoerbund. *Swedish Power Handbook.* S-KINNOR, Stockholm, 1994.

Sykes, Roberta. 'Obituary of MumShirl'. *Newsletter of the Black Women's Action in Education Foundation*, 1998. (Available from PO Box 1784, Strawberry Hills, NSW 2012.)

Tomasetti, Glen. 'Don't Be Too Polite, Girls'. 1969 song in Colin Tomasetti, *Songs from a Seat in the Carriage: 8 Songs for the Seventies by Glen Tomasetti.* R. A. Hulme & M. G. Dugan, Melbourne, 1970.

Trager, James. *The Women's Chronology: A Year-by-Year Record, from Prehistory to the Present*, Henry Holt, New York, 1994.

Truth, Sojourner. A contemporary report of her speech to the Women's Convention, Akron, Ohio, 1851. http://pacific.discover.net/~dansyr/truth.html

Tully, Kate. *Every Woman's Guide to Getting into Politics*. Office of the Status of Women, Canberra, 1995.

'200 Rich List'. *Business Review Weekly*, 26 May 1997.

'UN Report Slams Apparent Shift on Sex Equality'. *Age*, 20 March 1997.

Victorian Council of Social Services. *Planning: Knowing Where You're Going*. Melbourne, 1996.

Waring, Marilyn. *Counting for Nothing: What Men Value & What Women are Worth*. Allen & Unwin/Port Nicholson Press, Wellington, 1988.

——— *Women, Politics and Power*. Allen & Unwin/Port Nicholson Press, Wellington, 1985.

WEL Australia. *Women's Electoral Lobby, Lobby Kit*. Produced by Josephine Conway and Robyn Cotterell-Jones. Canberra, 1996. (Available from PO Box 191, Civic Square, ACT 2608.)

Windschuttle, Elizabeth (ed.). *Women, Class and History: Feminist Perspectives on Australia 1788–1978*. Fontana Books, Sydney, 1980.

Women's Education Development Organization Newsletter 1994. New York, 1994. (Cites Mary Robinson.)

Woolf, Virginia. *A Room of One's Own*. Harcourt Brace, New York, 1929.

FURTHER READING

No-one else's list of invaluable books can substitute for your own. We have learned from our own reading. We hope that our references listed above and the following suggestions will start you off on your own search for ideas, encouragement, information and allies in the community. Consult your local library, bookshops, newspapers, journals, magazines and the Internet – we strongly recommend you become proficient at using the Internet, if you have not already done this.

FOR AN UNDERSTANDING OF AUSTRALIAN FEMINISM

Bureau of Immigration and Population Research. *Gender Equity and Australian Immigration Policy*. AGPS, Canberra, 1994.

Australian Feminism: A Companion. Ed. Barbara Caine. Oxford
    University Press, Melbourne, 1998.

D'Aprano, Zelda. *Zelda.* Spinifex, Melbourne, 1977, 1995.

Kaplan, Gisela. *The Meagre Harvest: The Australian Women's Movement
    1950–1990s.* Allen & Unwin, Sydney, 1996.

Law Reform Commission. *Equality Before the Law: Justice for Women.*
    Report no. 69. Sydney, 1994.

Sawer, Marian. *Sisters in Suits: Women and Public Policy in Australia.*
    Allen & Unwin, Sydney, 1990.

Scutt, Jocelynne (ed.). *Growing Up Feminist: The New Generation of
    Australian Women.* Artemis, Melbourne, 1985, 1996.

Sykes, Roberta. *Murawina: Australian Women of High Achievement.*
    Doubleday Books, Sydney, 1993.

WOMEN IN AUSTRALIAN POLITICS

Caffrey, Cecilia (ed.). *At Home in the House: The Voices of Victorian
    ALP Women in Parliament.* ALP Victorian Branch, Melbourne,
    1993.

Phillips, Harry C.J. *The Voice of Edith Cowan: Australia's First
    Woman Parliamentarian 1921–1924.* Edith Cowan University,
    Perth, 1996.

Reynolds, Margaret. *The Last Bastion: Labor Women Working Towards
    Equality in the Parliaments of Australia.* Business and Professional
    Publishing, Sydney, 1995.

Sinclair, Amanda. *Trials at the Top: Chief Executives Talk About Men,
    Women and the Australian Executive Culture.* Melbourne University
    Australian Centre, Melbourne, 1994.

Street, Jessie. *Truth or Repose.* Australasian Book Society, Sydney, 1966.

Women, Power & Politics: Conference Proceedings. Women's Suffrage
    Centenary Steering Committee, Department of Arts and Cultural
    Development, Adelaide, 1994.

FOR HELP WITH THE PARTICULAR CHALLENGES FOR
WOMEN IN PUBLIC OFFICE

Commonwealth of Australia. *Australian Women Working Together: An
    Overview of the Activities of Australian Women's Non-Government
    Organisations 1997.* Parliament House, Canberra, 1997.

—— *Getting the Message Through: An Information Kit Prepared for*

Women's Groups. Prepared by Senator Jocelyn Newman. AGPS, Canberra, 1997.

Office of the Status of Women. *Every Woman's Guide to Getting into Politics.* 2nd edn. AGPS, Canberra, 1998. (Available from the OSW web site http://www.dpmc.gov.au/osw. Or email women@dpmc.gov.au.)

A Gender Agenda: A Kit for Women who Want to Stand for Local Government and for Those who Want to Assist Others to Stand. Stegley Foundation and the Municipal Association of Victoria. 1998. (Available from Stegley Foundation, 44 Garden Street, South Yarra, Victoria 3141.)

Haines, Janine. *Suffrage to Sufferance: A Hundred Years of Women in Politics*, Allen & Unwin, Sydney, 1992.

MEDIATION

Fisher, R., and Ury, W. *Getting to Yes: Negotiating Agreement Without Giving In.* 2nd edn. Business Books, Sydney, 1991.

MENTORING

McKenzie, Bonnie C. *Friends in High Places: How to Achieve Your Ambitions, Goals and Potential with the Help of a Mentor: The Executive Woman's Guide.* Business & Professional Publishing, Sydney, 1995.

Tye, Marian. *I Need a Mentor, Don't I?* Australian Federation of Business and Professional Women, Sydney, 1998.

DEMOCRACY

Rayner, Moira. *Rooting Democracy: Growing the Society We Want.* Allen & Unwin, Sydney, 1997.

LEADERSHIP

Sinclair, Amanda. *Doing Leadership Differently: Gender, Power and Sexuality in a Changing Business Culture.* Melbourne University Press, Melbourne, 1998.

RIGHTS

Kinley, David (ed.). *Human Rights in Australian Law.* Federation Press, Sydney, 1998.

Thornton, P., Phelan, L. and McKeown, B. *I Protest: Fighting for Your Rights: A Practical Guide.* Pluto Press, Sydney, 1997.

WEB SITES AND USEFUL INTERNET ADDRESSES

All political parties and most MPs now have their own web sites. So do many community-based activist groups. Web sites change quite regularly and what is useful and up to date this year may be out of date and less useful quite soon, so we recommend you use a good search engine on the Internet to seek out and update useful web sites for yourself. However, the following are good starting points.

AUSFEM-POLNET. An electronic network for activists, practitioners and scholars actively involved with policies that aim to improve the status of women, run from the University of Tasmania. For information on how to subscribe, go to their web page (http://www.utas.edu.au) or subscribe directly by sending a message to majordomo@postoffice.utas.edu.au. Your subject line should be blank and your message should read 'subscribe AUSFEM-POLNET *your email address*'.

ACTU. The web site's '1999 National Directory' is an excellent guide to unions, business, politicians and the media. http://www.actu.asn.au

National Women's Media Centre Activities homepage. http://www.isis.aust.com/nwmc

EMILY's List Australia. emilyslist@sydney.socialchange.net.au

Office of the Status of Women. http://www.dpmc.gov.au/osw, or email women@dpmc.gov.au

Index

community activism 51, 219–59
community advocacy 11, 221–4
  networking role 223
community ownership 44
community/team focus 43–4
compliments 54–5
confidence 39–42
contraception 22, 35
co-option of women to male-
  dominated meetings 151–3
corporate sector, women in 26
councillors (local government) and
  activism 228–30
courage 96–7
Cowling, Annie 174–5
Cox, Eva 15, 54
creative health 81
credit cards 92–3
criticism, dealing with 95
crying 45, 46, 205 6

decision-making 14, 108
  at meetings 133, 134
  exclusion of women at meetings
    135
decoration 265
democracy 265
Department for Women (NSW) 21
details, political campaigns 265
diaries 78, 265
disappointments, dealing with 98–9
disciplinary meeting 169
discrimination 27–8, 36, 170–2
  dealing with 173–8
  see also sex discrimination
doctors 81
Doe, Karen 88
domestic violence 21
Dunn-Dyer, Susan 27

education 22, 35
educational qualifications 156–7
EMILY's List 231–2, 249, 277
emotional health 81
employers, family-friendly policies
  148–9
employment 23, 155–6
  and experience 157–8
  and qualifications 156–7

in male-dominated areas 159
negotiating terms and conditions
  159–63
working with male managers
  167–9
workplace agreements 163–5
  see also workplace
employment contract 157, 158, 160
employment sectors, women in
  25–6, 54–5
empowerment 37
enterprise flexibility agreements 163
entertaining contacts or clients
  166–7
equal opportunity 102–3, 104, 170
Equal Opportunity Board 27
equal-opportunity laws 36, 169–72
equal pay 26, 40
equality 20, 21, 29–30, 35–6, 47,
  103, 104, 266
equity 266
ethics checklist 69–71
ex-office-holder 266
exercise 81, 82
experience 266

faction 266
facts 266–7
failure, living with 98–9
family life, and working life 148
family members, importance of 72–5
family structure 22
family-friendly workplaces 148–9,
  165–7
Faust, Beatrice 155
favours, asking for 120
fear 96–8, 99–100
feminism 18–19, 20, 102
feminist, being a 101–5
financial advisers 91–2
financial autonomy 23, 24, 34
financial management 66, 83
  attitudes and beliefs 83–6
  credit cards 92–3
  joint accounts 89–91
  where am I now? 87–8
  where do I want to get to? 89
financial needs 25
financial system, learning about 91–3